SCIENCE
for
PUBLIC POLICY

Edited by

HARVEY BROOKS

and

CHESTER L. COOPER

PERGAMON PRESS

OXFORD · NEW YORK · BEIJING · FRANKFURT
SÃO PAULO · SYDNEY · TOKYO · TORONTO

U.K.	Pergamon Press, Headington Hill Hall, Oxford OX3 0BW, England
U.S.A.	Pergamon Press, Maxwell House, Fairview Park, Elmsford, New York 10523, U.S.A.
PEOPLE'S REPUBLIC OF CHINA	Pergamon Press, Qianmen Hotel, Beijing, People's Republic of China
FEDERAL REPUBLIC OF GERMANY	Pergamon Press, Hammerweg 6, D-6242 Kronberg, Federal Republic of Germany
BRAZIL	Pergamon Editora, Rua Eça de Queiros, 346, CEP 04011, São Paulo, Brazil
AUSTRALIA	Pergamon Press Australia, P.O. Box 544, Potts Point, N.S.W. 2011, Australia
JAPAN	Pergamon Press, 8th Floor, Matsuoka Central Building, 1-7-1 Nishishinjuku, Shinjuku-ku, Tokyo 160, Japan
CANADA	Pergamon Press Canada, Suite 104, 150 Consumers Road, Willowdale, Ontario M2J 1P9, Canada

First edition 1987

Library of Congress Cataloging-in-Publication Data

Science for public policy.
Includes bibliographies.
1. Science and state.   I. Brooks, Harvey.
II. Cooper, Chester L.
Q125.S434314   1986   338.9'26   86–22654

British Library Cataloguing in Publication Data

Science for public policy.
1. Scientists in government
I. Brooks, Harvey   II. Cooper, Chester L.
351.007'25   Q125
ISBN 0-08-034770-3

Printed in Great Britain by A. Wheaton & Co. Ltd., Exeter

Preface

Since the turn of the century, and particularly since World War II, national and international policymakers have been confronted by a growing number of complex problems whose resolution hangs, to a significant degree, on scientific knowledge or technological insights. Yet, most policymakers have little or no background in science and technology. This puts a considerable premium on the quality and clarity of scientific/technical advice they seek and receive. And this, in turn, requires a high degree of mutual sensitivity and understanding between the policy and science communities. It is no wonder, then, that many national governments and international institutions have recently come to rely on "Science Advisors" to provide a bridge between the two communities in order to increase the effectiveness of Science for Public Policy.

In this volume, a score of authors from several countries, both East and West, and many backgrounds and "disciplines" examine Science for Public Policy. Environmental problems and policy provide much of the focus of the discussion.

From their vantage points as scientists, or policymakers, or science advisors, the authors examine the issue and explore ways to improve the quality and timeliness of scientific advice to decision makers.

Preliminary versions of many of the essays included here were presented at an international forum on Science for Public Policy held at the International Institute of Applied Systems Analysis (IIASA) in January 1984. Most of these were subsequently considerably edited and much new material was added. IIASA is a non-governmental, international research institute located in Laxenburg, Austria.

This publication was made possible by a grant from the German Marshall Fund to the American Academy of Arts and Sciences, the United States member organization of IIASA. The views expressed here are those of the authors, and are not necessarily endorsed by IIASA, the American Academy or the German Marshall Fund.

HARVEY BROOKS, *Cambridge, Mass.*
CHESTER L. COOPER, *Washington, D.C.*

v

Acknowledgements

The editors are indebted to Mr. Michael Dowling and Mrs. Roberta Yared, who edited the original proceedings of the Science for Public Policy Forum held at IIASA in January 1984.

They are also grateful to members of IIASA's publications division, who prepared and processed various versions of the manuscript.

Finally, they owe thanks to Professor C. S. Holling, Director of IIASA at the time of the Science for Public Policy Forum.

Contents

Contents

CHAPTER 1

Introduction and Overview

HARVEY BROOKS

The primary purpose of this Forum on Science for Public Policy was to review and synthesize our present understanding of the actual and possible modes of interaction between scientific findings and public policy decisions by both national and international decision makers. A hoped-for outcome was to be able to use the insights gained from this Forum to increase the relevance and usefulness of the research undertaken at IIASA to policy-makers in all the countries of its National Member Organizations and in International Organizations.

The Forum concerned itself with a quite restricted domain of the field known as "science policy". The agenda excluded decisions about the financing of research projects, or the methods of determination of priorities among various fields of science. Instead, it focused on the use of scientific evidence, data, and insights to illuminate public policy issues that are not primarily scientific, but that are strongly dependent on scientific and technological information. It also considered the use of science in the actual implementation of decisions about such public policy issues. As a result the discussion was not about areas of science or research, but about policy problems of human concern, such as food, energy, environmental regulation, health maintenance and improvement, hazardous waste management and disposal, arms control, methods of dispute resolution between institutions, social groups, and nations.

Although scientific and technological information may be quite crucial to the making of public policy decisions in such areas, it is still only one among many factors that have to be taken into account, something that is not always fully appreciated by scientists. One of the major challenges, therefore, is how to blend technical and nontechnical considerations in the final decision—how to act, for example, when scientific information is uncertain or there are large areas of scientific ignorance or wide disagreements among apparently equally respectable experts both as to the characterization of the technical problem and the implications of the data for political or other societal action.

We chose the problems of acid rain and carbon dioxide build-up as two concrete, illustrative issues—one relatively immediate, and the other of a

1

much longer time range—to exemplify the more general process and communication questions that we anticipated would be the main topics of discussion. The discussions in the Forum were not restricted to these examples, nor did the participants attempt to reach a consensus, either scientific or policy-oriented, on these two issues. The participants were encouraged by the organizers of the Forum to keep in mind the value of being as concrete as possible, so that generalizations would always be supported by examples of actual decisions, whether historical or prospective.

Some of the questions we hoped the Forum would throw light on were the following: How should knowledge be packaged in a form that is most useful to those faced with the task of using this knowledge in the making and implementation of policy decisions? What guidance should scientists reasonably expect from policymakers as they try to establish their research agendas in such a way as to be relevant to policy? What kind of guidance would scientists prefer and what kind would they consider inappropriate as, for example, compromising their independence as scientists? What is the advantage of international research institutions in comparison with their national counterparts working in similar fields? From what sources should international research institutions expect guidance on their research agendas?

Similarly, what kinds of answers can policymakers reasonably expect from scientists without attempting to push them to conclusions that simply cannot be extracted from existing data, given the current state of knowledge in the relevant technical fields? How do the findings of research get onto the agenda of policymakers, and what role should science and research play in establishing priorities among policy issues that should command the attention of the public and decision makers? What is the dividing line between keeping research relevant to policy and distorting the scientific process through excessive responsiveness to current policy needs or institutional and power structures?

IIASA provides an almost unique institutional setting for integrating experiences with the interface between science and policy in widely different political and economic systems. There is nothing as valuable as the opportunity to view a policy issue important to one society through the lens of an entirely different political and economic set-up; such a situation exists between the socialist countries and the market economies. One of the hopes is that problems which appear intractable when viewed from the habitual perspective of one society will reveal themselves as amenable to new, hitherto unconsidered, approaches when viewed from the standpoint of an entirely different social setting. The depoliticization of contentious social issues, which can occur in an institution such as IIASA, is certainly one of the most important benefits, to both Eastern and Western societies, of this type of research institution. We live in a world where more and more of the most important problems are either common to many societies differing widely in their political and social systems or stages of industrialization, or transcend the usual political boundaries and jurisdictions, so that they can be solved only by mutual agreement based on negotiation from a more or less agreed knowledge base.

A New Science?

A constantly recurring theme in the discussions was whether science for public policy should be regarded as a new and different kind of science, with its own rules and paradigms distinct from traditional academic science, and ultimately demanding a new kind of scientific education or apprenticeship. Nowotny referred to this new science as "managerial science", while Ravetz envisaged it as "a new sort of science, working in partnership with policymaking for the control of uncertainty and the management of ignorance". Brickman referred to policy science as "an effective tool of consensus", suggesting that consensus was the indispensable tool of effective social action, and that consensus on policy often made science unnecessary or irrelevant. In other words science for public policy should be looked upon as only one of the many kits of tools available to the policymaker or the policy "entrepreneur" for forging a political consensus on the appropriate direction for social action. Brickman pointed out that there *were* many cases where "compelling scientific evidence can reduce political controversy", and the search for such opportunities should be one of the principal goals for a research institution aimed at developing knowledge for policy. Nevertheless, one should be careful not to expect that scientific consensus should be a *necessary* condition for policy consensus, an expectation to which scientists tend to be too prone.

Others pointed to the hazards of "scientific relativism" inherent in the notion of a distinctive kind of science as a tool of public policy. Brian Wynne, for example, called attention to the large element of "craft judgment" inherent in the normal processes of science. He argued that the "temporary setting aside, on a judgmental basis, of many inconsistencies and anomalies" is essential to the progress of scientific research. Insistence in practice on the "tidy objectivity" and procedural rigor supposed to be the dominant characteristic of scientific work would, in fact, lead to stagnation in science. At the same time, these informal tacit understandings within the social system of science open science to attack by critics who are unhappy with the policy conclusions drawn from scientific knowledge. It is, indeed, true that the discretionary judgment accorded to scientists within the social system of science can be the vehicle by which, in the opinion of Charvat, "science as a social phenomenon absorbs to an increasing extent the features of the surrounding society and culture".

Generally speaking, the more centrally planned and managed the policy system, the more legitimate politically is the informal, discretionary evaluation of technical evidence and uncertainties by experts likely to be. In the American system, which lies at one extreme, with multiple channels of access to the policy process by diverse groups, any informal discretion in the exercise of technical judgment on scientific issues with policy implications tends to be hunted down and rooted out as an abuse, as emphasized by Brian Wynne. In defence against this attack, regulatory legislation and administrative rules, strongly reinforced by the judiciary, tend to be more and more surrounded with inflexibly specified inference rules, which narrow the scope of expert judgment and, indeed, supersede the customary social processes of science as pursued outside the policy context. Nowotny suggests that, as other political systems gradually become more open to public scrutiny, and more open and forthright in admitting uncertainty and tentativeness in scientific conclusions, the public may become increasingly doubtful of the legitimacy of science and adopt a sort of scientific "relativism" in which all scientific assertions can be considered equally legitimate, and the political system should be free to select whatever version of the truth best conforms to the political preferences of the democratic majority or of particular élites in a position advantageous to registering their views in the political system.

In short, the more the results of science are explicitly *designed* to function as tools in the policy process, the more knowledge is shaped by its intended function—which Ravetz suggests should be the criterion for policy science as compared to academic science—the greater the danger that not only the *form*, but also the *substance* of scientific truth will be distorted to fit policy preferences, not just policy needs. Thus, as suggested by Wynne, it is important that the "procedural ideals of science"—that is, of traditional academic science—be permitted to exercise a real quality-control effect over the science used to justify policy.

In summary, it is my own conclusion that, however much the agenda of research or the packaging of its results are modified to meet the requirements of policymaking, there remains, in the words of a well-known report of the US National Science Board, "only one science, only one set of standards for evaluating evidence".

On the other hand, there is bound to remain an inherent tension between the dynamic, provisional, and tentative nature of scientific knowledge in the midst of its processes of generation, and the need for some sort of stability and predictability in the policymaking process. Regulation cannot respond to each new piece of scientific information, let alone to public perceptions of that information, often dictated by the more or less random occurrence of the low-probability events that redirect regulatory or policy priorities.

Uncertainty and Ignorance

Another theme that dominated the discussion, closely related to the preceding one, was that of technical uncertainty. Indeed, it is frequently technical uncertainty that makes policy *problems*, as contrasted with policy *decisions* prompted by "compelling scientific evidence". Unfortunately, the latter are the exception rather than the rule in science for public policy. Although uncertainty or ignorance exists only at the "margins" of science (Ravetz), it is at these margins that most public policy problems involving science occur. One reason for this is that the consequences of the application of technology frequently carry us into domains where there exists no systematic or codified body of knowledge on which policy can be based. The present controversy over the management of hazardous wastes is a prime example (Ravetz). In the US there has been a whole series of new environmental laws, passed mostly in the 1970s, the implementation of which, in effect, presumes the existence of such a body of systematic knowledge, when all that we have, in fact, is scattered facts and empirical data with more gaps than information. Yet the possible consequences of what we do not know often do not allow us the luxury of suspending judgment pending the acquisition of more data and better theory, as would be the case in ordinary science.

Ravetz makes a distinction between ignorance and uncertainty, which is highly important for policy purposes. Uncertainty is an absence of knowledge that exists within "a completely articulated structure", a definite intellectual framework. It is simply a recognized gap in a systematic body of knowledge. In general, uncertainty in the policy context can be handled by well-developed analytic tools, such as decision theory, and various modes of statistical inference. In other words, it can be incorporated within the normal paradigms of science.

Ignorance, on the other hand, involves knowledge whose very existence may be unsuspected. Not only do we not know the numbers; we may not even know they exist or that there is something to measure. There may be clues lurking somewhere in the background, which, we would recognize later, should have alerted us to something important, but these clues are usually only significant in retrospect, after they can be fitted into an "articulated framework".

Actually, it is important to recognize gradations of ignorance. There is knowledge that, for all practical purposes, nobody knows exists, not even to look for it, never mind knowing where to look for it. There is also ignorance that is contextual: the knowledge actually exists, but the people—policymakers and experts—who are in a position to apply the knowledge are unaware of its existence and the few people who may have mastered the knowledge are not aware of its policy significance. In general, I think it is this second type of ignorance that is the more important in practice. For example, a few people were aware of the potential health hazards of asbestos as much as 50 years ago, but it was much more recently that this knowledge began to force itself into the general consciousness of the industrial hygiene community. One of the major aims of policy research institutions should be to insure that this type of ignorance does not persist too long, that "clouds no bigger than a man's hand" are spotted early and improbable clues are followed up. In many cases, those who should be aware of such knowledge are subconsciously reluctant to hear about it and tend to remain inordinately skeptical until cumulative evidence becomes overwhelming.

Wetstone has pointed out in his chapter how national studies on the environmental effects of long-range atmospheric transport and deposition of sulphur compounds were given little credence outside their own boundaries, as long as the main sources and victims were in different countries. Only when Ulrich put forward evidence that sulphur emissions might be affecting German forests was the "acid rain" issue taken seriously in the Federal Republic. This experience suggests the importance of key actors or events in bringing new knowledge into the everyday consciousness of policymakers, a topic to which the Forum devoted a good deal of attention, discussed below.

Although it has many disadvantages the system of adversarial science prevalent in the US has considerable advantages in bringing to light knowledge that might not otherwise come to policy attention because of "contextual ignorance", as discussed above. Such adversarial groups often overstate their case and present evidence selectively to bolster a particular policy position while ignoring other evidence, but the result is that new information is brought forward and debated as part of the mainstream agenda of policy. In more consensual systems, in which politicians and the electorate are more inclined to defer to recognized experts, contextual ignorance is more likely to persist for longer.

Differences in the social and cultural context of science for public policy in different national systems, when confronted with each other in the setting of an international policy research institution, may also accelerate the bringing to light of areas of contextual ignorance.

Although ignorance giving rise to surprise is a more frequent problem and more difficult to deal with than uncertainty, the latter also leaves large scope for the exercise of political or cultural bias in the interpretation of scientific evidence. This is particularly true with reference to decisions as to where the burden of proof should lie in whether or not to permit the introduction of new technologies. A useful device in this connection may be to force the proponents of various positions to identify what evidence or what narrowing of uncertainty would cause them to change their policy preferences.

Policy Formation as Structured Negotiation

The creation and implementation of policy is a complex process, which, in practice, involves negotiation among many actors and interests. One of the important functions of science for public policy is as an instrument for building consensus among these stakeholders. For science to play this role, however, it is necessary that there be agreement not only on the science, but also on which kinds of information entail which kinds of policy response. Generally, the higher the stakes perceived by the various participants in the negotiation, the less is it possible for knowledge alone to compel agreement on the appropriate actions. It is thus as important to understand the sources of disagreement on policy as it is to understand the reasons for scientific disagreement or to "get the facts right".

Conversely, when there is agreement in advance on the policy implications of various kinds of knowledge, reducing scientific uncertainties can be a potent instrument of consensus.

In addition, of course, the perceptions of various actors concerning their stake in a particular policy decision can be greatly affected by new knowledge—even reversed when the results of careful analysis of the evidence are "counterintuitive", as they frequently can be in complex situations.

The achievement of consensus can be more complicated when laymen or nonexperts are involved in the implicit negotiations that lead to policy formation. Studies of lay and expert attitudes on various issues indicate that the main difference between the two is that laymen may hold sets of preferences that are logically inconsistent among themselves, whereas experts tend to arrive at a greater internal consistency among their preferences [1].*
Thus, another important function of knowledge and analysis can be to demonstrate to lay participants the necessity for choice among inconsistent preferences—choices among competing "goods", rather than choices between "good" and "bad". At the same time, lay participation can force experts to take into account a wider range of value preferences or interests than would be the case if the necessity for negotiating consensus were restricted to the circle of experts.

The negotiation aspect of policy formation becomes more apparent when the implementation of policy involves co-operation among sovereign nations, as is the case for acid rain and carbon dioxide build-up, chosen as examples for this Forum. In the national context, government authority is available to compel agreement on policy in the absence of consensus, but this authority is much weaker in the international context. Thus, the role of knowledge can be relatively more crucial in the resolution of international policy problems. In

*Numbers in square brackets are to References at the ends of chapters.

principle, the universality of scientific truth can be appealed to in the international situation, especially if the truth has been agreed to within an international scientific institution. In practice, as Majone has emphasized, the universalistic norm of science is restricted to a few disciplines; the closer a discipline is to practical application, particularly public policy application, the more it is likely to be influenced by local priorities, traditions, research styles, and cultural contexts. Hence, the consensus-building capabilities of an international research institution in the near term may be less than one might hope, given the ideal of the universalistic norm of science. Nevertheless, in Majone's opinion, international research organizations have an important role to play in realizing a more universalistic ideal for the regulatory sciences through "the creation of a coherent cognitive basis and standardization of tasks and skills" across national boundaries, combined with the development of "a more sophisticated understanding of the dynamics of policymaking".

Setting the Policy Agenda

Much discussion went on, particularly in the three workshops, on how policy issues involving science and technology actually found their way onto the public policy agenda. There was general agreement that this was usually a long process, often requiring ten years from the first stirrings in the scientific community to gaining priority attention from national decision makers. Typically, a problem has to become both politically and scientifically "ripe", and has to have gained the attention of a considerable public outside policymaking circles. Several sources for placing items on the policy agenda were explicitly identified, although this list is probably not exhaustive:

(1) Scientific publicists (e.g. Rachel Carson).
(2) Public sentiment (e.g. the threat to German forests and endangered species).
(3) Legitimation by international institutions.
(4) Serendipity (e.g. research on ozone layer depletion from SST led to identification of fluorocarbons as a potentially more important source of ozone depletion).
(5) Random events (i.e. low probability, potentially high consequence events whose actual time of occurrence is unpredictable, such as Three Mile Island and Bhopal).
(6) Dissenting scientists who go public when they cannot attract the attention of their peers.
(7) Media attention to an issue, usually initially stimulated by dissident scientists, but becoming self-sustaining.
(8) Launching of a major public investment project (e.g. USSR proposed water diversion to Caspian).

The above plurality of mechanisms by which issues are put on the public policy agenda tends to be more prevalent in North America than in the other industrialized countries, where agenda setting takes place more within the relevant communities of experts and public officials formally charged with responsibility. However, this is only a matter of degree, and decisions in all political systems seem to be becoming more open to outside events and influences. The disadvantage of the highly pluralistic style of agenda setting is that it may establish priorities among problem areas for public attention that are not well related to the objective importance of the problem (e.g. the number of people potentially affected and the seriousness or irreversibility of the effects). Relatively minor problems may receive priority treatment because of attention from the media or influential lobbying groups, while more consequential problems remain on the "back burner" until public attention is drawn to them by some random, but well publicized, incident. An international research and analysis institution not tied to national economic interests may have a comparative advantage in helping all the participating countries to mutually set more sensible priorities among candidate problems for regulation, for example.

Dr. Jack Gibbons, Director of the Office of Technology Assessment (OTA) of the US Congress, suggested that all countries, as well as the international policy community, needed some sort of less politicized priority-setting mechanism. He described this as the "equivalent of an OTA process, a distillation, from many diverse points of view, of technical judgement about issues of policy relevance". An international OTA process, he thought, would also help sort out the influences of cultural, geographical, and historical differences on the approaches of both analysts and decision makers, thereby achieving greater consistency among the priorities of policymakers in different countries.

Conclusion

On the whole, I feel the Forum on Science for Public Policy achieved most of the objectives that the organizers hoped for. There was considerable discussion of possible follow-on activities, particularly in the nature of experiments with various modes and styles of interaction between representative decision makers and analysts. The Forum developed a very useful compendium of national experiences in problems involving science. These ranged from the very interesting activities, mostly related to social policy, of the Netherlands Scientific Council for Government Policy, described by Professor Quene, to the assessment of physical, climatic, and socioeconomic impacts of very large water diversion projects in the USSR, as described by Dr. Grygory Voroppaev. A constantly recurring theme in all these accounts

CHAPTER 2

Science and Government in the USA

DONALD F. HORNIG

The advance of science and technology has always affected the political fortunes of nations and at times influenced the conduct of affairs, but it is only in very recent times that science and technology have come to be critical elements of political power. It is only during and since World War II that the relation of scientists and technicians to government and the nature of their participation in the political process have become of serious concern.

In ancient times the successive development of bronze, iron, and steel weapons was paralleled by the rise and fall of nations. The long bow was used with great effect at Crécy and Agincourt against the classic weapons of the Middle Ages. The introduction of gunpowder, and with it muskets and cannon, marked the end of the medieval castle and the beginning of modern warfare. Firearms provided a decisive advantage to those who used them and contributed to the worldwide domination of Europe and Western cultures. Nonetheless, during all these ages scientific and technological development took place outside of the sphere of government. There were few systematic efforts to develop new technologies and, with few exceptions, scientists were not involved in affairs of state.

In most of the major powers, the military continued to absorb technological advances during the nineteenth century. Ironclad warships, the railroad, the telegraph, the machine gun—each contributed to the increasingly technological character of warfare. Still, as Sir Solly Zuckerman has pointed out [1], scientific and technological progress was accepted reluctantly by the professional military establishment. Change is difficult in a hierarchy dedicated to stability so it is not surprising that innovation was not fostered or even accepted without resistance. As far as I know, scientists were not taken into the military, other than as soldiers, or even consulted in any of the

Donald Hornig is Professor of Chemistry and Director of Interdisciplinary Programs in Health at Harvard University, USA. From 1964 to 1969, he was Special Assistant for Science and Technology to the President of the US and Director of the White House Office of Science and Technology.

countries with which I am acquainted. Their role was only to provide technical support.

The big political impact of the rapidly advancing industrial technology of the nineteenth and early twentieth centuries came through the economic power it conferred on the countries that espoused it. However, the industrialization process took place with little governmental participation. In fact, in the US laissez-faire was explicitly the order of the day. Under such circumstances, there was no need for scientists to be involved in government. Although the US National Academy of Sciences was founded in 1863 to provide scientific advice to the government, its advice was hardly ever sought before the First World War. The fruits of science and technology were adopted as they became useful, but the pace and magnitude of change did not yet pose critical political problems for any of the industrializing states.

Since then there has been a transformation in the role of science and of scientists. It is now commonly accepted that science is the major transforming force of our times. That it exerts a vital influence on political and social relations is also accepted. So it comes as no surprise that, in addition to their traditional role, some scientists and technologists now engage in conducting the business of government and in providing advice over a wide spectrum of governmental activities. They are involved in the machinery of government up to the highest "levels". It is with the growth of this participation and influence that the remainder of this chapter is concerned.

A problem which I have not been able to resolve is that a large part of the literature concerning the impact of science and policy concerns the American experience. Furthermore, my own experience has been as an advisor to the American government and, for a few years, as a participant in its processes. This chapter is therefore based primarily on what transpired in the US, although, wherever possible, I compare and contrast what occurred in the US with what was done elsewhere.

Despite this narrowness of outlook, I take comfort in the realization that for the most part governmental decisions that involve science and technology, either as a source of facts or to furnish a view of the future, have not differed greatly among countries. Despite apparently dissimilar mechanisms and structures in both economic and political systems, the outcomes seem remarkably similar. Therefore, I hope that observations based largely on the US are also applicable to others.

The Transition

Most discussions of science and government begin with the Second World War, and it is true that the war was a watershed. On the other hand, the intrusion of scientists and technologists into the bureaucracies on which the modern state is built started much earlier. The theoretical model of most modern states implies a political leadership that sets policies and a bureaucracy that carries them out. Long before World War II, it had become evident that governments had to concern themselves in a variety of technical areas which involved expertise remote from the capabilities and even the consciousness of political leaders or the traditional administrative class that staffed the bureaucracies. Scientists infiltrated the civil service in such areas as the Coast and Geodetic Survey, which mapped the wilderness into which the US was expanding (1832), and the Geological Survey, which located the mineral and fuel resources so essential to economic progress (1879).

Nowhere was the infusion of experts so apparent as in agriculture. There the federal government first created a net of universities, the land grant colleges (1862), which focused on science, agriculture, and the mechanical arts. Later (1887) it created agricultural experimental stations in association with the universities to conduct demonstrations, and an agricultural extension service to bring the fruits of agricultural research to the farmers. In parallel with these developments, the Department of Agriculture developed between 1880 and 1897, when it assumed Cabinet rank. Its scientific bureaus made it possible to furnish answers to new problems raised by the opening of lands in the West, to which traditional agricultural methods did not apply, and it gradually evolved a broad political base. By 1916 no other economic interest in the US, either in or out of government, could boast such a research establishment for the application of science. The land grant colleges were both a source of supply for the Department's personnel and its representatives in the states. Through its expertise the Department of Agriculture and its constituency formed a political system that was only partly responsive to external political direction, a system in which agricultural scientists and technologists played an important part.

In this same period initiatives were made, for example, in public health services and in natural resource conservation. However, the great impact of science lay outside the governmental sphere. Science-based technologies, such as the development of electric power generation, the telephone, the radio, and especially the chemical industry, emerged and became the prototype for the innovation-oriented growth industries of the twentieth century. An intricate web of connections bound scientific discoveries, technological innovations, and industrial expansion with structural changes in the economy, the work force, and other social institutions. Through all of these routes scientific and technological change entered politics but the effect on government was indirect at best. An effort by President Franklin D. Roosevelt, for example, to deal with problems created by the Great Depression (1932–8) through a Science Advisory Board chaired by Karl T. Compton, physicist and President of the Massachusetts Institute of Technology, which would advise him and members of his Cabinet, led nowhere.

Perhaps the first indication of the more basic role of science and scientists came in the UK as signs of impending war became more numerous. In 1934 a committee of scientists under Sir Henry Tizzard was set up to advise on how air attacks might be countered. In a paper prepared for the committee, *Detection and Location of Aircraft by Radio Methods,* Robert Watson-Watt set out the principles of radar, which was to prove decisive in the air war a few years later. This was the beginning of a new relationship between science and the military. Instead of trying to meet the needs of the military as the latter saw them, the scientists began to suggest what the needs were in terms that could be dealt with by science.

A similar independent influence came when Rudolf Peierls and Otto Frisch in 1940 outlined the possibility of utilizing nuclear fission to produce a bomb of unheard-of power. There was no military requirement for such a weapon. When it was called to the attention of Winston Churchill, he remarked that he was personally content with the power of chemical explosives but felt, nonetheless, that he must not stand in the path of improvement[2]. We return later to the subsequent role of scientists in shaping policy toward the development of nuclear weapons, on the one hand, and toward international control of nuclear weapons, on the other.

World War II

The trends we have been describing became important in World War II, especially in the US and UK. Radar, the proximity fuse, jet aircraft, rockets, synthetic rubber, penicillin, and the nuclear bomb not only affected the outcome of the war but of subsequent history. As a result of the wartime experience, science and the possibilities it introduced moved to the forefront of political consciousness in the advanced nations; when peace came the entire world was aware that science was a political, economic, and social force of the first magnitude. Most thoughtful people realized that the acquisition of political power by a new group, the scientists and technologists, and their participation in decision making posed new problems for a governmental system with little previous experience in responding to or coping with this new influence. This situation was presumably not unique to the US since all of the industrialized nations responded in various ways to it.

In the US, the break with tradition started in 1940 with conferences between President Roosevelt and four scientists: Vannevar Bush (President of the Carnegie Institution), James B. Conant (President of Harvard University), Frank B. Jewett (President of the National Academy of Sciences and an industrial research leader), and Karl T. Compton (President of Massachusetts Institute of Technology—MIT). Out of these meetings came the National Defense Research Committee (NDRC), whose aim was to bring the scientific resources of the country to bear on weapons research. While taking most of its projects from the armed services, the NDRC insisted on the right of its independent judgment concerning what to undertake as well as how to conduct its business. Lacking its own laboratories, it operated by contracts with whichever universities or industrial firms could best undertake each project. In this way it mobilized the best scientific and engineering talent; in the process it revolutionized the relationship of the government to the scientific community.

Its success led, in 1941, to the formation of its successor, the Office of Scientific Research and Development (OSRD). It remained under civilian leadership, reporting to the President himself. Under OSRD such organizations as the Radiation Laboratory at MIT not only developed radar but taught the armed services to use it and even to modify their tactics to obtain optimum results. Through the OSRD, the entire scientific community, especially in the universities, was drawn into a great effort in applied science. In a variety of ways, the UK also involved its civilian scientific community in the war effort, not only as technicians but as planners. However, I am not aware that the German government made comparable use of its scientific resources.

This wartime experience in dealing with both the military and the civil governments to make things happen, as well as to develop weapons, educated a cadre of scientists who were to continue to participate in public affairs for three decades to come.

Operations Research

Another transformation in which the role of science was extended beyond purely technical matters came about when scientists began to study military operations and to advise the military about the way in which operational problems should be formulated. This was the basis for what was called operations research or operations analysis during the war, a subject which has subsequently flowered, particularly since the computer has provided the means for modeling complex situations quantitatively. It has given rise to systems analysis, to cost effectiveness studies, and to other similar derivatives.

The "terms of reference" originally suggested by Sir Robert Watson-Watt were "to examine quantitatively whether the user organization is getting from the operations of its equipment the best attainable contribution to its overall objective, what are the predominant factors governing the results attained, what changes in equipment or method can reasonably be expected to improve these results at a minimal cost in effort and in time, and the degree to which variations in the tactical objectives are likely to contribute to a more economical and timely attainment of the over-all strategic objective"[3]. Most of the operational research carried on in the Second World War fits this description.

At the technical level, operational research is chiefly concerned with the technical description of operational needs in a way that can be incorporated into design studies. It considers weapons in relation to other weapons and other tactical problems. It considers the resources a weapon will demand and relates its effect to the diversion of resources which the development and production of a weapon will call for. It examines whether the technological effort is disproportionately large or small in relation to the importance of the operational requirement it is trying to meet and whether the overall effort is properly balanced between the various projects.

At the tactical level, operations research demonstrated its value by providing real information about what happened in operations so that changes in tactics could be based on fact rather than fancy. It made people realize that what happens in an operation is not necessarily what is reported as happening by those who took part. When the strategic bombing campaign was analyzed, for example, it was apparent that almost all aspects of its effect were exaggerated—the resistance of targets, the capacity to find distant targets, and the bombing accuracy under operational conditions.

A third type of research lay in the analysis of the way military plans—both strategic and tactical—actually worked out as opposed to how they were supposed to work. In this capacity it demonstrated, for example, the much greater effectiveness of a bombing campaign designed to destroy the German railroad network, not only to dislocate military movements, but also to bring German industrial activity to a halt by disrupting the flow of materials, as compared to the alternative plan, with which it conflicted, designed for the destruction of centres of population and industry.

The extension of this type of analysis to modern economic, social, and political situations is obvious. It has brought to statecraft not just the evidence science makes available or the products it provides, but the analytical methods of science. In one mode, social and economic programs are regarded as experiments, about which facts can be gathered and the actual outcomes related to the anticipated outcomes and the various factors entering the programme. However, another mode, the prospective mode, has assumed still greater importance. It is that of applying the dispassionate methods of analysis that are used in the scientific world to foretell the way events might unfold, given these or those circumstances. It is in this latter mode that scientists have contributed to policy formation with regard to nuclear testing, arms control, energy policy, and environmental regulation, to name a few areas of importance. It has been the conviction that scientific experience and an understanding of scientific principles gives them a unique vision that has led many scientists to become involved, either in the government or in public discussion, with the determination of the course of action.

Nuclear Weapons and Arms Control

The development of nuclear bombs was the biggest single factor in developing a political consciousness in the scientific community, on the one hand, and receptiveness to advice from scientists on the other. The history of participation by scientists illustrates both the strengths and the difficulties of their entrance into the political arena. I shall not examine the substance of the arguments, but rather the scientific participation itself for what it can teach us.

As early as 1944, Niels Bohr, the famous Danish elder statesman of physics then at Los Alamos, New Mexico, sent a Memorandum to President Franklin Roosevelt in which he prophesied that atomic energy would not only "revolutionize industry and transport" but would "completely change all future conditions of warfare". He went on to argue that since science would continue to develop still newer possibilities, the only route to the security of all nations lay in scientific openness and international control of atomic energy. At about the same time, a group at the University of Chicago headed by James Franck presented a Report, based upon "their acquaintance with the scientific elements of the situation and prolonged preoccupation with its worldwide political implications". Specifically, the Report argued that the principal aim of the US should be the prevention of an atomic arms race and that international control of atomic energy provided the only means to do so. Neither the Bohr Memorandum nor the Franck Report had any effect on policy at the time, but they were read by other Manhattan Project scientists, many of whom were engaged in intensive discussions on the use of atomic weapons during the war and on controlling atomic weapons afterwards.

As was so often evident later, the scientific community was not unanimous in its opposition to using the bomb. The Interim Committee that recommended the military use of the bomb to President Harry Truman included three scientists, Vannevar Bush, Karl Compton, and James Conant, and received the advice of a panel of scientific advisors composed of J. Robert Oppenheimer, Arthur Compton, Ernest Lawrence, and Enrico Fermi. Thus arose the first political cleavage among the scientists over nuclear weapons policy.

Immediately after the war a much larger proportion of the younger members of the scientific community coalesced in opposition to the May–Johnston Bill which was to give control of atomic energy to the military. It was defeated by rank and file scientists who set out to convince the Administration, the Congress, and the nation of the need for international control. This period saw the emergence of groups, such as the Federation of American Scientists, which are still in existence today. These convictions led to enthusiastic and fairly unanimous support by scientists of the Baruch plan for the international control of atomic energy that became the basis for US policy.

The experiences of this early period in dealing with the military, the Executive, the Congress, and the public led to the growth of a cadre of scientists who were willing to venture into the political arena, first in relation to atomic energy, but subsequently into arms control, space, international co-operation, environmental problems, and other areas. The experiences of this period also made it apparent that expert scientific opinion, especially when it involved projection into the future, could not be separated from political outlook.

The deep divisions which arose in the American scientific community over the question of whether to develop the hydrogen bomb, culminating in the Oppenheimer hearings in 1950, are well known and not reviewed here. The point to be learned, though, is that the ideal of purely objective scientific judgment on matters that also involve value judgment is not attainable, and that it is precisely through adversarial discussions that the relevant scientific, as well as political, considerations are aired.

By the late 1950s debates about whether to proceed were overtaken by events. The US and USSR both had substantial stockpiles of nuclear and thermonuclear weapons, and rockets with intercontinental delivery capabilities were being deployed on both sides. Weapons testing continued and the long-term health hazards arising from radioactive debris deposited by atmospheric nuclear tests aroused other elements of the scientific community such as the biologists and health scientists. This set the stage for a discussion of the conditions for a nuclear test ban and eventually produced negotiations involving scientists as well as diplomats. They have continued until this day. The central issues were (and are) typically mixed. One issue, which was internal to each nation, was the impact of a test ban on the respective weapons development programme, while another was the possibility of detecting violations of a test ban and the means that might be developed to do so. Note that these are questions with high technical content but they are not questions to which factual "answers" can be given to policymakers. They involve scientific knowledge and experience, to be sure. They also involve the use of natural laws to predict what might happen. Finally, they involve judgments as to the likelihood that ingenious men can invent ways to evade detection and what difference this would make. It is over these judgment questions that the American scientific community was divided and it seems safe to assume that parallel discussions took place in the USSR and elsewhere.

Nonetheless, in 1958 negotiations on a possible test ban were initiated in

Geneva, Switzerland, with a Conference of Experts; experts from the USSR, the US, and the UK participated. The hope of political leaders on all sides seemed to be that the political problems could be circumvented by a technical solution. The talks soon proved that the relationship between the political and technical is far more subtle than either American scientists or political leaders realized. In any case, the talks did produce what was known as the Geneva System to "make it possible, within certain specific limits, to detect and identify nuclear explosions". The experts also *recommended* the use of these methods in a control system.

However, intertwined with the technical discussions were questions of what lower limit of detection was desired, what number and character of on-site inspections, and others. When the Conference was concluded it became clear that many questions remained ambiguous or unanswered. Pro test-ban scientists such as Eugene Rabinowitch wrote: "The success of the Geneva conference of scientists . . . has confirmed the belief of scientists that once an international problem has been formulated in scientifically significant terms, scientists from all countries, despite their different political or ideological backgrounds, will be able to find a common language and arrive at an agreed solution"[4].

This, of course, is the conviction animating the Pugwash movement, formed in 1961, which continues to actively involve Soviet and American scientists as well as many others. However, this sentiment was not shared by anti test-ban scientists such as Freeman Dyson who noted that the experts "did not know to what extent artificial concealment of nuclear explosions was technically possible"[5].

In fact, in the following years such possibilities did arise to complicate the negotiations. Finally, some observers feel, as did Robert Gilpin, that "in the mistaken belief that one can separate the technical and political aspects of national policy, American political leadership . . . assigned to a group of inexperienced private citizens the task of negotiating the first part of what might have been an extremely important arms control agreement"[6].

The Geneva Conference was a beginning, and scientific advisors have participated in all subsequent arms control discussions. However, their role has become more complex. They have participated in the formulation of public opinion through public discussion and they have acted as advisors in the various agencies of the US government that participate in the formation of American policy. Most particularly, the President's Science Advisory Committee, formed in 1958, helped to shape the attitude of the President himself, at least through 1968.

Maturing of Scientific Advice

In the first two decades after World War II the main impact of scientists was on military, space, nuclear, and disarmament policies. The scientists involved included many with administrative experience and many more who had acquired an intimate knowledge and understanding of the mechanisms and functions of government. They were largely scientists who had served in OSRD or at one of the wartime laboratories such as the Radiation Laboratory at MIT or one of the Manhattan Project District Laboratories. Others were their students or colleagues who had acquired a similar outlook. The result was a group who knew each other, had shared experiences, and were supremely confident in their ability to deal rationally and analytically with almost any problem. Their wartime successes gave them enormous prestige which they utilized well in dealing with the Executive, the Congress, and the public. It was this group that best conforms to the "Scientific Estate" described by Don K. Price[7].

This group furnished most of the membership of the President's Science Advisory Committee from its formation in 1958 until 1980. It also furnished the first Director of Defense Research and Engineering (the third-ranking executive in the Department of Defense), two Secretaries of the Air Force, an Administrator of the National Aeronautics and Space Administration, and numerous officials responsible for scientific advice to cabinet officers.

It was this same "establishment" which founded the Committee on Science and Public Policy (COSPUP) in the National Academy of Sciences and provided the membership for important committees throughout the government. Its power and influence in the late 1950s and early 1960s led to President Eisenhower's warning in his farewell address that public policy might "become the captive of a scientific–technological elite". It also led to a much broader concern by social scientists and career administrators over the special character and biases of this influential input. Many of the analyses of scientific input written at that time reflect the special character of the group and the very special class of problems on which they concentrated[8–12].

Nonetheless, this cadre built a foundation that has led to the presence of scientists in every layer of the US government, as well as scientific advisory committees at many levels. As the original problems of defense and space were dealt with increasingly by in-house scientists, the attention of the broader scientific community shifted during the 1960s and 1970s to the environment and pollution, to energy related issues, to problems of Third World development, population and world food supply, and to the question of funding and priorities for basic research.

Consequently, the impact of science and scientists has diffused. A much broader set of issues is involved and a wider spectrum of scientific backgrounds included. One has only to look at the variety of reports issued under the aegis of the US National Academy of Sciences/National Research Council to appreciate the change which has taken place. A consequence of this evolution is that many more scientists are being involved, including a higher proportion who have less understanding of the workings of government. Another is that more bureaucrats are having to learn to deal with scientists. They are baffled that scientists cannot provide hard facts, that scientific "truth" changes over time, that different scientists arrive at vastly different conclusions, and that scientists make value judgments. Most of all, they are troubled by scientists wanting to deal with the "whole problem", including recommendations for actions to be taken.

In some ways the influence of scientists is less apparent than it was in nuclear and disarmament matters. That, it seems to me, is because the issues of health, economic development, and the environment, for example, are shaped much more by economic and political considerations and less by projections of sophisticated science. Whether this is true or not, there no longer exists the homogeneous core that formerly provided leadership. The scientists involved in health and in energy resource problems, for example, have little in common.

Still, there are long-term questions concerning the interaction of science and public policy that continue in the new context. Therefore, I examine briefly two of the areas in which interaction with scientists is currently important.

Energy

Typical of the problems that currently bring scientists and policymakers together in all of the industrialized countries is the long-range energy problem. The Arab oil embargo of 1973 dramatized a situation that had been evolving in any case. Although the world had gradually turned to oil and gas as a primary energy source, it was clear that the world supply of petroleum would be exhausted within the next century, if not in a shorter time. The question of alternative energy sources has challenged all of Europe and Japan, as well as the US.

The alternative that most illuminates the issues being discussed here is that of nuclear power and the development of breeder reactors. The scientific issues relate to safety and engineering design, but they are intertwined with questions of economics, public perceptions of hazards, and the siting of plants and waste depositories. The scientific community is deeply divided between those who see nuclear power as an inevitable requirement and those, such as the Union of Concerned Scientists, who find it completely unacceptable. Moreover, the attitude adopted colours deeply the technical arguments on which each group dwells, but it is not clear whether the political attitude precedes or follows the technical arguments. Nonetheless, there is a large body of analysis concerning reactors, safety, breeders, waste disposal, and so on, with which most of the protagonists can agree[13,14]. What the debate illustrates, though, is that some of the most critical questions involve projections that can never be settled by "science courts", consensus conferences, or other devices in the absence of new data or new insights.

Another major question is that of alternative energy sources such as coal, solar energy, windmills, tidal power or ocean thermal power. These have been the subject of many studies[15–18]. Since any change in the energy base of a country involves important economic and social questions as well as international problems, the interaction between technical and policy questions is intimate. For example, in the US a Solar Energy Research Institute (SERI) was created and subsequently abandoned, as was a programme to develop and demonstrate the production of liquid fuels from coal, after billions of dollars had been spent.

An example of the dilemmas facing the world is that in the absence of nuclear power the only presently foreseeable long-term source of energy is coal. However, conversion to coal on a large scale would enhance the acid rain problem and increase the level of carbon dioxide in the atmosphere. It is clear that analysis and debate will continue, but in the end some very large decisions will have to be taken.

The Environment

Although the provision of clean water and the disposal of sewage has been a recognized problem for a long time, the modern concern for the environment derives from the exponentially growing production of chemicals, their wide dissemination in the form of pesticides, for example, and the recognition that chemicals may be an important source of cancer, birth defects, and infertility. In the US it was Rachel Carson's book, *The Silent Spring*, that caught public attention and led to the banning of DDT after passionate arguments on both sides. By the early 1960s the dissemination of DDT was so widespread that residues could be found in the body fat of all animals and man, in glaciers and in oceans, although no adverse human effects were identified. Its damaging effects on birds and wildlife were well publicized. On the other hand, it was a very effective pesticide and for a long time the principal agent for the control of mosquitoes and hence malaria. The questions faced were great economic costs versus probable ecological damage and possible adverse human health effects. The balance was different in North America and Europe than in South Asia and Africa. Since the question was one of projection from animal to human models, the international scientific community was never of one mind.

The subsequent history of toxic chemicals in the work place and the environment is an extrapolation of the original history of DDT. In general, decisive data concerning the harmful health effects of chemicals at low doses are unavailable and probably will never be determined. Extrapolation from experiments on cells or small animals rests on an uncertain scientific foundation. And yet there is reason to suspect that thousands or even millions of human beings are affected. In this stituation many scientists are inolved in developing risk estimates and providing advice. The Environmental Protection Agency has a Science Advisory Board and employs large numbers of scientists. It contracts for Environmental Impact Analyses and other studies by private consulting firms. Basic scientific studies are undertaken at universities.

Nonetheless, there is no agreement on such basic policy questions as to who and what should be protected and to what degree. Nor is it decided whether (1) chemicals should be demonstrated to be safe before they are introduced or, alternatively (2) they should be demonstrated to do damage before they are banned. It is not possible, of course, to demonstrate absolute safety.

Against this background regulation proceeds. It seems likely that the number of scientists involved, not only in doing science but in developing regulatory policy, will steadily grow. Scientists feel that the only rational way to proceed is to establish the scientific foundations. On the other hand, political scientists have been heard to assert that the primary problems are political and that the attempt to base regulation on science is a diversion. For the present, no answers are in sight.

Other environmental problems, such as that of acid rain, pose great economic, social, and political problems since not only does emission control add great costs, but any change in the source of coal used to give a lower sulphur content will upset the economies of producing regions. Since sulfur dioxide and nitrogen oxides are transported across international boundaries, these are international issues as well. All of this is complicated because the atmospheric transformation and transport is only partially understood and the health and ecological effects are very uncertain[18].

Final Remarks

In this chapter I have tried to look at historical examples of the interaction of science and national policy questions. They point to the growing importance of that interaction, if for no other reason than because of the growing number of scientists and technicians in all of the industrialized countries and the growing importance of science and technology in national economies.

The historical examples do not demonstrate any obvious distortions of the political process. It is not clear whether scientists have insufficient influence, as they allege, or are exceeding proper bounds in the way they influence political decisions, as many political scientists allege. What can be noted is that the position of scientists is based on the special knowledge they possess.

In this they are like most experts in other areas. Non-scientist politicians have traditionally expected that the role of scientists is to answer questions and to provide expert technical advice. What I have been describing is the evolution of a much broader participation by scientists, which has raised serious questions as to the circumstances under which scientists can properly go further and suggest policy as well.

As a result of the impact of science on the war and their role in both nuclear weapons questions and arms control, scientists acquired enormous prestige, both in government and with the public. At the same time the scientists felt their ability to make contributions went beyond the provision of technical expertise. They felt that their background helped them define questions in better ways and to see policy alternatives which others might miss. The question then was whether their high public standing gave them undesirable power in areas for which they were not really equipped. These questions have been widely discussed and, in some circles, the intrusion of scientists has been resented.

What is important now is to obtain a better understanding of these problems by everyone concerned and to develop mechanisms for effectively utilizing the talents of scientists while learning to appreciate their limitations as well.

References

1. Zuckerman, Sir Solly (1966) *Scientists and War* (New York, USA: Harper & Row), p. 8.
2. Churchill, W. S. (1950), *Second World War*, Vol. III (London, UK: Cassel).
3. Zuckerman, *op. cit.*, p. 18.
4. Rabinowitch, E. (1958) Nuclear bomb tests, *Bulletin of Atomic Scientists*, **14** 287.
5. Dyson, F. (1960) The future development of nuclear weapons, *Foreign Affairs*, **38** (3) 461.
6. Gilpin, R. (1982) *American Scientists and Nuclear Weapons Policy* (Princeton, USA: Princeton University Press) p. 218.
7. Price, D. K. (1965) *The Scientific Estate* (Cambridge, USA: Harvard University Press).
8. Price, *op. cit.*
9. Gilpin, R. (1962) *American Scientists and Nuclear Weapons Policy* (Princeton, USA: Princeton University Press).
10. Gilpin, R. and Wright, C. (1964) *Scientists and National Policy Making* (New York, USA: Columbia University Press).
11. Skolnikoff, E. B. (1968) *Science, Technology, and American Foreign Policy* (Cambridge, USA: MIT Press).
12. Lakoff, S. A. (1966) *Knowledge and Power* (New York USA: Free Press).
13. Nuclear Energy Policy Study Group (1977) *Nuclear Power: Issues and Choices* (Cambridge, USA: Ballinger).
14. International Atomic Energy Agency (IAEA) (1982) *Nuclear Power, The Environment and Man* (Vienna, Austria: IAEA).
15. Ford Foundation (1979) *Energy: The Next Twenty Years*, (Cambridge, USA: Ballinger).
16. Committee on Nuclear and Alternative Energy Systems, National Research Council (1979) *Energy in Transition, 1985–2010.* (San Francisco, USA: W. H. Freeman Co.)

17. Wilson Carroll (Ed)   *Coal—Bridge to the Future: Report of the World Coal Study* (Cambridge, USA: Ballinger).
18. National Swedish Environmental Protection Board (1983) *Report of the 1982 Stockholm Conference on the Acidification of the Environment* (Stockholm, Sweden: National Swedish Environmental Protection Board).

CHAPTER 3

Science and Government: A European Perspective

JEAN-JACQUES SALOMON

The Old Continent often looks to the New for good ideas which could very well have been found at home, not only in the form of seeds but as full-blown fruit. This also holds true in the case of science policy, the concept of which goes back to the beginning of the seventeenth century. One has only to read *The New Atlantis* to see that, since knowledge is power, the relationship between science and the state has institutional implications: there is already the idea here of an established body side by side with the state institutions responsible for justice, the army, education, and finances, whose sole service would be scientific research. Bacon's utopia simultaneously implied that science is useful and that the state must support it. We already find most of the functions corresponding to the development of scientific research as we know it today: scientific attachés, information services, administrators, and counselors, up to and including advisory committees to evaluate research findings, to program research, or to decide which inventions must be kept secret.

When Europe, in the aftermath of World War II, borrowed institutional models from America such as the President's Science Advisory Committee (PSAC), the Office of Science and Technology (OST), and the Special Assistant to the President for Science and Technology, it was only to rediscover institutions, functions, and objectives that Europe had itself previously originated. After all, the function of the first Academies was to advise the political powers on research being undertaken and to propose "useful" research. On the other hand, if one speaks, as Professor Hornig does in this volume, of a laissez-faire attitude by the state toward scientific matters until World War II, this is true only of the US, not of Europe. From the eighteenth century, most scientists believed not only that knowledge would increase through the support of political power, but that political power itself

Jean-Jacques Salomon is Professor of Technology and Society at the Conservatoire National des Arts et Metiers in Paris, France. He is a former head of the Science Policy Division of the Organisation for Economic Co-operation and Development (OECD) in Paris, France.

is tied to contributions from science: from Maupertuis to Fontenelle and Lavoisier, the theme of a close alliance between science and government pervades throughout the Enlightenment, with the objective of assuring, through the progress of science, the progress of humanity.

Well Before the Twentieth Century

The idea of an alliance was there, but the services rendered to the state by science—and, by the same token, the support given to science by the state—remained too limited for the relationship to take on a deliberate, organized, institutional form. On the one hand, science still promised more than it could deliver (the onset of the Industrial Revolution owes more to technique and artisans than to science and engineers); on the other hand, the cost of scientific research activities was not such that it required huge public outlays. Science did not assert itself as a government structure until the time that technology established itself as the lever of transformation in economics, society, politics, and, above all, of course, military affairs [1].

With the French Revolution, this dream began to become a reality: for the first time, science took a direct part in the conduct of affairs of state. Under the Convention of 1793, the government relied upon the advice of a group of scientists to define and implement its policy: Lazare Carnot, Gaspard Monge, Claude-Louis Berthollet, and Jean-Antoine Chaptal joined "The Mobilization of Savants of the Year II", contributing to the war effort as scientists. Napoleon Bonaparte also surrounded himself with savants (not yet called scientists) to lead his expedition to Egypt (which failed).

In fact, the two functions of science policy, support of scientific research and the utilization of results from research within the framework of national objectives—science *for* policy and policy *through* science—were fulfilled in Europe well before the twentieth century. It is true that these two objectives were only *simultaneously* achieved during very limited periods of time, warfare giving scientists the opportunity to cooperate with the state rather than to directly influence the affairs of state. Once the wars were over, scientists could be recompensed for the services they had rendered to the state by new institutions (l'Ecole Polytechnique, for instance) and educational reforms, but the institutions established to advise the government in scientific matters were dismantled immediately after the crisis passed.

The experience of the French Revolution inspired scientists in many countries to plead for state support of science. Then, with the Industrial Revolution, came the successful example of the alliance of university and industry in Germany invoked (by Charles Babbage in the UK, Louis Pasteur in France) to put an end to the policy of laissez-faire. The development of technology—the joining of university laboratory and industry—raised the question of scientific research, in economic terms of international competition, and of challenges, the "technological gaps" to be bridged. As early as 1872, Lieutenant-Colonel Strange, a Fellow of the Royal Society and a friend of Babbage, proposed the creation of a Ministry of Science, the first project of a political nature recognizing science as an important national matter. However, the *reciprocal* commitment of the state toward scientific research and of scientists toward the state would still remain limited until the beginning of the twentieth century. As in the US, the institutions created during World War I to associate scientists with the war effort were abolished immediately after the conflict ended.

But the experience between the two world wars was to be different and, in Europe, marked by the interplay of ideological debate and political conflict (scientists took positions *vis-à-vis* Nazism and Communism) and by the example of the Soviet Revolution (which defined science as a public service, "integrated" into the social system as a productive force). While in the US laissez-faire remains an article of faith, it is much more easily called into question in Europe, particularly among the leftist scientists wishing a larger intervention of the state in favor of science (J. D. Bernal in the UK, Jean Perrin in France).

Thus, as early as 1936, France became the first country among the democracies to institutionalize the joint functions of policy for science and science for policy: the government of Leon Blum (the Popular Front) created a ministerial department for scientific research, first headed by Irene Joliot-Curie and then by Jean Perrin, both Nobel laureates, and established the National Center of Scientific Research (CNRS)—the first time ever in a noncommunist country that the government assumed responsibility for basic research. The laissez-faire days were over; even pure science became an affair of state.

A Different Tradition of Interventionism

The different political context explains why, well before the US, France was ready to carry out science policy. The institutional, social, and educational contexts also explain why the dialogue between scientists, administrators, and politicians was easier. As we know, it took Albert Einstein's famous letter to draw President Franklin Roosevelt's attention to the military importance of nuclear energy (the letter was actually written by Leo Szilard: it took a Nobel prize-winner, and that particular one, to act as a mailbox between the scientists and Washington). In France, relations between researchers and government officials was facilitated by the fact that both were products of the same "les Grandes Ecoles": a graduate of the Ecole Polytechnique holding an important position in a ministry (sometimes even being the Minister) speaks the same language as a scientist.

Hence, Raoul Dautry, Minister of Armament in 1939, had no difficulty in understanding what was involved when Frèdèric Joliot-Curie presented the patent applications for artificial radioactivity to the CNRS, in terms of civilian uses (power from reactors) and military applications (explosive charges). The alliance between science and government in the US occurred after a long apprenticeship (and many misunderstandings): before marrying, the two parties had to know each other. In France, the relationship was already one of concubinage! This is also seen in the fact that the political and military arrangements to produce a nuclear weapon were taken immediately (uranium stocks from the Congo and heavy water from Norway were mobilized as of 19 May 1939—9 days after Joliot-Curie's patent applications), while the time that elapsed between the transmission of Einstein's letter to Roosevelt by Alexander Sachs, a mutual friend, and the start of the Manhattan Project was more than one year [2].

More importantly, one must remember that the American dogma, both ideological and constitutional, of nonintervention by the federal government in matters of education and research extends the economic and political theme of the free market, summed up as that state is best which intervenes least. The Old Continent, with a majority of nations having centralized governments and education and research directly subsidized by the state, reflects a tradition of economic interventionism that has never been abolished despite the more liberal policies pursued from time to time. France could be considered, with a tradition dating from Jean Baptiste Colbert's financial administration under Louis XIV, as an extreme case of centralization and *dirigisme*; but many European countries show the same tendencies.

From the point of view of scientific matters and, even more, of industrial and technological issues, Europe has never had strictly drawn boundaries separating the public and private sectors. The New Deal provoked a shock in the US as if America had become socialist, while the nationalization of enterprises in Europe extended a form of interventionism present from the beginning of the Industrial Revolution. There is, it seems to me, a close link between the European model of a "mixed" economy, semi-liberal, semi-planned, and the kind of relationship that prevailed in Europe between science and government before World War II: science and the political power have been, long since, tied together.

After Vannevar Bush pleaded his case in *Science the Endless Frontier*, it took the American Congress five years to create the National Science Foundation and another ten years to provide it with significant appropriations. This type of intervention was taken for granted in Europe following World War II: not, as in the US, in the name of economic dogma by which leaving basic research "at the mercy of market forces" condemned it to a bare subsistence level of existence, but in the name of political considerations which made this domain as legitimate an area of state concern as any other.

The American Model

The aftermath of World War II, with the birth of nuclear strategic arms, forced all industrialized countries to recognize the importance of scientific and technological research activities. But while the US had a considerable head start gained from the contributions made by European scientific émigrés to the war effort, the European countries had first to reconstruct, heal the wounds of war, and modernize their research structures. Returning from America, certain émigré scientists (for example, Pierre Auger, Bertrand Goldschmidt, von Halban, and Lew Kowarsky in France) immediately alerted their governments to the priority that must be accorded to the development of scientific and technical resources.

The French CNRS had been in some ways inspired by the Soviet Academy system: an institution with the responsibility of supporting basic research, having at its disposal proper laboratories and researchers accorded a status and security similar to those of civil servants. (This status and security became identical in 1984.) But the American experience in mastering nuclear energy imposed upon the most industrialized nations the US model of a hybrid institution that falls between private and public sectors: the Atomic Energy Commission.

Nuclear research has grown to dimensions surpassing the resources of national universities; moreover, the secrecy associated with this type of research, even when it is not military, justifies outright intervention and state control. By the same token, scientists find themselves in positions of authority not only in advisory bodies but also in the management of public institutions whose aim is not exclusively scientific.

Yet, one had to wait until 1957–1958 before all European countries had established organizations specifically responsible for the elaboration and implementation of science policy. As the alarm raised by Sputnik forced the US to institutionalize these functions at the highest level of the Executive branch, the European countries borrowed, with some variations, the model of the OST, PSAC, and the Special Assistant for Science and Technology: first Belgium, then France, then the Federal Republic of Germany (FRG).

In this diffusion of mechanisms to orient the R & D effort, the Organization for Economic Co-operation and Development (OECD) played a leading role as a catalyst: the first Ministerial Conference on Science in 1963 was attended by only four ministers responsible for scientific affairs (they were still attached to departments of education or culture); three years later, the great majority of OECD member countries were represented at a new conference by representatives with ministerial rank responsible for both the support of scientific research and the utilization of research findings within the framework of "national objectives".

It is, however, appropriate to underline three important differences in the conception and operation of these new institutions in the US and in Europe. The first is that the American bodies have no direct managerial responsibility: the OST and the PSAC have information, advisory, and orientation functions but they do not run research programs, and it is not the duty of the President's Special Assistant to be responsible for research institutions. On the other hand, the European administrations responsible for science policy have at their disposal funds that permit the launching of research programs (for example, the "concerted actions" of the Delegate General for Scientific and Technological Research in France). The President's Special Assistant is both advisor to the President and, at the same time, Director of the OST, which is only a secretariat in the Executive Office of the White House; he is not the head of an agency or an "operational" department. In France, as in other European countries (the FRG, the UK), the Minister of Science (with varying titles, rank, and responsibilities depending on the time and the country) is often both the spokesman for the concerns of the scientific community and, as well, the manager of funds, programs, laboratories, and research teams.

The second difference lies in the membership of advisory committees whose duties are to counsel the top level of government on science and technology. Originally, the PSAC did not include any representative of the social sciences and they were, only belatedly, admitted in dribs and drabs (first a specialist in the science of education, then an economist). In Europe, on the contrary, from the very beginning of these institutions, the social sciences were represented in force on these bodies. This is because the continental conception of science is more extensive than that in the UK and the US: it includes "hard" and "soft" sciences: in French, as in German (*Wissenschaft*) or even in Russian (*nauka*), "science" is not limited only to areas where research is done with physical experiments.

By the same token, this cultural or epistemological difference carries with it a different perspective on science and technology policy; from the outset, the repercussions of technological change on social development are taken into consideration in policy making: repercussions on working conditions, way of life, culture, leisure. Moreover, the support to and development of the social sciences as such (even the humanities) constitute a domain of responsibility on the part of the state which is recognized within the framework of science policies as being as legitimate, and on the same level, as physics, mathematics, or the life sciences.

The third difference, even more crucial, deals with the very concerns and activities of these institutions. In the US, the agenda has been monopolized by national security problems and military research, while in Europe these questions were dealt with by other bodies (the scientific committees responsible for advising ministers of defense). The PSAC could discuss matters such as education problems, research in the civil sector, energy, or the environment, but its essential area of responsibility and influence was defined by the scientific aspects of strategic and armament problems. In Europe, the equivalent bodies have concentrated exclusively on the scientific and technological problems of interest to the civilian sphere: education, universities, basic research, and, also, technological programs of high priority such as those on space research, oceanography, electronics, and bioengineering; which places these bodies in an industrial policy perspective.

This difference in context explains why the European countries did not have to confront the kinds of political difficulties that American advisors had to face because of the military commitments of their country: the Vietnam War and questions such as whether to go ahead with ABMs not only divided the American scientific community, but also brought in to the PSAC points of view that clashed with the policies set by the President. All these mechanisms, challenged under President Lyndon Johnson, dismantled or abandoned under President Richard Nixon, suffered from being, according to the words of a commentator who closely followed events, "a classical case of responsibility without authority" [3].

"This Era of Contestation", characteristic of the late 1960s, certainly brought controversies to Europe similar to those in the US on the social functions of science (the birth of the ecological movement, the anti-nuclear campaign, the debate on the social control of technology, and public participation in decisions concerning science and technology). But these controversies did not consequently divide the scientific community nor their representatives on advisory bodies, nor did they call into question the influence of these bodies on political power.

This difference in content also explains why the bodies responsible for science policy in Europe became more and more concerned with technological problems from the viewpoint of industrial policy. There are, of course, European countries where the objective of science policy is the development and promotion of scientific resources *stricto senso* (higher education and basic research), without infringing on other ministries' territory. This is the case, for instance, in Switzerland. However, most European countries have progressively associated science policy with technological and industrial matters. While "there was a feeling in the White House and OBM [Office of Budget Management] that the OST/PSAC mechanism was 'input' rather than 'output' oriented," [4] the European experience shows a constant concern with projects that can be translated into industrial development.

When they were not dealing with strategic questions, the American bodies were naturally condemned to consider very long-term problems—purely scientific issues regarding which the scientific advisors were accused of being both judge and defendant, or, more precisely, making themselves the advocates of a pressure group concerned above all with increasing the budget for science. On the other hand, similar bodies in Europe are concerned with the long run, formulated primarily in economic terms: in the 1960s, it was a question of bridging the "technological gap" with the US, in the 1970s, to respond to the challenge of the energy crisis; since then, to face the double competition posed by Japan and the US. The European science advisors have never neglected, obviously, to plead the cause of raising the science budget; but this cause could be as little separated from the general concern with industrial and technological policy as science policy is institutionally inseparable from technology policy.

From the American Model to the Japanese Model

All these differences could be explained by, among other reasons, differences in concepts, constitutions, and systems of government. It is not easy in the US to define and implement an industrial policy: obviously, the state cannot intervene in business as it does in Europe. So, what can be the role and influence of advisory bodies responsible for science and technology in this area? The limits of authority and responsibility between the various bodies does not facilitate coordination, especially if this is the work of an advisory body whose influence on administrators, lawyers, military men, and politicians is reduced to an informal power. The American model of science policy was born in the aftermath of war, with structures inspired by strategic necessity and the technological race between the two superpowers. With the exception of this "strategic challenge", the OST/PSAC system was not intended to have a direct effect on events.

It was therefore always obliged to fight to convince Congress that support of basic research must become an affair of state since it fails to interest the private sector. Having accepted the strategic character of science, the American system was indeed forced to recognize the fact of the inevitable merger of the public and private sectors. As Don K. Price very early underlined, "the blurring of the boundaries between business and government was the earlier blurring of the boundaries among the sciences and between science and engineering; but the more urgent reason was the need to advance weapons technology in the interest of national defense" [5].

Although inspired by the American model, the European countries did not have to worry about such high stakes nor to question themselves on the risks or limits of this "fusion of economic and political power". Leaving the strategic questions to the bodies traditionally responsible for advising the military, they were not bound by the ideology of the market nor by a strong tradition of separating the public and private sectors: by giving the bodies responsible for science policy an "output-oriented" function in the economic domain, they were only extending into a new field of government responsibility a long tradition of interventionism (and, in the case of France, of *dirigisme*). To sum up, whereas in the US, to quote the excellent formula of Don K. Price, "the federal government had to learn how to socialize without assuming ownership" [6], most of the European countries already were, with their experience of nationalizations on the one hand and the availability of an important public system of higher education on the other, old hands at such socialization.

Was the American lesson learned and applied better in Europe? Much more space would be needed to evaluate the effective influence scientists have exerted on the political decision-making process, the difficulties they have met in the course of their dialogue with administrators and politicians, and the manner in which their advice was not only taken into consideration but also affected the entire political system by more references to scientific criteria. Surely, considerations henceforth have more weight in the setting and implementation of policy in general, and the scientific advisors of the government have become such a part of the political establishment that no European country can do without them.

To say, however, that science policy is more rational than other policies because it deals with scientific matters is a rash statement. It is even more rash to believe that the art of politics in general has become more scientific because of the contributions made by scientists!

Without falling under the spell of this "positivist" illusion, one can ask to what extent the European system of scientific advisors attached to the government has won, with all due allowances, a greater legitimacy in the policy establishment than the American system. The American OST/PSAC system, reconstituted after being dismantled in 1973, has had the greatest difficulty in regaining the legitimacy and influence it had in the days of Presidents Eisenhower and Kennedy. On the other hand, in the European countries where science policy as it includes technological policy is taken into consideration, the respective bodies have long since been part of governmental responsibilities, well recognized, well established, and, in many cases, perfectly integrated. For example, the national Colloquium on research and technology organized by the socialist government of President François Mitterand has amply demonstrated how scientists can influence government decisions and how the political establishment itself gives priority to scientific and technological matters.

But the institutional model itself has evolved. "How can we become like the Americans?" wondered the European scientists who, in the aftermath of World War II, envied the research structures and potential, the ability to rally the scientific community to large-scale projects, and the number of Nobel prize-winners in the US. "How can we become like the Japanese?" is the question asked today by both American and European politicians and industrialists who envy the vitality of Japanese firms, their ability to take advantage of advanced technologies, and their winning strategies in international markets. The institutional model has moved from Washington to Tokyo: it is now the Japanese Ministry of International Trade and Industry (MITI) that serves as the point of reference, a huge intersectoral department closely associating R & D, industrial policy, and foreign trade under the same administrative supervision. Thus a Ministry of Industry and Research was established in France in 1982, inspired partly by this example.

Whichever the model, there is no doubt that the basic concerns of science and technology policy makers have also evolved. The prestige conferred by the award of a Nobel prize in the Science Olympics or by the success of a major national project such as the Apollo moon-landing is of less importance to them than the value of new products launched to conquer international markets. Science and technology policy stands from the outset on the most sensitive front of the "economic war", namely, where the R & D effort is translated into industrial modernity and exports. MITI is so much a part of Japan's success story that many people are close to seeing its structures as the panacea for the modern state. From this viewpoint, in brief, there are no more differences between Europe and the US: the Old as well as the New Continent have their fascinated eyes fixed on the Japanese.

References

1. Salomon, J.-J. (1983) What is technology? The issue of its origins and definitions, *History and Technology*, **1** (2), 113–153.
2. Weart, S. R. (1979) *Scientists in Power* (Cambridge, USA: Harvard University Press).
3. Beckler, D. Z. (1976) Science in the White House, in Holton and Blanpeid (Eds.), *Science and its Public: The Changing Relationship* (Boston, USA: Reidel), p. 128.
4. Beckler, *op. cit.*
5. Price, D. K. (1965) *The Scientific Estate* (Cambridge, USA: Harvard University Press), p. 39.
6. Price, *op. cit.*, p. 43.

CHAPTER 4

The Netherlands' Scientific Council for Government Policy

THEO QUENÉ

Main Characteristics

One of the main instruments in The Netherlands in the field of science for public policy is The Netherlands Scientific Council for Government Policy (Wetenschappelijke Raad voor het Regeringsbeleid—WRR). The WRR provides information on developments which influence society in the longer term. It tries to indicate where particular problems or conflicts of interest may be expected to arise in Government policy. The Council also has the task of coordinating Dutch research of relevance to the future. The Council is an independent advisory body, but is nevertheless directly linked with the Prime Minister's Office. The Council was officially instituted by Act of Parliament in 1976, but it had already been operating in a provisional form for nearly four years.

From the outset it is important to stress the following characteristics:

(1) According to the Act of Establishment, all reports to the Government are published; the WRR does not have to obtain Government approval for publication. The Council's freedom to publish reports that displease the Government—should such a situation arise—is part and parcel of its independence.

(2) The Government has to publish a reply to the reports. Though the Act does not specify within what period this should be done, the Lower House submitted a motion requesting that it should normally be within three months.

(3) The Council works in support of Government policy and not simply for the Government of the day. When the Council was first established, some Members of Parliament feared that it would mean a further reinforcement of the executive branch of Government only. During the

Theo Quené is the Chairman of the Scientific Council for Government Policy of the Netherlands, The Netherlands.

debate on the Act establishing the Council, the Lower House then changed the word "Government" in the Council's term of reference to "Government policy".

(4) The word "scientific" in the Council's name includes the social sciences. The word refers to the method of work: the WRR must endeavour to provide information, and problem statements and policy alternatives, in as objective a manner as possible. It must supply a basis for policy that can withstand the test of scholarly criticism. This does not preclude social, i.e. political, choices, but it does mean that the Council must not let itself be guided by party politics or other biased points of view. Hence the Council has attached importance to the principle of openness. It makes accessible all the material on which its reports are based, so that all interested parties can follow the argumentation.

(5) The Council members are appointed for a period of five years, retiring from office simultaneously at the end of their term, and may only once be reappointed for a subsequent term. This rule serves several purposes: the curtailment of too strong a position of the Council *vis-a-vis* the central government; a term of office that differs from the four-year lifetime of a Cabinet; the promotion of a steady flow of new ideas; and the encouragement of a high production.

The question may arise as to how such a rather sophisticated institution could come into being and could find a generally accepted place within the governmental machinery. To understand this, it is first of all important to underline that many politicians in The Netherlands tend to have a fairly high opinion of the contribution science can make to policy. Politics and science are not two completely separate worlds. There is an influx of scientists into politics and vice versa; it is not abnormal that one-third of the members of a Cabinet are former academics. The idea that scientific insight is essential to long-term policy making is fairly widespread among responsible policymakers.

Second, there exists a long tradition of Government planning in The Netherlands. On the national level we have three planning bureaus, for physical, economic, and sociocultural planning respectively. Throughout Dutch history a major emphasis has been placed on the thorough preparation, planning, and programming of the infrastructure, for instance, to reclaim land or to develop cities in an orderly way, as seen with the Zuiderzeepolders and Amsterdam. The National Physical Planning Agency started in 1941. Nobel prize-winner Jan Tinbergen developed economic models on a national scale even before the Second World War. Immediately after the war he became the first director of the Central (Economic) Planning Bureau. This has become the backbone of economic planning efforts in The

Netherlands. Its staff of over one hundred econometricians calculates yearly short-term projections and five-year medium-term projections. In the early 1970s, the Social and Cultural Planning Bureau began to study trends in social life, social welfare, and culture. It is clear that such a tradition of planning upholds the whole idea of science for public policy and helps to break ground for a central overarching institution in this field, like the WRR.

Finally, the structure of the WRR as an advisory council of independent experts could also rely on experiences elsewhere within the Central Government. Such councils have existed for many years in the fields of housing, public works, physical planning, health, socioeconomic policy, etc. They have proved to be useful in providing the Government with scientific and practical experience from outside the bureaucratic system. Moreover, these councils play an important role as innovative stimuli, especially when a political impasse has developed. Through experience with these councils, Government and Parliament were familiar with independent advisory institutions before the establishment of the WRR.

The main question is whether the WRR is a success or not. During the twelve years of its existence it has certainly gained considerable prestige; nevertheless, the publication of every new report is an adventure. Most of them have aroused quite a lot of political and public debate and some have made a considerable impact on Government policy. Although the Council can rely on a certain amount of public confidence, we are fully aware of the need to maintain such trust constantly by the quality of our work.

Responsibilities of the Council

The Council's responsibilities are described in the Act of Establishment as follows:

(1) To supply for Government policy scientifically sound information on developments that may affect society in the long term and to draw timely attention to anticipated anomalies and bottlenecks; to define the major policy problems and indicate policy alternatives.

(2) To provide a scientific structure that the Government could use when establishing priorities and that would ensure that a consistent policy is pursued.

(3) With respect to studies undertaken in the sphere of research on future developments and long-term planning in both public and private sectors, to make recommendations on the elimination of structural inadequacies, the furtherance of specific studies, and the improvement of communication and coordination.

It is evident that these broad terms of reference leave room for interpretation and selection. During the first two terms particular attention was devoted to points (1) and (2) of its statutory responsibilities.

It is up to the Council itself to decide which subjects it wishes to study and report on. Here again there is a difference in emphasis from term to term. The determination of its own program of work is one of the aspects in which the Council's independent position manifests itself. Even if the Government submits a request for advice to the Council, the latter is under no obligation to submit a report (although there must be sound reasons for rejecting such a request, e.g. of a scientific nature or the difficulty of fitting it into the program of work).

The Place of the Council

The Prime Minister is responsible for seeing that the Council functions in accordance with the provisions of the Act of Establishment and that, in so far as this is dependent on the Government, it can fulfill its task under optimum conditions. The contact with the Prime Minister is of great importance for the Council's work. The Prime Minister informs the Council of the Cabinet's views on its reports. The Act provides the Council with the opportunity to be heard by the Cabinet with respect to its findings, but so far this right has not been exercised. During the second Council term two general discussions were held with the Cabinet concerning the Council's work, the second of these in the presence of H.M. the Queen. Another general discussion was held at the beginning of the Council's third term.

The Council has good working relationships with the various governmental departments. Once again—while preserving the Council's independent position—it is useful from time to time to hold discussions concerning departmental policy proposals. Care is, however, taken to avoid the Council's program of work being too heavily determined by the Ministries. On this point the importance of having timely and accurate information must constantly be weighed against the objection of excessive departmental influence. Naturally, The Council has extensive contacts with the scientific world, including research commissions.

A body such as the Council can easily become an ivory tower. For a Council whose activities must constantly be directed towards society, this would be fatal. The Council maintains direct contacts at home and abroad, with one staff member having special responsibility for communications. Of particular importance in this respect is the press. Press conferences are held upon the publication of reports and certain preliminary studies. Members of the Council and the scientific staff are repeatedly interviewed or themselves write articles for the general or technical press. A newsletter is published to record the Council's activities and symposia or conferences are organized from time to time to follow up published reports.

The Council occupies a unique position within the governmental framework. It operates at the interface between science and policy, so its products must be able to withstand critical scientific scrutiny while at the same time be of policy relevance. The Council seeks where possible to satisfy both these criteria in its reports.

A consistent guideline in the Council's work has been that its reports should be designed to render a contribution towards the public dissemination of important topics. Equally, this provides a measure of the Council's effectiveness. It may not assume that its conclusions or recommendations will always be accepted as they stand; this is a matter for the Government and Parliament. The Council may, however, assume that the Government will take serious account of its reports in formulating its policies, and the Council gears its work accordingly.

The Council sees as one of its tasks the mobilization of the expertise available in society in a particular field for policy formulation. In doing so, it seeks to comply with its statutory responsibility of providing scientifically sound information on developments that may affect society in the long term. Making political decisions with respect to those developments is not a matter for experts but for politicians.

The Composition of the Council

The Act of Establishment for the WRR mandates a minimum of five members and a maximum of eleven. At present the Council consists of nine members, including the Chairman; two economists, two sociologists, one lawyer, one political scientist, one physicist, one agricultural scientist, and one public administration expert.

The office of Chairman is a full-time position. The other members of the Council are, as ordained in the Act, available for Council work for at least two working days a week.

The members of the Council are appointed by the Prime Minister on a personal basis and are not departmental officials. The Council, therefore, is a fully external advisory committee, the members of which are appointed primarily on the grounds of their expert knowledge. The Government is further concerned that the Council's composition should be such that, within the limits of what is possible at the scientific level, it reflects the diversity of society as a whole.

According to the Explanatory Memorandum accompanying the Act of Establishment, advisory members are appointed to the Council to ensure efficient coordination between the Council and the major governmental institutions whose work is closely connected with that of the Council. At the moment the following officials are advisory members of the Council: the Director of the Central (Economic) Planning Office, the Director-General of Physical Planning, the Director of the Social and Cultural Planning Office, and the Director-General of Statistics.

Responsibility for its reports resides with the Council. The advisory members advise the Council on its activities but do not bear ultimate responsibility for the Council's reports.

The Bureau

The Council has a bureau, headed by the Secretary, to assist its work. The bureau is under the jurisdiction of the Ministry of General Affairs.

At present staff positions are held by scholars from the following disciplines: economics (6), sociology (4.5), political science (3), law (3), physics (1), environmental science (1), planning (1), and business administration (0.5). The staff also includes a computer expert, and the office has a reference library.

The Budget

The Council's budget comes under Chapter III of the Government Budget (General Affairs). Apart from personnel and other expenditures, the budget also contains a fund for scientific studies commissioned from other bodies. (All figures are in Dutch guilders; one US dollar is approximately three guilders).

Financial year	1984 (guilders)
Expenditure on personnel	4,425,000
Scientific studies	950,000
Other expenditures	720,000
Total	6,095,000

The amount of money available for scientific studies is rather modest if it has to be used for the collection of data or for original studies. In practice, this is not often the case: it is often possible to ask experts to furnish the Council with insights in a specific field, which they have already at hand.

Working Methods

Immediately upon taking office the Council sets about determining a program of work for the new term. Every Council member prepares a short paper with his or her personal proposal for new topics to be studied. After intensive and lengthy discussions the Council decides to concentrate on specific subjects. For the present term these subjects are:

(1) Revision of the social security system.
(2) Constitutional, political, and sociocultural margins for Government policy.
(3) Promotion of small- and medium-sized industrial business.
(4) Economic modeling, with special emphasis on growth-impeding factors.
(5) The Netherlands in the European Community.
(6) Basic education between 6 and 16 years of age.

After the initial selection of subjects, a provisional plan is drawn up for each study. Together these plans form the program of work; past experience is that this process takes about six months.

The program is submitted for comment to the Council of Ministers, to Government departments, Parliament, a number of social organizations, and some 150 experts in the research fields being studied. The Council seeks comments on both the selection of topics and the proposed design of the studies.

The Council attaches great value to external contacts with respect to the program of work. These contacts provide it with an initial reaction from the outside world, which enables assessment. The outside world, for its part, obtains the necessary information about the Council's activities, and can react accordingly and prepare for the reports to be published. An internal working group is set up at an early stage for each subject study. These project groups are generally chaired by a member of the Council, with a member of the scientific staff as secretary. As far as possible Council and staff members belong to more than one working group, in which they work on an equal basis. In practice, the working groups operate fairly independently. They act as a gateway to the Council, i.e. they prepare the publications, and submit draft decisions on program implementation and draft discussion documents to the Council. The work in the groups is characterized by intensive discussion and numerous drafts and redrafts, which thus gradually become the outcome of a collective effort.

The Council meets, on average, every two weeks. All of the basic steps forming part of a project are discussed in these meetings. Commissioned studies of any size are submitted to the Council for approval, and the Council also decides whether specific studies carried out by staff members or outsiders should be included in the Council's Preliminary and Background Studies Series. Final texts are always submitted for the Council's approval, with a report usually being discussed ten times or so by the plenary Council before publication. Council decision making is generally on a consensus basis. In many cases, the Council has unanimously supported the final text to be published; nevertheless, there are exceptions and these are readily accepted. It is more important to formulate the precise feelings within the Council than to reach agreement on a text that hides more than it reveals. The Council has ruled that minority views have to be argued on the same level as those of the majority, and that staff are also available to document a minority view.

In a body such as the Council, the relationship between the members of the Council and members of the scientific staff is an extremely close one. The results of its work depend to a large extent on the existence of a sound working relationship between members of the Council and the staff. By statute, the composition of the Council is constantly changing; the permanent staff is the major source of continuity provided for by the Legislature. In addition, the permanent staff provide the Council with an in-built repository of expertise. The Council should not, however, be regarded as some sort of governing board that does no more than examine staff submissions. The fact that Council members are required to make at least two working days a week available for Council work shows that they make their own contribution to its work. Some Council members, moreover, act as project chairmen, playing an important directing and stimulating role (although this does not provide them with any formal status distinct from that of other Council members: all decisions are the responsibility of the Council as a whole).

The Council meets several times a year with the advisory members. All reports for publication are submitted to them for comment. These formal contacts create important working contacts at staff level with members of the various planning bureaus in The Netherlands. The Council is kept up to date with current and proposed activities within the planning bureaus by the advisory members.

Reports

To date the Council has produced twenty-five Reports to the Government. Nine reports were produced in its seond term (1978–1983). These reports cover five sectors: the socioeconomic sector; the sociocultural sector; the physical planning sector; the public administration sector; and the international sector. In addition, surveys of future developments extending over a number of sectors have been undertaken.

Apart from reports, the Council also publishes a Preliminary and Background Study Series. These contain a good deal of basic material used in the reports along with material assembled by external experts or Council staff members in the context of specific projects. The Council's aim in publishing this material is to make it accessible to interested parties. However, responsibility for the content of the studies and the views expressed in them rests with the authors. Forty such studies were produced during the second term.

In principle all the information assembled for the reports is available to the public. Information not included in reports or preliminary studies is contained in working documents and may be obtained from the Council.

Some of the reports are primarily concerned with the provision of information and the submission of alternative policy options, whereas others are more specifically advisory and provide specific recommendations. The choice between the two is determined largely by the nature of the subject under examination. On the basis of the requirement that reports should be of policy relevance, there may or may not be a case for policy alternatives to be discussed. The Council has formed the impression that its advisory reports tend to have a more marked and certainly more discernable impact. At the same time, the effectiveness and impact of its reports naturally depend primarily on their quality and content and the subsequent reaction of the community at large and the communications media. The impact on the community at large is further reflected in the views and measures adopted by the Government in response to the reports issued by the Council.

It is impossible to typify all the reports in the context of this chapter. Nevertheless, some information about four reports may give an impression of the products of the Council and of the subsequent reactions of public and Government.

Place and Future of Dutch Industries

This Report provides an analysis of the strong and weak points of the structure of Dutch industry. It showed that the situation in The Netherlands is one of deindustrialization, with potentially far-reaching consequences for the continuity of the economic system. The economic and other aims of Government policy could only be achieved by a change of policy. Particular attention needed to be paid to the improvement of the economic structure, as The Netherlands has many middle industries that occupy an intermediate position in technological terms and are extremely vulnerable to international competition. It would be wiser to focus on industries with a future. A program to improve the economic structure would have to be designed to upgrade the intermediate sector (oil, chemicals, steel), revitalize sensitive sectors (clothing, footwear, furniture), and reinforce the equipment sector (machinery and appliances, electrical goods, transport, and instruments). The Council recommended the establishment of a Government committee together with sectoral committees and a National Development Corporation that would be established for the purpose. The Government would have to provide an annual budget of two billion guilders for a period of approximately five years.

From the outset the Report attracted a great deal of attention, with extensive descriptive and analytical coverage on television and radio and in the press. The Standing Parliamentary Committee for Economic Affairs discusssed the Report with the Council. The Government issued a preliminary and then a definitive reaction; the latter within six months. The Government proposed, among others, the following measures:

(1) An Advisory Committee of independent experts would be set up, whose first task would be, against the background of the analysis of industrial problems, to review current industrial policy and the package of measures proposed by the Council. This Committee would be required to issue its report within six months. After that stage, the Advisory Committee would be asked for advice on important questions of relevance to industry.

(2) Government procurement policy would have to be expanded in order to stimulate the regeneration of the private sector. A White Paper was promised on the subject.

(3) A further reduction of the burden on the private sector was promised, with an investigation to be devoted to the question of whether more flexible or new forms of procurement of risk-bearing assets was desirable.

In the meantime, the Advisory Committee—comparable to the Council's proposed Government committee—has produced many specific proposals that have been implemented; its first recommendation, the establishment of an Industrial Project Corporation, a variant of the Council's suggested National Development Corporation, has been implemented.

In summary, the Council's Report has contributed considerably to a reappraisal of industry in The Netherlands. The regeneration of the private sector is now one of the main aims of Government policy.

A Coherent Media Policy

This Report was written at the request of the Government for advice. The request placed particular stress on technical developments that might lead to new forms of mass communication or that would at least have an impact on the mass media system, especially the functioning of the broadcasting system and the press. In addition the Council was asked to examine sociocultural and societal aspects of these new developments, including effects on employment, and to make recommendations for Government policy on the basis of the constitutionally enshrined freedom of speech.

The Council decided that the growth of possible developments does not necessarily demand Government regulation. The growth does not, however, just open up interesting new possibilities, but also contains threats to parts of the system. This applies, for example, to the public service broadcasting system and to segments of the press. The question of compatability thus arises. This may provide grounds for Government intervention, and forms the reason for the emphasis in the Report on cohesiveness in Government policy. Public service broadcasting, the private press, and new cable services need to be examined in the context of a coherent policy.

A coherent media policy will have to be based on the constitutional right of freedom of speech and opinion. This calls for a diversified media system: broadcasting, new cable services, and the press will have to continue to exist side by side, as each of these serves a particular function that is worth preserving and developing. Diversity will also have to be maintained within each of these categories. Furthermore, the implementation of cultural policy is of relevance in relation to the maintenance and distribution of, and participation in, cultural values. Finally, considerations related to industrial policy and employment play a part. In order to achieve all these objectives, the Council would give priority to two points:

(1) The maintenance of achievements from the past.
(2) In principle, to allow new technical possibilities to be developed as far as possible.

On this basis, the Council made several dozen recommendations regarding the future development of the mass media. Among others, these included the liberalization of cable networks for local television and pay-cable television. The latter should be open to the press, to enable it to maintain its position. New rules were also proposed in order to reinforce the national public service broadcasting system, which is supposed to reflect the social and cultural diversity of the nation. In this connection, new admission rules should be fixed, and a third program run by a separate broadcasting organization should be set up.

Particularly because of the topic concerned, the Report, of course, prompted a flood of reactions in the media. The Government's reaction was published in the *Medianota*, in which it expressed its views on the future development of the mass media. It certainly does not follow all the Council's recommendations, but it nevertheless contains important changes in the traditionally tricky field of Dutch mass media politics. It is now being discussed in Parliament.

Prospects for Reforming the Labor System

The marked decline in the economic situation, the growing uncertainty about the prospects for a return to full employment, and the steadily increasing expectations to which the labor system has been subject prompted the Council to examine the possible solutions that might be employed in the future for tackling problems in the labor field. In its Report on the reform of the labor system, the Council elaborated a number of policy options for dealing with problems in the labor field, the choice depending on the political persuasion of the current Government and the nature of the problems. This report is based on two underlying premises, namely, uncertainty and control. Uncertainty relates to such factors as developments in world trade and the rise in energy and raw material prices. Control here means that the future development of society is partly determined by deliberate policy measures.

The Council's aim in this Report was to identify a variety of possibilities for changing the labor system, ranging over such differing concepts as a general reduction in working hours, differentiated wage formation, or a universal basic income. The selected policy options or concepts are of such complexity that their impact extends to many sectors and aspects of Government policy. The various solutions selected on the basis of this criterion thus afford scope for policy integration. Other considerations that played a part in the choice of options included the question of whether they enjoyed sufficiently wide support in society and the need to investigate a broad spectrum of ideas and attitudes. The Council did not aim at recommending detailed measures to be taken in the short run, as it was felt that neither public opinion nor the problems themselves were ready for that. The Report and the concepts developed in it have been discussed on various occasions in the socioeconomic scientific literature. The Report has been considered as an example of a nonconventional approach to employment problems. The Government's reaction in this case took the form of a contribution to the debate; except for the rejection of the idea of a universal basic income, it did not take firm stands.

Future Studies

A separate group of reports concern the Council's future studies. In line with its statutory responsibilities to provide information on long-term developments, the Council in its first term of office carried out a general survey of the future published in 1977 under the title *The Next Twenty-Five*

Years. This report depicted the most likely developments in society up to the year 2000. It relied partly on reports of external experts commissioned by the Council.

On the basis of the experience acquired with this study, the Council in its second term also undertook a wide-ranging survey of future developments. This second survey, *A Policy-oriented Survey of the Future*, has a completely different structure. Instead of asking, as the former study did, what the future will look like, this study is explicitly policy-oriented and concentrates on examining how the future would look if various policies were implemented. In its political orientation, the Report is concerned with illuminating political choices that are of relevance for future developments and with promoting a debate based on explicit normative assumptions. Its administrative orientation is concerned with the functions of the State, the position of the Government in the constellation of social forces, the level of Government activity, and the form of local government. These matters are viewed differently by the major political movements.

The above emphasis on policy relevance means that this survey of future developments does not give rise to a sketch of developments to which a certain degree of plausibility or predictive value may be attached. Instead, it juxtaposes six scenarios expressly based on explicit normative assumptions that enjoy a demonstrable level of support in society.

The ultimate aim of the undertaking is to place the conflicts and problems arising out of long-term developments in a context that enables them to come into their own in the formulation of political opinion, current policies, and thought on the role of Government.

Public reactions to the Report, published in two volumes, have been modest. The structure of the Report seems to be too complicated; the political parties are a bit embarrassed by the open discussion of their policies. The nature of the report is such that no reaction from Government can be expected.

External Contacts of the Council

In line with the statutory provisions, reports are submitted to the Council of Ministers through the Prime Minister. From time to time there are contacts between the Chairman of the Council and the Prime Minister. Contacts are also maintained with other Ministers if a subject taken up for study by the Council so requires, which applies particularly in the case of requests for advice. The Prime Minister is always informed of contacts with other Ministries. Occasionally meetings are held in full of the Council of Ministers and the WRR, for instance concerning the working program.

The contacts with the Second Chamber of Parliament are instituted through the Presidium of the Second Chamber. In practice, meetings with a delegation of the Second Chamber are held about the working program, and occasionally after the completion of a report. These contacts are consistently held in consultation with, and in the presence of, a representative of the Prime Minister.

The major forms of contact with the scientific community are the studies commissioned by the Council. The Council's reports, to a significant extent, draw on the results of studies carried out outside the Council. Preparing and seeing these studies through to completion involved intensive mutual contact. Fortunately, there is a general willingness in the academic world to assist the Council in its work.

The Chairman and the Executive Secretary of the WRR have regular contact with the chairmen and secretaries of a number of the major central governmental advisory bodies.

Contacts with social organizations, e.g. employers' associations, trade unions, research institutes of the political parties, are partly of a general nature, for instance, when the work program is being drawn up, and partly of a more specific nature as various studies are undertaken. In the latter case, this often consists of obtaining information or seeking their views on sections of completed texts. These contacts prove indispensable for effective operation within the matrix of forces within society. In many cases, it is these social organizations that provide the Council with the information it requires. At the same time, their comments provide the Council with an impression of the reactions its reports arouse in the outside world. Nevertheless, the Council tries to avoid situations that involve bargaining, because this could endanger the most important asset of the Council: its independent position.

Developments in The Netherlands cannot be viewed in isolation from trends in other countries. It is thus of vital importance for a body such as the Council to stay in touch with comparable institutions in other countries or with foreign institutions that are able to provide the Council with useful information. Of particular importance for the Council's work are its contacts with the Organisation for Economic Co-operation and Development (OECD) in Paris.

CHAPTER 5

Long-term Forecasting for Science and Policy: Experiences in Poland

ZDZISLAW KACZMAREK

Science and politics require long-term forecasting, as has been proved by the experiences of various countries at different stages of economic development and possessing different political systems. For this reason prognoses on global and regional scales and for groups of countries bound by political and economic alliances are frequently developed.

Long-term forecasting in the fields of politics and economics and—even more so—in the field of science and technology is a risky endeavor. Such forecasts lead to uncertain results and the authors of such prognoses have often been criticized or even ridiculed. The experiences of reports of the Club of Rome and the recent criticism of the well-known *Global 2000* report serve as interesting examples. Quite a number of disappointments occurred when previous optimistic prognoses of Polish scientific and economic development were compared with the actual situation in Poland. Nevertheless, long-term forecasting is an indispensable element for undertaking rational decisions. Thus it is worthwhile to devote more attention to forecasting both in politics and science; this chapter is devoted to this particular problem. It aims to present specific features of planning in science and politics, their inter-dependency, and the role of scientists in long-term political predictions.

The Aims of Forecasting

To begin, two kinds of forecasting need to be defined. Forecasting in politics means forecasting the social and economic development of a country or region, or the whole globe, and the changes in the political and economic

Zdzislaw Kaczmarek is the Scientific Secretary of the Polish Academy of Sciences. From 1972 to 1974 he was Deputy Minister of Science, Higher Education, and Technology in Poland. The author wishes to express his thanks to Professor W. Grudzewsk, Mr. M. Kazimierczuk, and Professor I. Malechi for their contributions to this chapter.

conditions. Forecasting in science and technology means forecasting tendencies of development in research and technology in the world and within a country, evaluation of possible scientific achievements, and the perspectives of new practical applications of such results.

Forecasting is not an abstract task, but usually has some definite practical aims. On the one hand, it is an important, though not the only, condition for making current decisions at various levels of management; and on the other, it helps to inform public opinion, decision makers, and scientists as to what the direction of development and results of decisions may be like. Since the future is always—to some extent—uncertain and difficult to foresee, I stress "may be" and not "will be" like.

Prognoses in politics and science should serve particular aims that result from practical and general needs and the differences and relationships of both fields. It seems that long-term forecasting in politics may help decision makers and society to understand long-term consequences of the decisions currently taken. The prognoses concern in particular:

(1) The impact of actions undertaken on political structure and institutions.
(2) Establishing preferences in economic development.
(3) Foreseeing intermediate consequences of economic decisions in terms of social changes, changes in the environment, or participation in international trade.
(4) Development of the demographic situation and, consequently, problems of housing, education, health care, etc.

These considerations may be important on a national, regional, or global scale. It should be noted that they are of interest to politicians, scientists, and journalists in both socialist and market economy countries. These problems are also within the scope of interest of many governmental and non-governmental international organizations that often confront the views based on different political systems and cultural traditions.

The particular aims of scientific and technological prognoses are different. They help the scientific community and decision makers to define:

(1) Tendencies of development in particular fields of science and prospects for new scientific discoveries.
(2) Preferences in developing research in particular countries, expressed by long-term research programs to solve essential economic, military, or social problems.
(3) Scientific personnel and material needs according to a long-term program of research activities.

The aims of social and economic policies and the aims of science policy are interrelated, but not identical. This results not only in methodological differences in planning and forecasting, but also in conflicts of interests between the social groups representing each of these fields, particularly conflicts between scientific centers and centers of political decision making.

The Problem of Time Scale

Political decisions in the field of economic and social relations should correspond to the needs and expectations of society. This is essential in those countries based on principles of socialistic development but also concerns other political systems. A far-sighted politician should, conditions permitting, make decisions for the current period taking into account some distant perspectives in time and long-term political predictions. However, he or she will constantly be under the influence of social opinion, usually awaiting quick results of political decisions. For political decision making centers this is not only a matter of being popular in society, but also an indispensable condition for ruling.

Science and its authorities, planning and sponsoring research programs, are in an entirely different situation. In the case of fundamental research, the problem of a time horizon is of secondary importance since both the contents of a scientific discovery and the time for its completion are difficult to precisely plan. In the case of research programs of an applied character, the problem becomes more complicated. The decision to undertake and financially support this kind of program should be based on hypotheses concerning the period of its completion, the expected results, and their practical application. Institutions undertaking such decisions are usually involved in the spheres of politics or economics and want to achieve results in the shortest possible time.

A contradiction often arises between the characteristics of the research process and the interests of scientists on one hand, and the regularities of the process of making political decisions on the other. In most cases, the possibility of obtaining scientific and technical results over a longer time period is not attractive to governmental and industrial organizations, since it is contrary to the usual rules of making political or economic decisions.

An economic planner initiating a novel undertaking expects science not so much to do research on new, unknown methods, constructions, or technologies, as to exploit the knowledge already acquired to solve given technological problems immediately. He or she is more apt to support practical applications of previous scientific results rather than to support new research on the problem of interest. Situations like these cause various difficulties in the cooperation of science with the political and economic establishment. We arrive at a conclusion, then, that research planning should be done well in advance, in time to respond to the practical initiatives of politicians and decision makers. For this condition to be fulfilled it is necessary to connect planning in science with political and economic plans which have long-term perspectives. These plans, however, are to a large extent uncertain and depend on many external factors. This is the most essential discrepancy between science policy and general politics.

Long-Term Planning Methods

Long-term planning in politics and economics is more complex than in research and technology. This is conditioned by various factors that influence actual political decisions and by the high level of uncertainty as to the future development of those factors. Forecasting socioeconomic development should be based on an analysis of a set of scenarios concerning, for example, the following problems: demographic processes, international political relationships (between variants of détente and armed conflict), international trade markets, discovering new sources of raw materials, country and worldwide scientific and technological development, and internal sociopolitical processes in the country.

The possibilities of correctly predicting all these factors over a long time span are extremely limited. Long-term planning in politics and economics should take account of this uncertainty to ensure the possibility of adjusting economic development to changing situations.

The situation in science is different. Fundamental research in particular countries is conducted under the influence of world trends. Planning fundamental research is a result of regularities in the development of particular branches of science and the willingness and readiness of countries to participate in it. In many instances, as in the field of nuclear physics or space research, the costs of research exceed the resources of a single country. Hence fundamental research is more and more frequently being conducted at international research centers or is organized as international programs, implemented by national scientific institutions according to coordinated research plans.

It should be stressed that the results of fundamental research are usually published in scientific journals or presented at international conferences. The results may be easily adopted by the world scientific community, no matter what the contribution of a particular country. From the point of view of a national scientific policy, it is more appropriate for a nation to undertake its own research programs, which in due time can provide results at a level comparable with that of the most advanced laboratories in other countries. This is an important clue in forming a national research program in the area of fundamental research. It should be stressed, though, that such a policy may not be accepted by scientific communities in the countries that have less chance of success in the world's competitive research market. This may become frustrating for scientists and create conditions for a brain drain process.

Long-term planning in applied research and technological development should be linked to general social and economic development. Applied research projects should be initiated, organized, and financially supported by government agencies or economic organizations as a basis for innovations in existing industrial processes or for new undertakings in the national economy. Long-term plans for applied research and technological development should become an integral part of economic policy and be well advanced before industrial and agricultural projects are undertaken. It is obvious that new technological inventions are usually not presented in a routine way by scientific information systems.

Planning and developing applied research depends on the level of technological advance of a country. In the most developed countries the aim of scientific and technological policy is to search for new technological solutions in order to undertake the manufacture of new products; to improve the already existing production processes so as to increase the product's attractiveness and decrease the cost; to protect the environment from different forms of pollution; and to increase competitiveness in international markets.

Here the connection between fundamental and applied research is of the greatest importance since applying new scientific discoveries opens up new possibilities in technology and the economy. Examples of such interrelations may be found in the research programs of biotechnology, genetic engineering, microprocessors, etc.

The situation is different in less developed countries where the technological lag may be as great as ten to twenty years. The economic and technological development of these countries should be based, on the one hand, on extended scientific cooperation with technologically highly advanced countries and, on the other, on their own applied research programs in some fields of their economy. The task of overcoming the technological gap is extremely difficult since it is undertaken by countries of low national income level and limited financial sources for research. Such a situation demands precise forecasting and research planning to make the best use of limited financial possibilities.

The above considerations lead to certain conclusions concerning interdependencies in long-term planning in science and economics.

First, this relation is much stronger in applied than in fundamental research; in the latter case the development of particular scientific disciplines results from the evolution of science itself as seen from worldwide perspectives.

Second, the differences in time scale used in science and politics should be considered; research projects should precede economic undertakings since the time lag between scientific discovery and its application may be many years.

Third, planning for applied research and technological development should become an integral part of long-term economic planning; this is particularly important in economically and technologically less developed countries with large disproportions between the necessity for fast development and limited financial resources. It seems that the above conclusions concern both socialist and market economy countries.

Concluding this part of the chapter I would like to stress that the connection between planning in science and planning in economics is two-way: long-term political and economic projects influence the directions of the development of science, but, on the other hand, the achievements of science may modify plans and decisions in socioeconomic policy. In scenarios of political forecasts, the influence of the possible application of technological innovations should be considered. The experience of the last 50 years provides numerous proofs of the thesis that science and technological development enormously influence life and work style, as well as social relations. Nor is this influence always beneficial.

Politicians and Scientists—Cooperation Mechanisms

In his work *Science and Technology for a New Social Order*, A. Rahman pointed out that we are witnessing a specific agreement between a knowledgeable scientific elite and decision makers in politics who are the contemporary science supervisors and take decisions about its progress. According to Rahman this agreement serves only small groups and does not help in solving important social problems [1].

It seems that this opinion is too general and quite unjust, though it is true that some scientists consciously or subconsciously influence tendencies to divide our world, to increase social inequalities, and also contribute to military threats. It is not, however, a prevailing phenomenon. Contemporary science deals with important global problems, including environmental protection, improvement of life and work conditions, fighting disease, etc. In all countries scientists and politicians cooperate in establishing plans and directions for development.

One may ask how science and scientists contribute to political forecasting or long-term economic planning. It seems that the following areas of cooperation are essential: scientific analyses of the present state of economic and social relations that are objective and politically unbiased; real evaluation of the possibilities of obtaining and applying new scientific discoveries and technological solutions both domestically and abroad; working out variants in demography, social relations, international politics, etc.; and complex evaluation of the long-term social and environmental consequences of political decisions.

In order for scientists and politicians to cooperate in establishing long-term plans for development, mechanisms for joint action must be formed. Such mechanisms are difficult to generalize and undoubtedly differ in particular countries. Scientists may be involved with political and decision making authorities, for example, through participation in the activities of parliaments, governments, or political parties. Thus they pass on their knowledge and scientific way of thinking acquired at universities and research laboratories. Scientists may serve as advisors or participate in expert groups to suggest alternative solutions to decision makers or to evaluate suggested plans and methods of development. Expert reports may be prepared in scientific institutions, initiated by either decision making authorities or the scientific community. The value of scientific advice depends on the precise formulation of problems, on the objectivity and comprehensiveness of scientific opinions, and on the mutual trust of experts and decision makers.

Proper cooperation of science and politics is also important in formulating long-term programs for applied research and technological development. It seems that in the case of planning in the field of fundamental research, science is relatively independent of politics and economics. This is not possible, however, in planning research activities with definite practical aims, due both to the high costs of research and the necessity of investments indispensable for the practical application of research results.

Long-term Science Policy: Polish Experiences

Poland is a medium-sized country at a medium level of economic and technological development. Before the crisis of 1980–1983 expenditure on research and development was about 2% of national income. At the universities and research institutes, there are some 75,000 scientists and about 105,000 engineers and technicians.

Basic research in Poland is done at the Institutes of the Polish Academy of Sciences and at universities. Long-term programs of fundamental research are prepared by the Congresses of Polish Science organized by the Polish Academy of Sciences. The first Congress was held in 1951, the second in 1973, and the third will take place in 1985. Scientific priorities are thus established by the scientific community based on an evaluation of trends in science, the general tendencies of social and economic development of the country with a long time perspective, and personnel and material opportunities of Polish science. Operational plans for basic research are calculated for a five-year period in the form of over sixty research projects accepted and financially supported by the Polish Academy of Sciences and the Ministry of Science, Higher Education, and Technology. Universities and institutes, as well, may introduce and run their own research projects, based on their own financial means.

Planning applied research is more complex. The Ministry of Science, Higher Education, and Technology chooses research projects in close cooperation with the State Commission of Planning, which is responsible for the preparation of plans of social and economic development in Poland.

Practically, operational plans in the fields of both the national economy and science are done for the same five-year period, which does not allow time for proper coordination between research results and economic undertakings. It is obvious that research projects carried out in a given period may influence technology and production several years after their completion. Rational programming of scientific activities demands economic planning for the next ten or fifteen years, with serious risk and uncertainty.

To overcome these difficulties, several governmental development programs concerning the power engineering industry, housing, and coal processing have been undertaken in Poland. They include appropriate research projects, technological work, and investment plans. These programs are directly coordinated by the responsible government agencies.

In the last thirty years, since the first Congress of Polish Science, much effort has been devoted to introducing and verifying many solutions in planning research activities. The results are not encouraging. We have not succeeded in constructing a system that could harmoniously combine research projects with social and economic plans. As a consequence, a large number of research results have not been properly used in practice. It seems that in a situation of quickly changing conditions in economic activities, a greater flexibility of research programs is indispensable.

Social Implications of Scientific Policy

This problem has been considered for many years at various international conferences, and many publications have been devoted to it. While working out plans for research activities one should always ask: "What may be the social consequences of applying scientific results?"

Particularly drastic problems arise in connection with research for military needs, as well as basic research in biology, physics, and chemistry where the potential military applications are difficult to foresee. Questions are often formulated concerning the limits of scientists' responsibility for the utilization of their results to achieve goals not in conformity with social ethics. There is no doubt, however, that direct involvement of a scientist in the development of particularly severe armaments is generally highly criticized by society.

Any results of a research undertaking, applied in practice, brings about some definite social consequences, whether positive or negative, which are not always easy to identify. Research that led to the development of the automobile industry has indirectly brought about serious changes in the organization of social life, development of living settlements, and ways of spending free time. Another result is the deterioration of the ecological situation in highly developed countries. The research on genetic engineering will probably bring about some positive changes in world nutrition but its far-reaching consequences are hard to foresee. Progress in microprocessors and related equipment will probably have a great impact on the organization of production processes but, on the other hand, it may cause increased unemployment and social disturbances.

Critical views on the goals of science and the social consequences of research are indispensable. In the past, too great a priority has been given to research projects undertaken only to increase the profit of an economic organization. It seems necessary to subordinate scientific policy to basic social needs in the contemporary world. For example, the problems of human nutrition, the use of nonrenewable raw materials, the problem of environmental protection, and other similar questions.

Long-term programming of the development of science and technology should contribute to create a new, more rational and humanistic vision of the future.

Reference

1. Rahman, A. (1979) Science and technology for a new social order. *Alternatives, a Journal of World Policy*, **4** (3).

CHAPTER 6

A New Branch of Science, Inc.

HELGA NOWOTNY

The Separation of Science from Public Policy

Those responsible for scientific policy occasionally run the risk that a piece of unanticipated reality may be lurking behind the metaphorical imagery they have constructed in order to accommodate a broad spectrum of different ideas. As the organizers of the Science for Public Policy Forum remarked, the conventional link between science and public policy is to think in terms of public policy for science—a long-standing concern among a small circle of experts drawn from the natural sciences, the policy sciences, and politicians as to how to find optimal ways of funding research and of guiding the innovative process of scientific–technological development. The Forum organizers asked us, however, to consider the converse combination: science for public policy. This has, as I will try to show, both an obvious ring of familiarity, asking us to restate and perhaps clarify the directive mission contained in the pronoun, but at the same time a more provocative meaning inviting us to overcome the *de facto* separation of science from public policy.

Let me first consider the obvious meaning: science for public policy as the outgrowth of the oldest social mission of science—for the public good. Ever since the inception of modern science in seventeenth-century England, with the incisive formulations of Francis Bacon, scientists and technologists have conceived their activities in terms of noble aspirations. By linking their work to an increase in welfare—first of their own nations, but ultimately of the entire human race— they sought to reduce suffering due to the lack of means, to satisfy material wants, and to alleviate degrading labor. The collective purpose of science conceived in these broad terms has hardly changed. In the latter part of the twentieth century the common good is still on the public agenda and policies are still directed towards tangible results. As Harvey Brooks has reminded us, the standard list of fundamental human needs to which science and technology are expected to contribute is still remarkably unchanged: food and energy supply, health needs, transportation, shelter,

Helga Nowotny is a Lecturer at the University of Vienna and Director of the European Center for Social Welfare, Vienna, Austria.

personal security. Later additions seem to be the remaining items: a cleaner environment and a social system which, in the words of Harvey Brooks, facilitates rapid adaptive change while restraining the possibility of violent conflict[1].

Such additions to the standard list already signal the shift from the tangible results of science and technology, from their expected direct contributions to economic growth and welfare, to the more intangible, indirect, and mediated ones. Today, science for public policy can no longer concentrate on accelerating the rate of innovation as an aim in itself. Rather, it has increasingly become preoccupied in dealing with the unwanted and unintended effects of its direct contributions. The quest for a cleaner, safer environment is a case in point. The secondary and tertiary effects, the as-yet unknown consequences, of our interaction with the environment have become the source of our main concerns. There is an equal quest for a social system that would facilitate adaptive change and yet not be overturned by it. The expected contributions of science for public policy have shifted from the operational to the symbolic realm. Utilizing its cognitive capacities, putting knowledge as the most precious resource science has to offer at the disposal of policymakers thought to be in desperate need of it, scientific knowledge and information has become the key for managing a future whose existence is threatened by the interventions made in the past. Science, so far, holds an absolute monopoly on this kind of knowledge and, as other previous monopoly holders, it had to maintain its claims by guarding its institutional boundaries, in this case, its autonomy in the production of knowledge. This is one reason why the dividing line, separating scientific facts from values, ordinary everyday knowledge from scientific knowledge, scientific expertise from lay participation, and science from politics, is so entrenched. What science had to offer—according to its own definition of its social mission— was advice: advice held to be clean from political considerations, free from values and mere opinions, from interests and control over its later applications. Science was disinterested and neutral, committed solely to its own impartial and context-independent conception of Truth. This, at least, was the ideal.

But is such a formula sufficient? Is this what science for public policy is all about, when the pressure of taking action mounts in areas of genuine scientific uncertainty, and when the roles of what once were thought to be "hard" scientific facts amid "soft" human decision-making procedures, as Jerome Ravetz has pointed out [2], are becoming reversed and we now are confronted with the necessity for making "hard" decisions in the face of "soft" scientific evidence? While science for public policy is firmly ingrained in the social mission of science, both in the sense of tangible, instrumental results and the more intangible resource of providing information for guiding the policy processes, the lines separating science *from* public policy are also sharply drawn. Harvey Brooks states this very clearly: science and technology, he writes, cannot provide a solution by themselves. They can only generate the conditions in which a society can develop a solution[3].

But does the policy process really live up to the expectations put into it? Who does the translation from one field to the other in the first case and what happens (as invariably it does happen) if scientific findings get transformed, distorted, subject to political bargaining in the translation process? Is it really true that science "only" creates the conditions in which society can develop a solution? Are not both science and the evolution of an institutional societal framework geared towards the production of certain types of solutions, linked to each other through a common historical ancestry? Are not both, as Max Weber suggested a long time ago, embedded in the process of ongoing rationalization that happened to be both a precondition and the most important consequence for capitalism to evolve, bent on achieving a high degree of predictability and calculability, of efficiency in the domain of nature as well as within the social and economic order? While the spillover effects of the scientification of everyday life, including political institutions, has been enormous, one ought not to lose sight of the tremendous changes that science, its organization, and the concept of science have undergone in this very same process.

Thus, the innocuous looking line that restates the obvious—that science is for public policy—while at the same time separating science from public policy—by claiming that it only creates the conditions for society to develop solutions—opens up a dilemma which is becoming more acute under the pressure for new solutions on the part of science for public policy.

How Rational is the Policy Process?

The impact of the process of rationalization has been uneven: while the organization of scientific knowledge became the model of rational organization *per se*, the political process is generally viewed as lagging far behind. It is worthwhile to recall the great appeal that the scientific method once commanded as a way of settling disputes, and the futile hope that was expressed again and again, in scientific and political utopias alike, that it would be possible to arrive at similar rational procedures for solving conflicts in the political realm[4]. The dominant view of science for public policy shares some of these elements, since it rests on the implicit assumption of an underlying structural similarity of mutually converging rationalities. This assumption has been elaborated in two directions: one is the still dominant model of rational decision making that was devised especially by policy analysts, and the other one is the view that a great number of scientists hold about the nature of their input into the policy process.

This picture of a rational or, perhaps better, over-rationalizing model of the policy process has not failed to repeatedly attract well-founded criticism. Majone, among others, has pointed to an underlying deeper commitment to a teleological, end-result conception of policy making and the reliance upon a number of fictional constructs which follow from the model[5]. In a thorough review, Aaron Wildavsky highlights the essential difference that exists between puzzles—to be solved once and for all—and (policy) problems that may be alleviated, eventually superseded, and finally redefined. He declares that the "rational paradigm" is simply mistaken. It fails to adapt to the ways in which decisions are actually made, where available answers determine the kinds of questions that are asked and objectives are never the products of the seat of rationality, but dependent upon available resources[6]. Others, like Peter House, have systematically questioned the assumptions by which policy analysis was supposed to be brought into the policy process, by comparing a number of actual cases with their analytical foundations[7]. In attempting to explain why policy-oriented research seems to have had little or no direct impact on policy making, Björn Wittrock has suggested that the mismatch between the supply and the use of policy-relevant social knowledge can be traced either to a highly rationalistic conception of the policy process—the "social engineering" model—or to an "enlightenment" model that assumes that social science research does not so much solve problems as provide an intellectual setting of concepts, orientations, and empirical generalizations. He argues in favor of a third model—a dispositional one—a conception of knowledge utilization: the process is neither arbitrary and haphazard, nor entirely pre-programmed; important policy research must be there to be utilized and if conditions are propitious and important actors available, its findings might well have an impact[8].

While some of these commentaries and criticisms pertain more to the utilization of social science knowledge, there is widespread recognition of the enduring and conflicting nature of public policy issues in general which have increasingly come to include environmental and technological issues[9]. In such an enlarged view of policy analysis, the question of the epistemological foundation is also receiving renewed attention. Thus, in a recent review of policy research and a rejoinder undertaken in defense of the policy sciences as science, one consistent theme of contention between the authors was that one of their models would follow an outdated positivistic conception of science, while the policymaking process should be viewed as resting on a much broader epistemological basis[10].

While some of this ongoing dismantling of the Received View can be interpreted as a necessary correction of the immature field of policy analysis, I think that the reasons lie somewhat deeper. The Received View has been adopted not only by its proponents—over-confident about rational problem solving and about the extension of methods and tools from one realm—that of military and industrial operations—to the much more complex and ambiguous arena of political and social issues—but also has its adherents among actual decision makers and scientists alike. It conformed to the Enlightened View that science and public policy were either slowly converging in their inherent rationalities or that public policy, in order to be receptive to scientific advice and improvement, had to come to resemble more closely what a scientific model of the policy process demanded it to be. This was a highly convenient way of thinking about science for public policy, as long as it remained the exclusive concern of a relatively small circle of public policy officials and scientists involved as advisors in certain policy arenas. It fitted into an institutional arrangement, moreover, that defined public policy as falling within the competence of a relatively closed administrative-scientific coalition.

Not surprisingly, the correlative view held by many scientists involved in the policy-making process as experts or advisors carries an equally strong faith as to what good public policy is all about. It is to be guided by scientific expertise which claims authority also over the definition of good government: one that admits to strong scientific guidance in how to conduct political affairs. There was a recent reanalysis of the testimony of some 130 expert witnesses who stated their views on the necessity and desirability of creating a US Congressional Office for Technology Assessment. Most of these witnesses were of the opinion that technology is to be equated with effective intelligence which they considered to function as a substitute for an otherwise failed sense of history, of logic and purpose in the unfolding of events[11].

Although expressed in a particular context and referring explicitly only to technological expertise, such views probably accurately reflect the confident attitude of a scientific–technological élite involved in the public policy process so long as their equally held belief in the impartiality of their expertise remained unchallenged. Good science and good public policy would meet as long as both would conform to the underlying assumption of the growing convergence in their rationality. The shock and disturbance which came with public contestation were accordingly great.

Science Contested: Science for Whom?

As long as public trust in science and technology was still high and undisturbed, as long as it was a small circle of a scientific élite that functioned as advisors to governments and administrative officials, as long as the public image of science would reasonably cover what scientists themselves projected their activities to be for society—science for public policy was what good scientists did for a rational policy process[12]. The internal hierarchy of the status system was sufficiently strong to carry its weight in the public arena and the internal status system determined who a good scientist was. Looking back to the time before public contestation seems almost like looking back at a bygone age. Science and public policy have long since ceased to be bound by a relationship consisting simply of a few representatives of science and a few policy makers and officials. The public has intruded in public policy and is, so it seems, here to stay, even though it is not always easy to say who the public is. Most observers would most probably agree that a new set of political actors and new social movements have come to the fore in the stream of an altered public awareness of the impact of science and technology. They have done so, first by questioning what has been taken for granted so far, namely that science always works for better public policy; then by protesting that their concerns were not taken into account properly; and finally by claiming that science for public policy should be subject to participatory scrutiny like other inputs into the political process. Since it had become obvious that science and technology could sometimes have negative side effects and even potentially cause great harm, the assumption valid from the seventeenth century onwards that science would inevitably produce results for the public good has definitely come to its end.

Among the many repercussions that the protest phase had on the relationship between science and public policy, I want to single out those that illustrate the changes of the context in which science for public policy is defined today. This changed context reflects a new balance of the tensions inherent between science and public policy.

The first outcome is the undermining of the alleged rationality of the political process, which turned out to be far less rational than depicted by the champions of rational policy analysis. There was not one unitary decision maker but a multitude of conflicting parties. The political process showed itself to a certain degree receptive to protests, and new forms of political intervention were designed to distort, disrupt, and alter the way politics was routinely conducted. The high standards of rational decision making quickly dissolved under the eyes of the empirical observer, yielding their place to a mixture of power games, arduous negotiation processes of political bargaining, and recourse to already institutionalized conflict-solving mechanisms, such as the courts. While nothing in this is surprising to political scientists, it came as a surprise nevertheless to those who had thought that scientific advice was exempt from these ordinary forms of political rationality. When confronted with scientific advice and expertise, the policy process did not display the rationality expected. Scientific expertise was treated like any other input into the political process: as a political resource to be used by both sides, negotiable, and not necessarily "true"; in any case not endowed with higher political credibility than other inputs.

The second outcome is related to the first. It underlines the inherent difficulty in reconciling the idea of scientific knowledge, generated in accordance with its own methodological canon of objectivity and intersubjective validation, with demands of popular participation. What can be shared to a certain extent—"popularized" as the term has it—comes after scientific facts have been established and a body of knowledge validated. It is the diffusion of knowledge and, to some extent perhaps, its application that can be opened to public participation, but not the process of producing and validating scientific knowledge as such. Yet, in the public contestation phase, the objective findings of facts, their precondition as well as political consequences, were challenged. Thriving on the open disagreement of experts in public, a more transparent model of science for public policy was proposed, an adversary system that would allow for some kind of representational system of comparing scientific findings and methods of arriving at them. By juxtaposing experts and counter-experts, each chosen as trustworthy from the opposing parties, science was to become more democratic. Underlying such a proposal was of course the expression of a deeply-seated distrust of science functioning as an objective enterprise and standing above vested interests. In the public contestation, science was charged with taking sides with other powerful interest groups in society and therefore discredited as not being truly for public policy.

The other two changes affecting the dominant conception of science for public policy arose out of internal reflection and critical evaluation, notably through sociological studies of science. They show science not to be as neutral, objective, and free of social interests as the positivistic ideal of science affirmed for a long time, and claim that all scientific knowledge is socially constructed and negotiated[13]. Scientists were shown (in their own accounts of how they arrived at results) to oscillate between a usually informal context of contingency, in which they admit the uncertainty and provisional nature of the knowledge in question, and an empirical, formal context in which they justify the conclusions reached by emphasizing solely the certainty and absoluteness of the results they obtained[14]. Both of these themes represent revisions of the official model of science, the standard model confirmed by the public rhetoric of science. Although the critical dismantling of some of its features came from inside science, so did public controversies throw open the not-so-objective sides of objectivity and add the weight of context-dependency to the process of scientific inquiry. Among others, Brian Wynne has noted that it is important to see clearly that such criticisms and invitations to self-reflection are not to be taken as an all-out assault on science; nor is it a question of deliberate bias and willful distortion on the part of scientists that needs to be publicly exposed. Rather, the all-pervasive message of such studies and detailed critiques is to make a much more general point: that the definition of a scientific problem is never isolated from the political context in which it occurs, nor can political implications be completely eliminated from the course of the analysis and policy conclusions derived only at the end[15]. Put in another way, I would add: we have to recognize and accept that all scientific analyses tied to a given policy context anticipates and reacts to the often unstated assumptions of policy outcomes. The use of concepts, the substantive implications of methodological procedures, the utilization of any kind of data cannot but be impregnated with different policy meanings. To claim anything else would be utterly naive and could not be upheld in the face of overwhelming empirical evidence to the contrary. How to utilize this knowledge for better public policy purposes is, however, still another matter.

In the period of public contestation and its aftermath, science for policy has been turned into the question of "science for whom?" While the policy arena has been potentially elarged by a wider public that wanted to be heard, the lessons to be drawn from the demystification of the over-rationalized political process and the over-rationalized image of the internal workings of science are by no means clear. If we admit that policy-prone types of scientific analysis inevitably bear the marks of their contexts of justification, of contingency, and of political relevance; if we admit that the informal process of scientific reasoning, of the utilization of data, and their interpretation include much stronger doses of intuitive judgment, implicit values, and tacit procedures of persuasion—are we set on a course which leads not directly to hell, but to something akin, namely scientific relativism? Or, as many scientists (who still uphold the ideal of no science-in-public) would maintain, would a greater degree of honesty and modesty about the internal workings of the scientific process lead only to a further decline in public trust or increase public apprehensions, perhaps willfully distorted even further by the media? Is there a way out from haughty retreat behind a formal position and from apologetic relativism alike?

Between Orthodoxy and Reformism

The orthodox response has been to reassert the traditional separation of science from public policy, arguing that only then can it be *science* for public policy. Similar statements abound in the policy field dealing with risk analysis, risk assessment, and risk management. A recent study prepared by the National Research Council of the US Academy of Sciences makes an explicit distinction between risk assessment and risk management: risk assessment is to be based on scientific judgment alone and has to find out what the problems are; it should therefore be protected from political influence. Risk management, on the other hand, is defined as the process of deciding what to do about the problems. It involves a much broader array of disciplines and is aimed towards a decision about control[16]. Perhaps more clearly than other policy studies, risk analysis has been confronted with the problematic situation that is inherently at the heart of most of them: while the intention is to provide as clear and careful a basis for action as possible by diligent scientific scrutiny of the hazards that can be subject to analysis, the selection and implementation of intervention measures generally involve balancing scarce resources, political goals, changing social values, and sometimes a somewhat unpredictable public opinion[17]. Another study published by a group of the UK Royal Society, equally devoted to methods and approaches to risk analysis, reached a different conclusion in which the whole process, including risk estimation, risk evaluation, judgments on acceptability, and taking account of public opinion, is referred to as risk management[18]. The respective roles of these two parts of the process are treated differently.

The chances for a successful application of the relativistic strategy are even slimmer. Not only is relativism a highly contested philosophical position within the theory of science[19], it has few, if any, friends among practicing scientists. Even if we would leave aside the deeper philosophical issues and concentrate on a reformist plea for greater public openness about the internal side of science in which subjective judgments have their place, uncertainty abounds, and room is even made for errors—would this alone provide a better basis in the face of pressure for political action when confronted with incomplete and uncertain scientific knowledge? Although the public image of science is in urgent need of correction in the reformist vein, no miracles can be expected from this strategy if nothing else changes.

This takes us back to the questions raised at the outset of this chapter. If science only creates the conditions in which a society develops solutions, we may ask from a sociological point of view which kind of solutions are likely to emerge. If science itself takes proper notice of the increasingly recognized realm of uncertainty, due not only to the human condition of ignorance but to the knowledge gained about the interacting secondary and tertiary effects of scientific and technological interventions in the natural and social environments, the conditions are created for science *and* society to develop new kinds of solutions. On the epistemological side, this can be an intellectually exciting venture; for the policy process it might reveal some unexpected results.

So far, the historical conditions have favored one particular type of solution: the utilitarian–instrumental one. Utilitarian solutions have pressed for the increased applicability of scientific knowledge, for its industrialization and more efficient organizational forms, and for its relevance to continued innovation. The concomitant societal mechanism aiming for the distribution of the surplus thus created, for motivation of the work force, and for the smooth functioning of societal institutions has been an instrumental type of rationality concerned only with efficient and hierarchical means–ends procedures that have become the guiding principle of how social affairs are conducted in the industrialized West. Yet, we have also come to realize recently that the conditions created by science and technology have increasingly cast doubt on the adequacy of these solutions as a guide for policy. The discussions about accelerated economic growth in the face of environmental damage and the threat to the overall balance between nature and man have been only one facet of growing uneasiness. Discussions within the scientific community on how to cope with uncertainty under the outside pressure for action have underlined the limits of the utilitarian–instrumental solution.

The Rise of the Managerial Conception of Science for Public Policy

The utilitarian–instrumental solution allowed for a clear-cut separation of science from policy while maintaining at the same time a strong (utilitarian) link of science for public policy, based on a means–ends relationship. While the production of scientific knowledge needed its autonomous space, it was assumed that it would lead more or less automatically to its social utilization since this was the in-built direction for scientific technological development to take. Steering clear of too-close a contact with the political system, "not meddling in politics", science became closely enmeshed with the industrialization process and its aftermath.

Science is now confronted with new demands from the political process. As with the industrial system, the question is not so much one of direct influence or control. The scientific system has guarded surprisingly well the core of its institutional autonomy. It was at the height of industrialization in the latter part of the nineteenth century that major industries in Europe became science-based, and the split between basic and applied science was successively introduced. I see something similar occurring today, with science yielding to the powerful and all-pervasive political context that demands new scientific solutions for dealing with problems that science and technology have helped to create. An institutional split—which is also epistemological, concerning methodologies, substantive content, and professional self-understanding alike—is likely to occur within the sciences— between a public policy branch and an academic branch. But there is no ready-made kit of tools and recipes, of techniques, nor computer simulation models which can easily be drawn upon to fill the knowledge gap. Rather, the epistemological and practical basis for this latest branch in the differentiation of the sciences is yet to be created. In order to be successful, it has to have a strong epistemological tradition within at least some of the sciences themselves; it has to be ideologically attractive; it has to be politically feasible. It has to hold out the promise of conceptual power and clarity and, at least, a methodological armory that is adequate for the types of problem to be addressed. In short, it has to embody a vision of being able to meet the demands of the policy process without relinquishing its own social and cognitive identity, and without giving up its strong claims to institutional autonomy from direct political interference. In order to keep its position as monopoly holder of the most cherished type of knowledge and to be trusted by the public, confidence in its impartiality has to be restored. These criteria are met by a new conception of science for public policy which I call the managerial conception of science.

The development of the managerial conception occurred gradually and on several levels. At the height of environmental concerns, when the limits of growth and exploitation of natural resources became a newly perceived part of reality, resources were suddenly seen to be finite—to be managed for the interest of all. When technologies were threatening to get out of hand and in urgent need of new kinds of control, we started to speak of managing them. When it became clear that the new problems created through scientific–technological interventions, with their unknown, unintended, yet potentially harmful effects, could not be solved in the accustomed way—if ever at all—we switched in our rhetoric from solving problems to managing them. This is a reasonable adaptation to a new situation in which too many variables were interacting under highly uncertain temporal conditions and in which the resilience or robustness of systems had yet to be determined empirically and theoretically. The thought of management comes easily to systems thinking, as this is one of its more precisely defined roots.

The managerial conception of science for policy also contains an implicit plea for shared responsibility at a time when individual responsibility has lost all ground in the modern organization of science. It is no coincidence that it alludes to a corporate style: management of problems which cannot be solved; management of uncertainty rather than a quick and unfounded (irresponsible) hope that it disappear quickly. This contains an appeal to a multi-leveled hierarchy of responsibility adequate for the new kind of situation we are facing. In contrast to a notion like "muddling through" which Charles Lindblom proposed, with very moderate success, to explain the political process, the scientific management of problems proclaims a relatively high degree of control in the face of a sea of external uncertainties. It contains the promise of exploiting new opportunities, should they arise, and of ways to "identify and carry out actions that will allow us to change the rules of the game"[20]. In short, management, and especially scientific management, is a respectable, orderly procedure with a high degree of success in economic life, particularly within large-scale organizations. It implies a certain type of rational behavior since it is goal-oriented, but also takes account of unavoidable constraints. It has a formal and an informal side, as every student of organizational behavior knows and good management is apt to utilize both to the fullest. Contrary to the political model of accountability, defined as the electorate in Western democracies, managerial accountability rests on the assumption of a built-in hierarchical structure of duties and liabilities which is only ultimately responsible to a distant and abstract entity (the "owners") who are not supposed to interfere. Thus, one of the strong appeals of the managerial model over a kind of political model lies in the high degree of autonomy it promises to the managers—in this case, to scientists. While it has remained problematic to defend the autonomy of science in the face of its role in the political process, the managerial conception promises a way out: while not denying the need for a built-in system of responsibility, its exact nature remains shrouded in a veil of competence in the double sense of the word; competence of those who are capable to handle scientific policy matters and of those who are officially charged with handling them.

The new conception of science for public policy—as distinct from academic science research—reduces the old question of how to maintain the boundary between science and public policy to irrelevancy, since by definition scientific management of policy problems stands above the need to protect science from political intrusion. It has all the evocative power of a new mediating institution and of a new social invention in the face of otherwise unsurpassable contradictions. It is an elegant solution and I predict that it will work successfully. It can incorporate the orthodox response and the reformist strategy described above: the former by interpreting the protective line being drawn between scientific fact-finding and political decision-making as being merely an administrative procedure; the latter by proclaiming greater honesty about inherent biases in the way science works as being part of the informal side of the management process.

The new ethos of science for public policy will be that of scientific managers, and good management is for the sake of the company. The only drawback I see is the question that remains open: who is the company and who controls it?

Commentary: *Hans Landberg*

The purpose of this section is to comment on "A New Branch of Science, Inc." by Helga Nowotny; it is not an attempt to write a new section on the same topic. Her chapter presents a specific analytical perspective—a perspective which I think is both important and fruitful. I would like to divide my comments and questions into three parts to follow the general structure of her chapter. In the first two sections she characterizes and analyzes the "ideal" relation between science and society and the "ideal" model of political decision making. In the second part of the chapter Helga Nowotny deals with what she sees as a revolution—and the somewhat shocked reaction from the scientific establishment to that revolution. In the last part of the chapter, she concludes that a new "managerial" concept of

Hans Landberg is the Secretary General of the Swedish Council for Planning and Coordination of Research, Sweden.

science for public policy is growing, which will be as important, and successful, as the split between basic and applied science in the late nineteenth century—whatever she means by "successful".

Nowotny argues that the conventional approach to the link between science and public policy is to think in terms of "public policy for science". Yes, that is so: that is why "Science, Incorporated" is one of the biggest and strongest lobbying machines that ever existed. We also know of discussions that first concerned what science could do for society in a specific area, but later changed character, and ended up as discussions of what society could do for science. Usually, more money for basic research was requested, and more openly pressed, as the complexity of the policy problem increased—leading to the paradox that the most important results of science for public policy have often been policy for science.

The purpose of the first part of her chapter is to make clear that there still are problems involved in the relations between science and public policy; and obviously there are. Helga Nowotny demonstrates that there are different concepts of the relations and/or interfaces between science and policy that are disputable or, at least, could be further elaborated. A question I would like to raise, however, is whether the different concepts Nowotny discusses are really mutually exclusive. "Science, Inc." is a rather giant conglomerate and the relations and separations between science and policy are manifold.

More interesting than the fact that different theories have different epistemological bases is that all of them have been used, and have been useful, in the dialogue between the leaders of "Science, Inc." and the leaders of society. This leads me to reflect on the political process and its rationality.

The pedagogical approach in her chapter is obvious. The critique of the naive, over-rational model of the policy process is important—and perhaps especially important in the context of systems analysis and an institution like IIASA. I must confess that I wonder if this critique does not have some elements of overkill, but I will leave that question. My reaction here is perhaps only a reflection of my wholehearted support of the views expressed by Nowotny. It leads, however, to a different question, which I believe ought to be addressed: Why has the over-rational model Nowotny speaks of been accepted at all in political circles or among the political decision makers themselves? They ought to know better. For they, the real users of scientific foundations for decisions, should have a realistic understanding of the conditions governing political decisions for public policy. In her chapter, the only comment on this issue is, "This was a highly convenient way of thinking about the relationship of science for public policy, as long as it remained the exclusive concern of a relatively small circle of public officials and scientists involved as advisors in certain policy arenas. It fitted into an institutional arrangement, moreover, that defined public policy as falling within the competence of a relatively closed administrative–scientific coalition." It would be fruitful to reflect on this problem as a case of mutual benefit for two different establishments, the scientific and the political. For one establishment (in the very broad sense), it gives more resources and access to the decision-making arena, for the other, it gives "legitimacy" in the eyes of political constituencies. (An added benefit is that scientific uncertainty could even legitimate a political decision not to act.)

Such a hypothesis is hard to prove and I will certainly not try to do it here, but I do think it fits well into the interesting discussion in Helga Nowotny's chapter where she dwells on the "phase of public contestation".

She concludes that the shock to the system was great, and she is obviously right. Nowotny's remarks that the public has invaded public policy and probably will stay there, and her observations on what happened during the invasion are important and relevant. It ought to be stressed, however, that the interest of the public was directed primarily towards *policy*, not towards science. The criticism of science was a consequence of a more general skepticism toward public policy and the fact that public policy received so much of its legitimacy through science.

With this perpective I want to make a more precise comment on what Nowotny calls "the second outcome" of this period of protest on the relations between science and public policy. Here Nowotny discusses the possibilities and restraints of an extended public—or rather, popular—participation in science. She is somewhat pessimistic and underlines the difficulties of opening up the process of producing and validating scientific knowledge to outsiders.

This may be true but the point is—and it is implicit in her chapter—that what the public demanded, and needs, is not to be a judge in any internal scientific battles, but to be informed of the ambiguities, uncertainties, and, thereby, the potential of scientific results to contribute to political decisions. From this point of view, the meaning of "scientific mediation" and "popularization of science" is to point out those kinds of uncertainties. It is not to find the "united front" or a unanimous scientific standpoint, but to explain, in general terms, how science works and why scientific uncertainty is a legitimate part of the scientific process and not "bad science".

Science itself can, perhaps, not be more "democratic" in terms of scientific work itself, but the understanding of the general conditions for scientific work can certainly be more widely understood.

Her conclusion that "we have to recognize and accept that all scientific analyses tied to a given policy context anticipates and reacts to the often unstated assumptions of possible policy outcomes", must be publicized and widely understood if there will ever be a sound use of science for public policy.

The chapter ends with the key question: Well, what do we do now? Is there a way back to the old solution of a distinct separation between science and public policy, or are there possibilities in the reformist attitude (which is also called relativism)?

A brief analysis of the first alternative shows that there is no return. The discussion of a reformistic alternative is somewhat more complicated and so the answer to the key question is: managerial science is here, and is here to stay.

Is it necessary, as Nowotny does, to rank reformism and relativism in the same category and then label them as something akin to "hell"? I cannot see that an increased openness and a greater degree of honesty and modesty about the internal working of the scientific process (which is the core of the reformist program) should inevitably lead to, in philosophical terms, an unacceptable scientific relativism. I hope that her view is not based on the assumption that an increased openness would lead to "further decline in public trust or increase public apprehensions". What do we have to lose? And who expects miracles?

Finally, when Helga Nowotny presents the solution to the problem—the managerial concept of science—she describes a set of qualities among which are not only epistemological traditions already present in some of the sciences but also ideological attractiveness and political feasibility. Public confidence in the impartiality of science has to be restored if it is to be trusted by the public, summarizes the author who concludes that "these criteria are met". She describes the good qualities of managerial science in almost lyrical words and states almost in triumph that it will work successfully—without much empirical evidence to prove it or even make it probable. So lyrical that you hear a tone of irony even here. Whatever it is, Helga Nowotny has put a break on the triumphal wagon by posing the question: Who does managerial science serve and who controls it? This means—to put it another way—that the question is whether or not managerial science will be trusted by the public; and that was one of the important criteria.

If managerial science shows the image, and demonstrates the aspirations of a "multinational" Science, Inc., it will not be trusted. And then we will have to start the discussion all over again.

References

1. Brooks, H. (1981) Some notes on the fear and distrust of science, in A. S. Markovits and K. W. Deutsch, (Eds), *Fear of Science—Trust in Science* (Cambridge, USA: Oelschlager, Gunn, and Hain Publishers).
2. Ravetz, J. R. (1985) Uncertainty, ignorance and policy, this volume, Chapter 7.
3. Brooks, H. *op. cit.*
4. Mendelsohn, E. and Nowotny, H. (Eds) (1984) *Science between Utopia and Dystopia: Yearbook in the Sociology of the Sciences*, Vol. 8 (Dordrecht, The Netherlands: Reidel).

5. Majone, G. (1984) Shortcomings of the policy science approach to the analysis of the public sector, in F.-X. Kaufmann, G. Majone, and V. Ostrom (Eds) *Guidance, Control, and Evaluation in the Public Sector* (Berlin, FRG: Walter de Gruyerter).

6. Wildavsky, A. (1979) *Speaking Truth to Power* (Boston, USA: Little, Brown, and Co.).

7. House, P. (1982) *The Art of Public Policy Analysis* (Beverly Hills, USA: Sage).

8. Wittrock, B. (1983) *Policy Analysis and Policy-Making: Towards a Dispositional Model of the University/Government Interface*, Report No. 29 (Stockholm, Sweden: University of Stockholm, Sweden, Group for the Study of Higher Education and Research Policy).

9. Coates, J. (1978) What is a public policy issue? in *Judgements and Decision in Public Policy Formulation* (Washington, DC, USA: American Association for the Advancement of Science Selected Symposium 1) pp. 34–69.

10. Schneider, J., Stevens, N., and Tornatzky, L. (1982) Policy research and analysis: an empirical profile, 1975–1980, *Policy Sciences*, **15**, 99–114; Brunner, R. (1982) The policy sciences as science, *Policy Sciences*, **15**, 115–135. See also Brewer, G. and de Leon, P. (1983) *The Foundations of Policy Analysis* (Homewood, USA: Dorsey).

11. Doughty Fries, S. (1983) Expertise against politics: technology as ideology on Capitol Hill, 1966–1972, *Science, Technology, and Human Values* (Spring).

12. Nowotny, H. (1984) Does it only need good men to do good science?, in *Science as Commodity* M. Gibbons and B. Wittrock (Eds) (London, UK: Longman).

13. A good sampling of the literature can be obtained in *Social Studies of Science*.

14. Mulkay, M. (1983) Scientists theory talk, *The Canadian Journal of Sociology* **8** (2, Spring).

15. Wyne, B. (1983) *Models, Muddles and Megapolicies: the IIASA Energy Study as an Example of Science for Public Policy*, Working Paper WP–83–127 Laxenburg, Austria: International Institute for Applied Systems Analysis).

16. National Research Council (1983) *Risk Assessment in the Federal Government: Managing the Process* (Washington DC, USA: National Academy Press); Ruckelshaus, W. P. (1983) Science, risk and public policy, *Science* **221**, 1026–1028.

17. Coppock, R. (1983) *The Integration of Physio-technical and Socio-physical Elements in the Management of Technological Hazards*, mimeo (Berlin, FRG: Science Center, International Institute for Environment and Society).

18. The Royal Society (1983) *Risk Assessment. A Study Group Report* (London, UK: The Royal Society).

19. For a glimpse of an ongoing debate see Roll-Hansen, N. (1983) The death of spontaneous generation and the birth of the gene: Two case studies of relativism, *Social Studies of Science*, **13**, 481–519.

20. Clark, W. C. (1980) *Witches, Floods, and Wonder Drugs—Historical Perspectives on Risk Management*, R–22 (University of British Columbia, Canada: Institute of Resource Ecology).

CHAPTER 7

Uncertainty, Ignorance and Policy

JEROME R. RAVETZ

Introduction

My topic here is uncertainty, as it affects communication between scientists and policymakers. We can see this as a defect in the information provided by science to policy; and our task is to see how, and to what extent, this defect can be remedied. Because I believe that the problem is a serious one, and not a simple absence of the desired and normal completeness of information, I should start by putting it in perspective.

Generally, our system of provision of scientific information for policy works very well. The success of our highly sophisticated, complex, and integrated technological system depends crucially on information being available at the right place and time, and of the right quality. Not merely production and distribution, but also innovation, generally proceed in a harmony where the discords are conspicuous only because of their rarity.

The problems of scientific uncertainty and the errors of policy that result are on the margin. Generally they involve the "externalities" of the system, its interactions with its human and natural environment. But in recent years this margin has grown, both in size and significance, as unintended effects spread. Thus, the problem of disposal of hazardous wastes has become a serious nuisance for conventional industry, and threatens to cause quite serious difficulties (on top of all the others) for civil nuclear power. In these areas, revelations of uncertainty, or, still worse, ignorance, have caused a loss of confidence in those who manage industry among important sections of the public. This is most visible in the US, but it is a problem that affects all the industrialized nations.

A most salient case of ignorance is the problem of hazardous waste dumps. As the recent report of the US Office of Technology Assessment says, "The inadequacy of data on hazardous waste management is of such magnitude

Jerome Ravetz is a Professor of History and Philosophy of Science at the University of Leeds, UK.

that it obscures the scope, nature, and complexity of the problem" [1]. There is no standard definition of the term "hazardous waste"; and little information on where it is and what it does. Hence, it would appear that any realistic attack on the problem, starting now, would have a long way to go before reaching square one: the best starting point could well be a discussion of the principles of a scheme of description and classification, before drawing up such a scheme as a preliminary to the data-collection that precedes the policy-formation that guides the essential action. A bit like the house that Jack built!

All this will take time and resources, and in the meantime the policymakers must cope with the practicalities of a problem of ever-increasing intensity and aggravation. The idea that the policymaker can simply open a drawer and pull out the right scientific information, or at least the right panel of advisory scientists, is in this case extremely unrealistic.

I think that this sort of problem, where we must learn to cope with the results of past errors, and do so in the absence of effective information, is the problem most worth serious attention just now. Although it is still on the margin of our information-rich technological society, it is already sufficiently serious, and also likely to grow, that it cannot be relegated to insignificance.

Before embarking on an analysis of the problem, we would do well to consider the range of possible solutions. These may be classed as technical, political, and moral. And we may be sure, in advance, that there are no quick and easy solutions; otherwise this whole Forum would not have been necessary. On the technical side, we need science that is "better", not so much in its internal criteria of quality, but in which problems are chosen and results presented with a view to their use in the policy process. In order to achieve this improvement, there needs to be more dialogue between the two sides, and perhaps new administrative procedures to supplement the present various peer reviews. Some may think that to find still more sorts of review in the American agency system would be quite difficult. But the US National Research Council has done it, with its recent recommendations for "Managing the Process" of risk assessment in the federal government [2]. I discuss this later.

However, attempts to improve the quality of science by administrative means may suffer from the same sort of reaction that has recently afflicted attempts to improve the quality of life in general. Without commitment by those affected, or clarity of goals, such endeavors might accomplish little beyond creating another set of committees for the gratification of those whose ambitions lie that way. Hence we must include, in our analysis, the sorts of broader understanding and commitment that must be diffused among scientists and policymakers if any real improvement is to be achieved. Of course, when we depart so far from tangible problems and solutions, we are in danger of dealing in moral uplift; but I see no way of avoiding such a course, with all its known hazards to the intellect.

My own approach here is to consider the information problem as a structural, or, perhaps in the new terminology, a "generic" problem of modern high-technology civilization as it has evolved up to now. I shall concern myself not so much with policy for information in the process of production and development, but rather on the still-marginal problems of policy for its unintended effects.

Our Present Dilemmas

To explain why I'm concentrating on the nasty problems instead of the nice ones, I shall indicate some of their effects, on science and on society.

First, we have a *confusion*, what some scholars call a "cognitive dissonance". As we look about us and experience our technological environment, its airplanes and televisions, it is genuinely hard to imagine how anything could be seriously wrong. The existence of large areas of material poverty can be seen as a *negative* phenomenon: an absence of all those good things caused by some imperfection in the system of distribution. If only there were a way of taking the cash registers out of the supermarkets, poverty (in America at least) would no longer be a problem.

Yet, usually somewhere else, but made vivid to us by TV, are the things going wrong: Seveso, Love Canal, and such-like. And the invisible specter of dread disease now haunts people who were exposed at some time or another to some sort or other of industrial garbage. How can all this be? The scientists should have seen this coming. "There must be some mistake."

Out of this confusion comes *conflict*. If evil has occurred, someone must be to blame. When startled administrators and bewildered scientists must cope with a sudden crisis, they are all too easily seen by an aggrieved public as perpetrating muddle and cover-up. As whole industrial systems find themselves in crisis, such as civil nuclear power, the temptation is for everyone to blame someone, or even everyone, else. Managements, scientists, engineers, operators, legislators, regulators, environmentalists, and NIMBYs (Not-in-my-back-yarders)—all join in a merry-go-round of recrimination. A loss of confidence in the central institutions of our technological society, hard to quantify but easy to discern, is an inevitable result.

In America at least, there is a roughly quantitative measure of the conflict that results from such a breakdown: the extent of litigation. Now that the operators of the Three Mile Island plant are facing *criminal* charges for the falsification of safety and reliability records, and the default on bonds by the utility in the Pacific Northwest brings a rash of civil actions to pass the debt-parcel around, we can say that the nuclear power industry is in real trouble. And when firms manufacturing chemicals or other possibly dangerous substances take out tort-liability insurance in the half-billion dollar range, or even try to bankrupt themselves, we can say that the loss of confidence is not restricted to the nuclear industry.

Popular discontent with professions and institutions is an old story; but at present this can lead to a serious *paralysis*. For the "consent of the governed" is nowhere so necessary for government as when people's own homes and families are endangered by activities of the state. NIMBY politics may be most visibly effective in the US, because of the extreme localization of regulatory powers and the availability of the courts for campaigns of obstruction and delay. But the same phenomena can be seen elsewhere. As a result, we face the prospect that crucial sectors of industry, first nuclear power and then others, may soon approach the state of choking in their own wastes. This would *not* come from a general public disapproval of their work, but from a combination of Barry Commoner's axiom: "Everything has to go somewhere", and (in a time of breakdown of trust in governments and their experts) the universal application of the slogan "Not in *my* back yard."

This crisis in toxic-wastes disposal manifests itself in the growth of quasi-legal or illegal practices in response to a shortage of proper facilities and stringency of regulation. "Midnight" dumping and export of wastes to more accommodating territories become standard practice. The toxic-wastes trade, providing a service to which many desire access but to which few accord respect, will (rather like gambling and prostitution) be vulnerable to the influence of the irregular or illegal sectors of the economy. The fate of the drums of dioxin-contaminated soil from Seveso is one dramatic example; and the tendency for the Mafia to "adopt" toxic-wastes firms in some parts of America has been well documented.

Because of all this, I see the problems of scientific uncertainty and ignorance in policymaking as most crucial in this urgent area, what we might jocularly call "garbage-science". But we must all learn that garbage is no joking matter; and to this end I shall develop my analysis.

The Problem

Let us start with an optimistic assumption: that among policymakers, old attitudes of carelessness or rapacity toward the environment are dwindling fast. Just as previous generations learned to accept that all humans are really human in spite of differences in race, creed, or gender, now we all know that we have only one earth, and must begin to tend it properly before it is too late. The process is far from complete, of course; but as environmental problems become the focus for bruising conflicts, in politics and (in America) the courts, the lesson is brought home even to the least enlightened.

What we have to deal with are therefore survivals from the past, the attitudes, practices, and devices that have produced our present comforts—

and also our future difficulties. Among the attitudes, I need only mention briefly a few items. There is the very pervasive faith, traditionally opposed only by conservatives on the far margin of mainstream culture, that science can produce nothing but Truth, and that its products and technology can produce nothing but Good. Also, attitudes to the environment described as "good husbandry" were considered mere survivals of preindustrial society; one has the classic joke, "What's posterity done for me lately?"

A consequence of such attitudes regarding technical problems was the belief that the externalities of production are but minor problems, easily fixed—preferably by someone else. The old Yorkshire saying, "Where there's muck there's brass" expresses it well—the price of prosperity was paid by nonhumans and by lesser humans; and this was not merely in direct exploitation but also in their being uninteresting as problems, social or scientific, to the prosperous and successful. In scientific terms, corresponding attitudes were confidence in simple fixes: magic bullets for unwelcome species, and dispersion and dilution for unwelcome substances.

Even as these old attitudes die away, we will still have to cope with the structural problems of the science of unwanted things. First, and contrary to common assumption, the scientific expertise that *creates* an external problem is *not* usually adequate to its solution. Mechanical engineers, designing boilers that use radioactive fuel as a heat-source, have no expertise in the chemistry of reprocessing, or in the biological effects of radiation. Nor even do scientists using recombinant DNA techniques necessarily possess skills in pathogenicity or in microbial ecology. One might quote the 1960s slogan, "If you're part of the problem, you're not part of the solution," even though this insight may produce irritations among scientists who naturally want to maintain full control over their work and its products.

To compound the difficulty, these urgent problems frequently lie outside any single recognized branch of science. This is partly because of their novelty but also (as problems) of their inherent complexity, both scientific and social. As a result, there is always likely to be radical disagreement, over methods and even over the basic competence of participants, in a policy debate. I have defined a sort of science I call "policy science", where, typically, facts are uncertain, values in dispute, stakes large, and decisions urgent. A policy maker may say "that's life", but a traditionally trained scientist could well react, "that's not science". Whatever it is, that is the sort of problem we now confront in our attempts to manage our technological system for the best.

The problem as now presented to policymakers is a curious inversion of the traditional dichotomy of "arts" and "sciences". Then, the "hard" objective facts of science were contrasted with the "soft" subjective opinions of the literary studies. Now, by contrast, we have a need for hard decisions by politicians and administrators: "precisely how much to permit?", for which the only factual basis will usually be a mass of abstruse and strongly contested, and hence "soft", scientific evidence.

In such situations, there is a need for a new conception of science, as a basis for expectations, attitudes, and methods that are appropriate to its new role. Rather than seeing science as banishing ignorance and simply telling the policymaker what to do, we should envisage a new sort of science, working in partnership with policymaking for the control of uncertainty and the management of ignorance. I sketch some ideas on this in the following sections.

Ignorance in Technological Development

The heart of the problem of "uncertainty" is the impotence of science in meeting challenges created by the success of science-based technology. This is usually only relative and temporary, but it can be no less crucial for that, as it appears repeatedly in one crisis after another. Such limitations, one might say failures of science, are a relatively recent phenomena of public comment; and so far there is very little systematic discussion of them among scholars, educators, or publicists involved with science.

Hence it will be useful to analyze the problem from several approaches. First, we should distinguish between uncertainty and ignorance. Decision making under uncertainty has been recognized for some decades, and it has been subjected to empirical and theoretical studies that demonstrate the possibility of its being rational by certain demanding criteria. However, for uncertainty in this sense to exist, the problem as defined must have a completely articulated structure, with precise quantities, representing either values or probabilities, available at every mode. So even in this sort of uncertainty, there is little that is vague.

Ignorance is a more severe condition, though, of course, never absolute or total. A decision-problem involves ignorance when some components which are real and significant are unknown to the decider at the crucial moment. They are discovered retrospectively, when errors or pitfalls of practice are detected through things going wrong. One can imagine elaborate arrays of types of ignorance, and of responsibility for it. A possibility might actually be known to exist, but be deemed beyond credibility and so excluded from further considerations, or there might be contingencies so novel that they could not even be imagined until they occurred. As to the state of ignorance, it might be fully justified, or (at the other extremity) culpable under criminal law.

All our lives we are coping with our ignorance, sensing and processing signals from our environment that warn us of new hazards. How we do this depends on our expectations and values; the anthropologists speak of "bounded rationalities" whereby we apply filters so that our environment makes sense to us and is manageable. In these terms, persons with radically different, even conflicting, pictures of the world in general or of some policy problem can both be rational; that is, they can be coherent in their knowledge and honest in their actions. By means of such concepts we can escape from the naive scientist's faith that truth about nature is simple and uniform, and so all who disagree with him or her are either intellectually or morally sick. In this way, the contrast between the life of science and that of politics is reduced. Although the public cannot normally witness debates on problems involving mixed ignorance and knowledge in basic science, they are on open view in policy science questions. The main difference is that, in research science, participants in a debate have the luxury of suspending judgment, an option not freely available in policy science.

Indeed, for the proper management of our technologies, coping with ignorance may turn out to be more important than applying knowledge. The point has been well expressed by David D. Collingridge in his "dilemma of control" [3]. This has two horns. The first is at the birth of a new technology. At that point, its effects on its natural and social environment cannot be realistically estimated. So much depends crucially on such unknowable aspects as the rate and direction of growth, that all scenarios are speculative, with little to distinguish among them. Hence, for policy purposes, they are not probability-based uncertainties but only thinly disguised ignorance. So social control is impossible because of ignorance; then the technology grows, and eventually some effects are revealed. *Then* some might want to step in, but by that point the technology is realized in a collection of institutions, with inertia, vested interests in growth, and means of keeping critics in some degree of ignorance about their activities. Hence, social control is now impossible because of impotence; the technology rides high. Only much later, when scandals or disasters arouse public concern, can critics begin to claw their way into a position based on some knowledge and commanding some power. By then, waste of resources and damage to the environment may be considerable or even irreparable. As Collingridge presented his dilemma, it was rather stark; usually (and more so recently) the two phases are not so distinct, but as an analytical device drawing our attention to symptoms of our present state, it deserves serious consideration.

Given this inescapable, irreducible ignorance concerning the impact of new technologies, Collingridge presents an approach to a remedy. This is to apply to technology the Popperian theory of science; advance through criticism and testing. To facilitate this, not merely administrative arrangements but technological systems themselves must be specially designed. The various tendencies to entrenchment, whereby it becomes difficult or costly to replace or modify technologies, should be mitigated. Diversified and flexible technologies are in this respect preferable; though of course such a style has its own costs.

As important as anything else in Collingridge's analysis is the point that ignorance in the planning of technologies is *not* a cause of embarrassment. It is inherent in the sophisticated, powerful, rapidly evolving systems we have now developed, and on which our civilization has come to depend. When we come to terms with this, we will be better able to design systems of scientific communication whereby the information we do possess can be utilized to best effect.

Towards a New Understanding of Scientific Knowledge

In my list of the elements of a solution to the problems of uncertainty, I mentioned the improvement of the scientific information that is provided to policymakers. This is not so much a question of the results being derived more rigorously (as by tests with larger samples, more rigid protocols, more peer reviews, etc.) but rather of results being *designed* more appropriately to function as *tools* in the policy process.

I think that this new understanding of science in the policy process is a prerequisite for a genuine reform of practices, either among individual scientists or in the decision-making process. Hence, I feel free to concentrate or this rather abstract end of the problem for my contribution.

This new understanding may require a rather radical change in our common-sense image of the materials provided by science. Traditionally, we have assumed that science provides solid facts; we may use the image of hard nuggets of truth, discovered by researchers and then made available for all to use. This was the impression conveyed by nearly all philosophers of science until very recently. Those involved in research know from their experience that it never works quite that way; but there is only now beginning to emerge an explanation of scientific information that reflects that experience. Also, the nuggets image of science is reinforced by the example of the classic discoveries made by the great scientists, such as Copernicus, Galileo, Newton, and so on. As to these, I have come to see that each such discovery was as roughhewn and plastic in its early stages as the results of any other research. But they became "standardized", so that what were later considered to be their essential features were displayed in a simplified form; their actual content, as imperfect solutions to obsolete problems, was dropped from the folk-memory of science.

For examples, we may recall first that the sun-centered system of Copernicus ran counter to astronomical science (absence of stellar parallax), physical science (absence of discernible effects of earth's motions), the unanimous agreement of philosophers and Scriptural commentators, and against common sense as well. Galileo's later telescopic discoveries rendered the Aristotelian system of the heavens very implausible, but proved nothing for Copernicus. His attempt at a theoretical proof, explaining the tides on the analogy of water swishing around in a rotating bowl, was a complete failure, totally obscure in argument and predicting a single, daily tide. Newton's work was of course acclaimed as a very powerful description; but his universal gravity provided no explanatory mechanism, and was therefore considered by many to be not quite scientific. Also, some important problems were beyond the reach of Newton's conceptual and mathematical tools; later progress depended on the mathematics of Leibniz and the mechanics of Huygens. In each case the original achievement is rendered for later generations in a smoothed, standardized form, so that its difficulties and imperfections are either neglected or even made impossible to convey.

The recent reaction against the old nugget image uses metaphors like "construction" and "negotiation" to describe the processes whereby information is produced and accepted. Such terms have the connotation of denying all objectivity in scientific knowledge, and this is deliberate among scholars in this new tendency. I find this objectionable; for civilized debates on science–policy problems require the common assumption that there is something involved beyond special interests and power politics.

I therefore wish to suggest that we consider scientific information, in this context at least, as a sort of *tool*. To academically trained minds, this may seem a vulgarization of science; should we reduce scientific knowledge to the level of, say, a screwdriver? But anyone with practical experience is familiar with the "objectivity" of tools; a good tool is one which performs many functions, is robust in use, and can be adapted to new functions. A screwdriver may not look much like a "Fact", but it is certainly not merely a "relative" or "subjective" sort of thing.

By using the metaphor of "tool" for this information, we are reminded of its function, and also (most important) of its *design*. A fact may seem (especially when standardized) to have a content completely independent of the circumstances of its origin, and even of possible constraints on its range and applicability. But when we keep design in mind, we know that our information has been *shaped*, not at all necessarily by prejudice or caprice, but by some intended function. Its applicability to new functions (as, in the most salient case, physiological results combined with epidemiological information) is then an open question, that needs to be tested by experience rather than being expected to happen in the natural course of things.

Although the idea of scientific information being designed around a function may be new in theory, it is quite familiar in practice. For example, every statistical result is (or should be) stated with relation to a confidence limit; how high this is will depend on the policy context. We may put the decision on this aspect of experimental design in terms of the following question: How large a sample do you need, in order that when you say, "There's no significant evidence that A causes B, the odds against your being wrong are sufficiently high?" The higher the required odds against a false negative result, the larger the sample, and the more expensive the test. How high is sufficiently high depends on the policy question; 20–1 (95%) is common, but 100–1 (99%) may be required in particularly sensitive cases. Setting the odds against error, or setting the significance level, is therefore a policy decision in which the costs of possible error (human or environmental) are balanced against the financial and resources costs of the larger sample required for a more rigorous test.

Of course, these tools are not material devices for the accomplishment of tasks on material objects. They are part of a *system* that includes the material world, information about it, and decisions concerning actions to be done to it. We know from experience that there is no single absolute resting-point in such a system. Science only sometimes produces facts which entail a policy decision (as in the manifest danger from a particular hazard); and usually this occurs after a lengthy and complex debate that serves to stimulate and guide the research by which such conclusive facts may eventually emerge. This is doubtless a cause of inconvenience and aggravation; but with this new understanding of scientific information it should no longer be a case for confusion or lament. The removal of uncertainty in policy-related science is a hard-won result; it is achieved by the eventual production of those tools that are appropriate to the job at hand.

Further, in these terms we are enabled to recognize the essential role of *values* in the process of producing and incorporating scientific information for the decision process. We need not expect scientists to come to their research, or to their advisory roles, with minds wiped clean of commitment and prejudgments. The research they do will be guided in its choice and even in its shape by its functions for them as professional and political beings. But results that are *robust*, in being capable of withstanding criticism and being applied in new contexts and to new problems, gain the status of genuineness.

For this, they do not need to be assumed to embody some timeless truth, nor do their creators need to be devoid of human interests and concerns. The communal processes of criticism and application are sufficient to validate the objectivity of results, and the skill and integrity of those who achieved them.

Coping with Uncertainty and Ignorance

Let us now see how this new understanding can enhance our analysis of our present discontents in the application of scientific information in the policy process. We can appreciate the task as one of *design*, albeit of a new and demanding sort.

The complex system of policy formulation consists of a variety of components, each involved in tasks specific to themselves, with their own goals, institutional constraints, languages, and styles. Among them we can identify the sociotechnical systems that create the problem at hand; the research that investigates the problem; the information system that digests and presents the results of that research; the decision process that determines policy on the problem (even, at the outset, recognition of its existence); the regulatory agencies that mitigate the problem; and finally the sociotechnical system of devices used for amelioration and monitoring.

In each of these systems, the same basic facts are in play; yet in each context they are used as tools, performing special functions and taking their shape accordingly.

In any problem area, even one under relatively good control, there will be real problems of *translation* of materials from one subsystem to another. With the image of tools rather than nuggets, we can see why this is inevitable; and hence a case for self-conscious work rather than confusion or regret. If specialists in any of the subsystems were systematically aware of the necessary transformation of scientific information as it passes to them and from them, then much misunderstanding and error could be avoided.

Further, when we encounter policy problems involving severe uncertainty and ignorance, we should immediately appreciate that we have not merely an absence of the necessary information but also a problem of creating a new *design*. Any scientific results that will be produced to order will inevitably lack full conclusiveness for the problems of decision and implementation. Hence an assignment of what we may call the *burden of proof* will have to be made at each phase of the process. This is not a simple affair, in technical matters any more than in jurisprudence. Each solved scientific problem is a complex structure of evidence and inference, of which every element is shaped by the field's accepted standards of what is adequate for its functions. In different contexts, different criteria and standards are appropriate, depending on the expected or intended function of the solved problem. Hence the translation of results from one phase of the decision process to another is not merely a matter of finding equivalent technical terms; it essentially involves a reinterpretation of the "rules of evidence" from one context to another.

For example, in the case of acid rain, there are man-made processes of generation, then environmental transport and deposition, reactions in soil and water, reaction by flora and fauna, secondary effects on ecosystems, consequences on the man-made sociotechnical system, and necessary responses by units of government. These last will filter all information through the exigencies of politics. Thus it is entirely natural that information cast in terms of kilograms per hectare of deposit should be less salient to politicians; and it is therefore entirely legitimate for the media to dramatize the issues, as did *Der Spiegel* on this issue among others.

If we understand politics to include the established scientific institutions, with their various explanatory paradigms of subject-divided science, then it is also natural for the early scientific warnings to be ignored or rejected; a bit of public agitation would seem to be as necessary (and therefore as legitimate) in this context as in the other more familiar one. We should reflect on the historical fact that it took some fifteen years to spread awareness of this problem, even among scientific communities, from Scandinavia to the rest of Europe to North America. We must seriously ask how much longer the problem would have lain in dogmatic slumber if left to the academics and administrators.

As a further example of the varied uses of scientific information in the policy context, we may consider a fine-scale map that shows changes in soil acidity expected to result from continuing depositions. As such it is of ecological interest; but if its information were appropriately translated so that it presented a pictorial hit-list of doomed forests and lakes, then no matter how imprecise or even inaccurate the conclusions, such a map would have great influence over land-use predictions. It would then be an instrument of great power or value to anyone possessing prior knowledge of it. Thus, by changing one array of numbers, by simple mathematics, into a form with direct meaning for policy, the scientists would have totally transformed their report as a social possession.

The task of designing scientific information to be capable of effective use all through the policy process is a large one, whose importance and urgency has just recently been realized in the case of Risk Assessment in the Federal Government of the US.

In a pioneering venture, the Commission on Life Sciences of the National Research Council (of the US Academy of Sciences) appointed a Committee of the Institutional Means for Assessment of Risks to Public Health. In March, 1983, it issued a report: *Risk Assessment in the Federal Government: Managing the Process*. They produced a plan for the design of scientific information at that crucial phase of the policy process. The details of that plan need not concern us here; it is sufficient that the problem has been recognized by some, and with attention to all its complexities I think that a close study of that plan, applying the insights of those experienced in the relevant sciences, in methodology, and in administration would be a very worthwhile endeavor for the improvement of the processes of decision making under radical uncertainty.

Considering that study as an exercise in administration, we find some important lessons for the design of policy processes in which scientific information is used. The plan set out in that report accommodates two features of the patterns of scientific inferences: their strong dependence on context and their continuous modification through ongoing experience. The proposed system for setting inference guidelines therefore includes a mechanism for considering exceptions, and another for continuous review.

It would be useful if, in their approach to new and difficult environmental problems, agencies could accept and utilize the inescapable fact that there is no immediate or definitive solution to such problems; that the tasks of framing regulations will recur, whether planned or not. Agencies might then adopt a Plimsoll line approach; the first such "line" could only prevent barges sinking at the docks from simple overloading; gradually it becomes a more stringent and sophisticated marker for safety. In this way, the small and indeed largely symbolic advances that are inevitably the first to occur (as with acid rain) can be appreciated as prerequisites for the next, more substantial phase, rather than as merely partial victories and hence partial defeats. This is not to advocate complacency, but rather a realistic perspective for the long haul. With that, management of policymakers might be accomplished with greater skill, as they are led more gently into the frightening areas where science produces not solid facts, but only more uncertainty and even the confirmation of irreducible ignorance.

The perspective on carbon dioxide and the greenhouse effect given by Thomas Schelling would make this an ideal problem for such an experiment in long-term administrative strategy [4]. Lead times are likely to be comfortably long; mechanisms for monitoring and for less inexact forecasting can be set up without haste and panic; so that there might even be sufficient time, and sufficient general awareness of the problem, for mankind to react in a way that embodies both technical effectiveness and humane sympathy for those most at risk.

When policymakers and scientists alike develop the new common sense of scientific information as a tool, needing to be self-consciously shaped so as to be robust in the performance of its various functions, then we may see a dispelling of the confusion and acrimony that afflicts the process now, and the more effective application of science as a means for the service of mankind.

Commentary: *Ronald Brickman*

Modern industrial societies have entered a disconcerting phase in their development where scientific and technological progress seems to present governments with as many problems as it solves. The old assumption whereby any innovation issuing from scientific and technical enterprise was automatically deemed a social boon, with the proper role of government confined to nondirective promoter and client, is no longer operative. Instead, public authorities must now deal with an ever-broader array of difficult issues which science and technology raise but do not solve.

Ronald Brickman is a Public Affairs Fellow at the American Enterprise Institute in Washington, DC, USA, serving on the staff of the US Congress.

Professor Ravetz is correct in stating that the key problem before officialdom today is not applying knowledge, but managing uncertainty. Uncertainty is more than ignorance. It is also knowing what we are ignorant of. In this respect, uncertainty has increased, rather than diminished, with scientific and technological development. As the scale and sophistication of technology have grown, so have both its ability to produce multiple and far-reaching effects and our awareness of them. Science is able to establish linkages between what previously seemed remote and unrelated phenomena. But these newly discovered linkages and effects, by their nature, are often less amenable to precise scientific assessment or purely technological control. Appropriate safeguards can less easily be factored into the design of the technology itself, either because the effects are too far removed or because affected publics do not trust the technology's progenitors to make the proper adjustments. Governments are called upon to make the necessary choices just at the point where technology's impact becomes more apparent but less manageable.

If the problem were only one of the inadequacy of existing knowledge and information, the task facing public authorities would be fairly straightforward. Their principal recourse would be the reduction of these inadequacies through more and better science. But the real problem is that their choices so often entail political as well as scientific uncertainties. The scale and impact of modern science and technology now activate fundamental value conflicts within society, and the political fallout stemming from these value conflicts is what our political leaders must attempt to assess and resolve. The issue is not just determining what is known and unknown, but also determining what is acceptable and expedient.

We cannot understand the role of scientific uncertainty in public policy unless we understand the relationship between scientific and political uncertainty. To some extent, the relevance of one in deciding upon a course of action is a function of the other. Where there is social consensus, the need for scientific certainty is less important. There is little reason to establish with precision the hazardous properties of a waste dump if everyone agrees that it should be cleaned up. In turn, compelling scientific evidence can reduce, if not always eliminate, political controversy and indecision.

The real dilemmas of public policy occur where there is both scientific and political uncertainty—when neither science nor social consensus provide public authorities with clear policy prescriptions. In these cases, officials must go beyond the search for purely scientific and technical solutions. They must create institutions and procedures for reconciling scientific uncertainty and political conflict in ways that maximize the credibility and legitimacy of public action.

There are two basic strategies for attempting this reconciliation. One stresses science by developing programs of information generation in the hope that improved knowledge will overcome political controversy. The other stresses politics by developing institutions and procedures to further consensus when science is inadequate or irrelevant.

In the final pages of his paper, Professor Ravetz advocates one variation of the first approach. He stresses the need to structure the quest for scientific information in terms of the policy purposes to which it will be put. He properly points out that standards of conclusiveness and the adequacy of information cannot always be as rigorous in seeking policy solutions as they are in seeking scientific solutions. (In some cases, however, standards for policy purposes may be more rigorous, as the relationship between cigarette smoking and lung cancer would seem to illustrate.)

But Professor Ravetz's approach does not deal squarely with the problem of value conflicts. He recognizes that different value positions can distinctly shape the production and use of scientific information. But he seems to believe that whatever conflicts ensue can be resolved through the normal processes of scientific validation and cross-examination, or dissipated through the information's adaption to different uses.

I doubt, however, whether the problem of value conflicts is so easily disposed of—especially in the highly controversial and scientifically uncertain cases that are the most important in public policy. If policy-relevant science is to be an effective instrument of consensus—and this should be its primary function—then more is required than directing the attention of the scientific community to useful areas of inquiry and translating the results into policy terms. Agreement must also be reached by the principal social actors on what kinds of information entail what kinds of policy response. Procedures must be found that foster consensus on the policy implications of different stages of scientific uncertainty and on the appropriateness of alternative research strategies to overcome uncertainty. The generation of policy-useful science, in other words, should be just as much an output of, as an input to, the political process. If this is not done, the information produced will either be ignored, or will be less a tool of consensus than a weapon of confrontation.

The deployment of scientific artillery in the service of particular and often opposing political ends has become an inevitable corollary to the appearance of controversies with technical components on government agendas. When the stakes are high enough, areas of uncertainty will be sought and invaded by armies of conflicting experts. And it is these battles, not the more numerous instances where science is incorporated into the policy process without dissension, that catch the public eye. The more decisions hinge on the outcome, the more hotly contested the point, the more publicly exposed is the inability of science to fashion an agreement. This scenario, played out repeatedly in many societies over the past several years, does not augur well for the prospects of policy-relevant science, no matter how well designed, to deliver public authorities from their quandaries. As the relevance of scientific information increases, so does its propensity to become an object of dispute. The recent debates over cost-benefit analysis in the US provide a useful illustration.

In situations of conflict, scientific analysis cannot substitute for legitimate political authority. Accordingly, we should perhaps be less concerned about the design of scientific information than about the design of consensus-building institutions. Science and scientists also have an important role to play in this regard, which goes beyond providing policymakers with useful information and advice; it also requires lending their scientific stature and social authority to the decision-making process in order to improve public acceptability.

Despite surface similarities, different governments have evolved very different institutions to assimilate the scientific and political components of decision making. Their institutional choices reflect different trade-offs between expert and political judgment, rationality and expediency, and peer and public accountability. Moreover, their choices are not random but the product of different political histories and circumstances. And they show a varying aptitude for dealing with the dual demands of political and scientific uncertainty.

An adversarial culture such as that of the US gives to science a different policy status and dynamic force than do more hierarchically organized polities like those of Western Europe. These differences are readily revealed in a number of concrete indicators: the substantially greater resources in technical expertise of US agencies, their greater expenditures on R & D, the obsession with policy analysis and evaluation, and the apparent need for any serious actor in the political process, including Congress and interest groups, to have an independent analytical capability.

The reason science and analysis loom so large in the US context is the relative absence of other legitimate sources of authority on which to base an acceptable course of action. The American political system is remarkable for its failure to give any single political entity sufficient stature and power to act in the public interest. Enmeshed in a complicated web of checks and balances, the American polity turns to science to deliver the policy solutions that its political processes are unable to provide.

Other governments, although they use science, do not need it to the same extent. This is because they have greater access to other mechanisms for resolving issues. These include a strong bureaucracy enjoying considerable public deference, a politically compatible governing cabinet and legislative majority, fewer opportunities for judicial court review, and a continuous cooptation into decision making of the most powerful groups affected. In this context, there is less need to formulate and defend policy positions in rationalistic terms. By the same token, scientific uncertainty is less of a liability, since the political system has alternative means to compensate for its effects.

By elevating science to a more central position in public debate and policy deliberation, the American system places a premium on the generation of information relevant to the analysis of technical issues. Its open, adversarial processes are well suited to distinguish fact from value and to prevent the appropriation of political power by those in control of relevant knowledge. European governments are often able to limit the politicization of the scientific debate but also often leave the respective contributions of science and politics to policy outcomes more a matter of public ignorance or ambiguity.

We should try to focus on how science can be a better servant of public policy, not on how public policy can be a better servant of science. Toward this end, we must examine not only the limitations of science but also the limitations of our policy-making processes. Unlike the former, the latter vary from country to country, and are thus subject to comparative examination and appraisal. With a better understanding of the fundamental constraints under which these processes operate and evolve, we can make more enlightened choices in marshalling the resources of science to serve public purposes.

References

1. Office of Technology Assessment (1983) *Technology and Management Strategies for Hazardous Waste Control* (Washington, DC, USA: Office of Technology Assessment).
2. National Research Council (1983) *Risk Assessment in the Federal Government: Managing the Process* (Washington, DC, USA: National Academy Press).
3. Collingridge, D. (1980) *The Social Control of Technology* (London, UK: Frances Pinter).
4. Schelling, T. (1983) Climate change: Implications for Welfare and Policy, in Carbon Dioxide Assessment Committee, *Changing Climate* (Washington, DC, USA: National Academy Press).

CHAPTER 8

Uncertainty—Technical and Social

BRIAN WYNNE

Life is a process of drawing adequate conclusions from inadequate premises.
Samuel Butler

Uncertainty *as such* is not a problem. After all, the human race has survived for a long time, and uncertainty has been around for at least as long. So why should it be a fashionable issue at present—and to whom is it so?

Uncertainty becomes a problem when we *interpret* it as a problem. And once the fever takes hold, there is an almost unlimited amount of uncertainty to be found. This is true even in science when we find informal interventions at all points in the difficult business of constructing systematic, technically useful knowledge. External images of formal, objective decision rules obscure more uncertain real processes of scientific influence and judgment. Expectations that society and technology (like science it was thought), were proceeding in an inductively checked fashion, are shattered when new areas of ignorance are "revealed"—the effects of thousands of commercial chemicals or wastes, the dynamics of climate change once new perturbations are introduced, the mechanisms of cancer, etc.

Yet sometimes institutions and people embrace uncertainty or even amplify or generate it—for themselves or for others—in the furtherance of their legitimate roles and concerns; sometimes they try to suppress it; sometimes they just ignore it; sometimes they may amplify *and* ignore it. On any given question, there is not a fixed level of uncertainty "out there", but different interacting perceptions of how much, and of what shape and meaning it has. Since uncertainty has always existed without there having been such a song-and-dance about it, defining when uncertainty does or does not exist may be better seen as a tacit exercise in evaluating what is a tolerable level of uncertainty. "It exists when it is intolerable." But tolerability must be measured by someone, in relation to some *commitments*, be it lifestyle or environment, which the uncertainty is thought to threaten, and which it is felt should be protected and protectable.

Brian Wynne is a Lecturer in the School of Independent Studies, University of Lancaster, UK.

Thus what we count as uncertain seems to be connected not only to conventional factors, such as the scale and subtlety of the effects of modern technology or the resolving power of science to see more of those effects on a finer and finer scale, but also to the scale of our commitments and of our cultural expectations about what we or our expert representatives should be able to control. What are the commitments we feel to be threatened? If the climate may change, is the uncertainty this generates more significant for its physical effects, or its threat to familiar social arrangements?

If technical uncertainties in knowledge for policy seem to loom so large at present, is this because there is really more uncertainty than before; or because we have artificially stretched our social demands of knowledge to a degree where it is no longer that uncertainties pervade a tissue of knowledge, but that all we have are fragments of knowledge adrift in a sea of ignorance? In comparison with the past we seem to have as much, if not more, technical knowledge as ever, even in relation to our expanding commitments. Therefore the question poses itself: Is the more important kind of uncertainty with incomplete technical knowledge *per se*, or with problems of what social values to implement to give that technical knowledge practical policy meaning and effect? Do facts and premises, which are after all chronically incomplete, only become *problematic* when the social values and institutional processes which convert them into adequate conclusions become problematic?

We are already into some big questions, but that is where the issue inevitably leads. In this chapter I want to diverge for a while from questions about how to deal with uncertainties of various kinds, and first discuss where they might be coming from. If it encourages others to improve on this attempt, better understanding of the processes of uncertainty *generation* should help eventually to improve our ability to live with or reduce uncertainties.

A New Concept of Science?

J. R. Ravetz's central concept of scientific knowledge for policy as robust tools rather than brittle nuggets [1], involves a fundamentally different understanding of science than traditionally dominant. Although Helga Nowotny has examined it at greater length [2], it is worth giving this new concept at least an explicit outline here, to make some later arguments and implications more clear. The new model sees science as:

(1) Influenced strongly by intuitive judgments and implicit, negotiable principles rather than precise and explicable rules of inference and method. Following Michael Polanyi [3], Ravetz himself was one of the earliest to point out some of the implications of this craft dimension for science in public policy [4].

(2) Founded upon a socially achieved consensus, using technical realities as part, but not all, of the determination of valid knowledge.

(3) A selectively nonfalsified construction amongst a web of ignorance. This context is conceived as natural and given, hence secure, but may be a source of radical surprise.

(4) Permeated by socially *transmitted* authority as well as independently, empirically tested authority.

This new model revises our perspective as to where the strengths and weaknesses of science lie. Much of its productivity and coherence is a result of the social achievement of consensus and of the temporary setting aside (on a judgmental basis, not by objectively prescribed rules) of many inconsistencies and anomalies. Much of its flexibility and creativity lies in the room, indeed need, for intuitive leaps, which can become institutionalized as pragmatically useful, even if no more basic rationale can be given for them.

However, set in a context of expectations created by its previous image (of being empirically validated through pure scepticism following clear rules of method and logic) the informal reality of science is vulnerable, in an infinite number of ways, to the destruction and undermining of its authority. These traditional expectations are unrealistic, and they reach their most extremely unrealistic pitch in one of the most frequently used and influential policy settings (in the US at least), namely legal cases [5]. However, it is vital to recognize the great depth of this contradiction and the ensuing vulnerability, before going on to ask where it comes from. As I later discuss, it appears to arise in large part from the unselfconscious way science presents itself in public, as a natural extension of the way it presents itself in regular internal discourse within science.

Ravetz has neatly linked the practical and theoretical issues surrounding uncertainties in the role and content of science for public policy. His key proposal is to redefine our normative frameworks and expectations for science in policy, toward a more robust policy tool concept. This moves us away from the previous notion that science is a common medium and does not need basic translation into meaningful frameworks for policy actors (whether these be singular or plural groups). From the entrenched notion of science as an objective substratum detached from but controlling any possible policy options [6], we would move to a view of science as organically embedded in the process of *persuasion* and *justification*. The trick is to do this without falling into untrammelled relativism. I fully support Ravetz's attempt to encourage epistemology (and thus the public soul of science) to catch up with practical realities that have been apparent and causing concern for some years. Of course, his proposal is no panacea. The object of the Forum and this volume is not some ultimate solution but a pause for reflection upon relatively recent changes both in the social roles of science and in our understanding of science as a means of generating authority through knowledge.

As usual, history encourages such modesty. For as Ravetz reminds us, the tensions in science's relationship with the public sphere are not new—they reflect a continual conflict between the role of construction, of generating or supporting public authority, and the opposite role, of restraining the overreach of authority via necessary criticism [7]. If criticism seems currently to be enjoying a field-day in some places, it is worth remembering that the emphasis has varied hugely over time, and varies between political cultures on the same issue, or within the same political culture on different issues. Indeed it is this variety, and the conceits which accompany many worthy policy causes with which science is often married, that creates the need for a new ethos of science. In depicting science as playing a legitimate advocacy role in policy, this ethos would articulate a new normative image that might realistically eschew claims to definitive *content* in the aim to provide procedural rules and guarantees. It is therefore interesting to note that social analysis of science has shown how strongly the intrinsic objective of persuasion and justification inspires and influences the whole process of creating knowledge—and legitimately so—even in the most rarefied of academic disciplines [8].

There are therefore some good precedents available if we care to examine them sensitively, without becoming overheated by either relativism fever or its twin, relativity paranoia.

Implicit and Explicit Languages

As with the translation of scientific knowledge itself into policy, however, so with models of scientific practice and communication. When sociologists of science first began to find that science was not actually like the idealized descriptions given in existing influential accounts, there was a tendency to imply that some kind of cosmic fraud had been unearthed. It sometimes appeared as if the informal unruly practice of science—its many dead-ends, failed experiments, leaps of faith, dogmas, and petty human jealousies—had been more or less deliberately concealed by insiders while they expressed an idealized rhetoric for external consumption.

Thankfully this tendency soon mellowed into a realization that scientists like others communicate in multiple-level descriptive language. The apparent arbitrariness of much scientific practice is recognized by scientists, yet the idealized normative language is also used *descriptively* as a way of gaining *prescriptive* purchase on scientific practice, so that even though they are not fully achieved, the precedural ideals do have a real quality-controlling effect. This does not mean they tie practice down so tightly that no freedom of thought is left, but that *excesses* of arbitrariness or bad practice can be avoided [9].

Thus scientists, even within their private culture, tend naturally to express a model of scientific practice, and of knowledge, which appears to be controlled by tidy processes and objective rules. Like many well-functioning communities they have a *tactit* understanding of many regular problems, mistakes, and pragmatic compromises, but this does not need to be repeatedly spelled out. Indeed, it needs not to be, because it would otherwise undermine concentration on more rewarding things. The point of recent work in the sociology of science here is that in their own professional practices, scientists routinely handle the complex balancing act, between self-description judged legitimately to blot out an essentially unimportant arbitrariness of process, and self-description which is felt to exaggerate this purification exercise. This continual balancing is part of the craft judgment of a science, a largely tacit, socially maintained skill for which no explicit rules can be given internally, let alone handed to the outside world for justification.

Here we see the same kind of justification and self-description of *process* as for substantive knowledge claims themselves. They too are evaluated by a rich complex of explicit rules and situational interpretations that may be nonexplicible. Indeed the two processes are really the *same* process— *substantive* and *procedural* claims and evaluations are united. But while scientific *insiders* may tacitly appreciate the limitations on knowledge and process and evaluate descriptions and claims accordingly, outsiders will not, unless a deliberate effort is made to explicate the implicit self-knowledge of the insiders. Without this effort, the natural extension of the implicit language inevitably tends to understate uncertainties and other limitations in the knowledge. If this were only a problem of individual politicians or scientists willfully trying to obtain credibility by deception it would be realtively simple. The *structual* process I have tried to outline makes the situation more complex. It is not that scientists have been concealing their inside implicit knowledge, just that they have been quite naturally operating with their own style of knowledge in a different set of social relationships

When we enlarge the context of relationships to the policy sphere that style of knowledge is no longer appropriate, because the social relationships are very different. In the policy arena the language of tidy objectivity and process no longer receives insider informal interpretation, and instead creates images and expectations of science that have led us astray. Hence the paradox noted before, of increasing reference to science and scientific paraphernalia, with decreasing credibility.

So we have two fundamental problems intertwined:

(1) There are explicit and implicit uncertainties.
(2) There are dislocated social *expectations* that make uncertainty such as recognized in incomplete knowledge problematic when perhaps it should not be.

As emphasized later, robust knowledge requires more than new character-istics of science. It also requires new properties of the institutional contexts and processes in which it is to be used.

The Biogenics Corporation Love Canal study of residents over a hazardous waste chemicals dump was a classic case of technical knowledge being dragged into a policy issue "before its time" [10].

This illustrates two points for the present discussion: first, the point about context and expectations. To be robust, knowledge must not only have certain intrinsic characteristics in terms of its explication of assumptions, methodological shortcomings, and other conditions affecting its status, but it must also enjoy a certain *institutional context* of use, particularly with what is expected of technical knowledge and how it is used in social argument. Thus the notion unites *substance* and *institutional context* or *process*.

Second, that even if we can achieve a correspondence on the preceding question, there remains the question of correspondence between the *provisionality* of policy commitment suggested in the very idea of robust knowledge, and the very real need for *commitment, as if certain*, in many policy situations. It cannot be too strongly stressed that *certainty* of belief is not merely a construct of politicians and/or scientists conniving to get what they want; it is a natural prerequisite of necessary action. Thus the authorities had to decide immediately whether or not to evacuate (and later compensate) Love Canal residents, on the basis of an inevitably hurriedly conceived and conducted study (mainly of chromosome damage to some residents) in a cauldron of urgent public controversy. They could not sit and wait for more definitive knowledge of the health effects, nor was there any evident provisional move they could make short of evacuation. Sometimes it is true that decisions can benefit from simply sitting on the fence and waiting, but not by any means in every case. Sometimes commitments can be evolved incrementally and reversibly, as knowledge evolves, but often not.

In those places where the critical function of science does seem to have so swamped the constructive function as to have nearly paralyzed authority, the problem seems to be symptomatized by the irony noted by Martin Greenberger, that scientific models are being used more and more in policy, yet believed in less and less [11]. Yet the latter seems merely to feed the former. As Bernd Marin expressed it [12], science is a problem for policy makers.

> ...because it is, paradoxically, an increasingly scarce resource, despite the fact of its exponential growth. Like legal codifications, the more science expands and the more rapidly it grows, the more it is needed. Science, like law, creates its own demand; its scarcity as a political resource comes about with an abundance of research, not its lack. That again is why politicians simultaneously face know-

ledge overload as well as a lack of sound scientific information on both the input and the output sides of politics. The problem for them is to know in time what to know at all [12].

Incidentally this characterization also indicates why many scientists on the edge of policy express frustration about not being able to squeeze onto the policy agenda. But the present point is to note the paradox of increasing policy use and yet decreasing credibility. Every concern it seems has to be expressed in the language of science, but adversary confrontation only destroys the credibility, leading in a vicious circle back to the source of more elaborate scientific weapons to try again.

This would not seem to bode well for an epistemology of science-for-policy like Ravetz's which champions science's inherently justificatory role. Is that not just asking for more trouble? But the crux is that a different *vision* of the nature of scientific knowledge is being called for. This would radically alter public policy *expectations* for scientific knowledge in the public sphere, and thus alter the standing of, for example, unashamedly incomplete knowledge, or normative knowledge.

Technical and Social Uncertainties

Of the many complex factors driving the modern concern about uncertainty across many issues, two seem to be common:

(1) A concern about the quality of data and understanding (even identification) of key dynamic relationships, in comparison with the size of commitments that could be ruined by having that understanding proved wrong.
(2) Perplexity as to how to actually *implement* solutions even if we can identify (technically) optimal or feasible solutions.

These two are self-evidently connected by the fact that if we are badly misunderstanding a problem or generating bad data on it, we are not likely to be implementing effective solutions. However, my point here is to draw connections between explicit perceptions and the usually implicit social uncertainties, to suggest that we pay more careful attention to the latter.

One approach to protecting incomplete knowledge has been to keep it private within an elite circle of policy deliberators. This is equivalent to keeping an issue off the public agenda until options have been evaluated and prepared, away from the noise and urgency of public controversy. Yet this privatization has its own costs in terms of producing a more socially brittle policy process, wherein public expectations are encouraged wildly to exceed the realities of knowledge, with devastating results upon credibility and implementability of any policy.

Indeed it may be that the *style* of scientific policy input itself influences these broader public expectations and thus the level of uncertainty around and the damage it can create for authority. Thus, for example, an epistemology of policy-oriented science that expressly upheld the legitimacy (and even value) of empiricism riding with an explicit lack of understanding of underlying mechanisms would automatically recognize an honest lack of control. This in turn would disallow policies that imply or require such control and would emphasize the necessary adaptability to unexpected eventualities. The cultural tendency at present is precisely the opposite—an elaborate scientific effort towards modeling mechanisms and dynamics conceals the importance of empiricism as an epistemological–technical policy and thus undervalues the dimension of *provisionality* in policy commitments. The kind of public epistemology we use is itself a kind of moral choice, influencing at a basic level where we pay respect to uncertainty as a legitimate and necessary part of our policy awareness, and where we suppress it.

Concern about uncertainty usually focuses heavily upon technical uncertainties—as Ravetz puts it, "defects in scientific information". However, whilst one doesn't wish to dismiss these, it is worth considering whether this technical focus overlies vaguer, less explicit, but deeper kinds of uncertainty about human behavioral underpinnings of policies, their consequences, and further responses to those perceived consequences. This suggestion is indeed supported by the fact that Ravetz's notion of *robust* knowledge requires something not only of the *knowledge*, but of the institutional context of its use, as he is aware. For example, public fear of nuclear risks is well known to be exaggerated as a technical question, but is widely interpreted to be a vehicle for expression of more important but less precise concerns as to whether nuclear decision-making *institutions* will deal adequately with an expanding industry, the problems of nuclear proliferation, the institutional side of adequate safety control, waste disposal, etc. [13].

Hazardous waste policymaking often appears to focus upon the *technical* questions (of toxicity, degrees of hazard, environmental pathways, and health effects—all of which, of course, raise a rich diet of genuine uncertainties) at the expense of even more difficult *behavioral* questions. These are about the behavior of the countless autonomous actors who are generating those risks and uncertainties, and who cannot be closely controlled (indeed they are by no means even fully known) [14].

The uncertainties surrounding the health risks of environmental pollutants such as 2,4,5,-T have usually been defined as purely technical, for example through controlled laboratory-type studies, neglecting the social realities of usage on the farm or in the forest [15]. These social uncertainties of *enactment* may completely alter the real risks involved. They may thus transform the *technical* framework of uncertainty and its meaning for policy, by changing the technical parameters assumed to be involved (e.g. degree of exposure, or chemical composition of toxic material).

Thomas Schelling's discussion of the possible responses to climate change illustrates the same general point [16]. Schelling points out that the range of likely climate changes due to the build-up of carbon dioxide and other gases in the atmosphere will fall well within that range large sectors of the population already routinely and voluntarily experience in travel, migration, etc. But what he fails to discuss is that the latter occurs from one relatively stable zone to another, and the differences may matter less than that each is more or less stable. Surely an underlying fear in respect of climate change is that it may produce new human dependencies, such as massive migration, or dependence on others' weather modification as the only feasible solutions to unpredictable forms of destabilization of the physical system.

As Schelling does point out, some technical fixes such as weather modification—leaving aside uncertainties around their second order technical effects—may be used as adaptive alternatives to *human* negotiation of joint mitigative or preventive responses such as reallocating national territory or wealth. Here we welcome back a familiar question, that of technical fixes which have often been attempted to short-circuit and avoid more apparently intransigent problems to do with social negotiation, or the trustworthiness of social institutions or individuals [17]. This has often been done by controlling symptoms rather than tackling causes of social problems, e.g. by using sophisticated police surveillance and data banks to control crime and political disloyalty. That is, implicit social uncertainties have been redefined as technical ones, apparently controllable through available technologies.

We have to work hard to remind ourselves that is is not *self-evident* that throwing more scientific resources at an issue through major international efforts is the natural or best approach to a problem if (as it often appears to) it leads to the belief that solutions can only be defined and enacted via the resolution of the technical uncertainties identified through that effort, and through associated global decision making and planning institutions (e.g. international conventions).

The climate change issue, for example, may be more appropriately dealt with through free, adaptive responses by institutions and individuals (who, of course, should be as well informed as possible) rather than megapolicies (which often mean a technical fix) that may be, in the abstract, more optimal but are not so in reality. Acid rain may be an opposite case (and so might climate change) where no amount of decentralized adaptive diversity or ingenuity can help once we have physically passed a certain point.

Energy policy is an area where assumptions built into analysis as to its natural scope and level assume a certain kind of policy process, and a certain menu of central uncertainties which may not be relevant to an alternative way of defining the policy process, analysis, and problem. To *assume* that an issue naturally exists as an analytic problem at a certain level implies that it is a *decision* problem at that level, even if it does not *necessarily* entail this. It thus suggests intervention or response at a certain level, which in turn biases our attention towards some classes of solution (and uncertainties) and away from others. Thus, the very style of analysis (institutional and cognitive) may correspond with a certain style of policymaking or power structure, and the degree and kind of uncertainty expressed may be a *symptom* of that style and its latent social anxieties as much as a justifying cause of it [18]. The greatest uncertainty perhaps is in judging the extent to which attention to reducing technical uncertainties is overrunning and undermining our perception of related social uncertainties and responsive opportunities that do exist.

Social Interpretations of Necessary Uncertainty

I pointed out at the beginning of this chapter that the amount and meaning of uncertainty is a social construction, not an objectively existing thing. This is true within science itself. Uncertainty is not always and repeatedly stressed within science because, although it may be perceived, it is—rightly or wrongly—felt to be under the interpretive and technical *control* of the relevant disciplinary community. A large proportion of the uncertainties in the body of knowledge and in the surrounding processes of experiment, observation, or communication, are part of the implicit discourse of that community—they are socially backgrounded in order to throw coherent light upon a limited selection of well defined problems and putative solutions [19]. Other uncertainties may be well known to insiders but only informally discussed because it is not especially useful to keep explicating them in day-to-day practice—indeed, it may be harmful. It ought therefore to be no surprise that when they enter, or have their work dragged, into a policy issue, scientists are often accused of understating uncertainties in their knowledge. That is the natural (and functional) character of their internal expert discourse. Indeed (as we noted) the formal public *expectations* of scientific knowledge, and the informal, socially constructed reality, means that there are an infinite number of ways of embarrassing scientists in public policy areas by exposing uncertainties in their knowledge. This is most extremely the case under exaggerated institutional rhetoric of empiricism and inductivism used in legal processes.

However, there is an extra dimension which adds to the potential for misunderstanding on a large scale. As Ravetz notes, there are social assumptions, often value-laden, in technical statements of statistical confirmation of correlations. The statistician effectively makes a decision about the needs of his audience as to the levels of confidence required to make an inference (and thus, perhaps, a material commitment). More accurately, the scientists may be enacting an *already taken-for-granted evaluation* of whether the practical policy meaning following the observation of such a correlation requires a 90%, 95%, 99% or 99.9% level of confidence. Although the evaluation of acceptable confidence will vary according to social values, etc., this may be buried in the technical knowledge, as part of its implicit discourse. Another example is the choice of absolute versus relative risk frameworks for stating risks, e.g. in epidemiology, and the use of natural background exposures as a yardstick. Thus the same individual exposure to, say, a toxic chemical may be represented as a 10^{-6} cancer risk per year, or as a 5% increase over natural background rates (if natural background were here assumed to produce a risk of 2×10^{-5} cancers per year). The former expression of the same risk makes it appear much less than the latter. This kind of difference in expression *may* be due to deliberate choice, to evoke desired public reactions; but it may, like the confidence limits question, simply follow the natural form of the internal scientific discourse.

Examples of other neglected uncertainties are too numerous to cite but one particular kind is worth mentioning. This occurs, for example, when scientists specify a linear functional relationship $Y = kX$, and this becomes embedded in a surrounding web of technical knowledge so that it cannot be isolated from surrounding parts and its validity independently evaluated. What other experts, even experts in the same field, may not know is, what was the *meaning* of $Y = kX$ in an opportunity costs sense? Was it because the function went through the origin (not $Y = A \pm kX$), or that it was linear, not quadratic (not $Y = kX^2$), etc. etc.? This may be part of the tacit knowledge of a small handful of specialists, yet the sensitivity of the term may end up as important in a policy context, where its interpretation may be controlled by other scientists or policy experts not party to the tacit knowledge that is aware of its sensitivity towards alternative formulation.

A given scientific field will have more than one way of representing its knowledge, according to the different forms in which it normally operates. Those of us who went through graduate research degrees in science will be familiar with what at my institution was well recognized as second-year blues—when you began to learn painfully that there are various unanswered questions, or inconsistencies, in bodies of knowledge you thought were complete, and nobody could give you an answer. Or when you failed to reproduce an observation by a method recorded in the literature, until you heard (maybe through direct personal contact) of all the informal experimental wrinkles that were never reported in the published papers [20]. These were parts of the operating knowledge that were not articulated in the textbooks, lectures, tutorials, or scientific papers. They were uncertainties it was necessary to learn by direct experience, and to have as an insider practitioner.

Most of us learned our physics at school through Newtonian mechanics, with a degree of assurance and certainty about its accuracy that usually left us dizzy when confronted later with quantum mechanics and its radically different mathematics and conceptual apparatus. Yet even this was taught at undergraduate level with a degree of solidity that did not prepare us for the second-year blues of graduate research. The specialty had interpreted our cognitive needs in that particular setting and articulated corresponding degrees of uncertainty. The same process occurs for other settings, including informal conversation with colleagues; more formal, but still internal, communication as in journals; and different kinds of policy setting from privately given advice to courts of law [21].

One of the problems has been that the process of interpreting receiver needs in terms of the level of required uncertainty is so routinized for the usual scientific fora as to no longer be an active self-conscious judgment, but taken for granted. Thus when scientists encounter different audiences in public policy settings, their inherent familiarity with their own expert context and its routine habits lets them down. Thus to outsiders they may be concealing uncertainties, thereby losing credibility, while to other insiders they may be showing so much that they also lose credibility, but for the opposite reason. These different reactions may occur at the same time within the same issue.

Decision Rules—Formalism versus Informalism

One of the areas in which differences occur in the level of institutionalized need for uncertainty in policy-related science is whether to operate formally or informally in the policy system. As Ronald Brickman and colleagues have recently shown in comparative detail [22], following Brendan Gillespie's earlier work, different political cultures place science and scientists in different institutional roles, and this has a basic influence upon the particular level of acceptable uncertainty in what is useable knowledge in each system.

Gillespie *et al.* [23] showed that essentially the same body of science (the environmental affects of aldrin/dieldrin) was used by different regulatory systems, the US and the UK, to produce opposite conclusions over the carcinogenic risks of the chemicals. Thus the US banned them whilst the UK found them acceptable. Of more interest to us here than the substantive correctness or otherwise of each decision was the analysis of the translations that each system gave to the science as it was moulded into policy science. In the UK, the scientists were much closer institutionally to government, and operated in a more personal network with the decision makers, with less process for formal review and explicit justification of scientific (and political) judgments. In other words, the decision rules for going from a scientific front, still full of various anomalies and uncertainties to policy knowledge of risks, were private to the elite scientists and policymakers. They could, and did, have the relevant uncertainties under *their* social control, so that such uncertainties for them were a *resource*, not a problem; while for outsiders the fact that they did not influence the interpretation of the technical uncertainties became a social uncertainty of equal or greater importance.

In the US, on the other hand, scientists operate in a much more decentralized, pluralized, and adversary setting, formally and informally. Although, as Peter Hutt has eloquently described it [24], there is still some room for informal discretion, this is hunted down as a public "bad". Thus, in the US explicit, formal decision rules are dragged out of science, often where they do not exist, by judicial demands for accountability and by political attempts to establish particular rules of inference, e.g. on carcinogenicity, which will objectively support one set of political values (as reflected in a given regulatory policy) rather than another.

The particular outcomes described by Gillespie *et al.* (and by Ronald Brickman *et al.* [22] and by Steven Kelman [25], amongst others) are less important than the processes they describe; these vary in different countries according to the role they give to science and the levels of acceptable uncertainty they tolerate in the hands of different policy actors.

Thus, for example, in the field of hazardous waste management, a UK scientist described the use of concentration thresholds in other countries for defining hazardous wastes as "a system that could be administered by monkeys" [26], indicating the degree to which in the UK it is felt proper and necessary for (the right) scientists to control the interpretation of hazard on a case-to-case basis, according to their judgment. This was unspecifiable in programmable recipes and rules like concentration values. The other countries' use of apparently simple criteria (actually less than appears since scientists can disagree even over sampling, etc.) reflected the greater purchase of the administration and courts, and the lesser discretionary power of scientists in the policy system.

Before giving an example of specific political demands for certainty and controllability of science's outputs by trying to explicate and control its rules of inference, emphasis should be given to the points made above that uncertainty may be good rather than bad, if defined to be under one's control, and that uncertainty as a problem combines dimensions of technical and social uncertainty, e.g. lack of control of others' discretion. Technical uncertainty will appear more threatening if its interpretation is not under one's social control. Also, technical uncertainty will be less of a problem in a system where trust still prevails in expert judgment and its driving motivations, even if there is lots of discretion.

In more centrally planned systems, the distinction between scientists and decision-making roles may be even less strong than, say, in the UK, and the informal discretionary evaluation of technical uncertainty may be more routine and efficient, at least at this level, than in other systems. Equally the external social uncertainty created as a corollary of this discretionary freedom may be stronger. This may be good for authority but bad for implementation.

Carcinogenicity Decision Rules

One of the well-known problems of regulating chemicals is being able to know their health effects at low but chronic doses, as data, if it exists at all, is for higher doses, shorter times, and often from other species such as laboratory tests on rodents. Thus to estimate low-dose effects on humans for regulatory standards either of no-effect thresholds, or acceptable risk levels of exposure, extrapolation is required from other conditions and species. This has long been a notorious point of conflict, for example, amongst radiation effects scientists [27]. The rules and premises adopted for extrapolation are open to different scientific views, often according to particular specialties, and themselves rest upon further theories or methodological traditions that are part and parcel of the cultural resources and useful skills of that specialty.

Cancer policy and regulation have been a major focus of public and political leadership concern since the 1970s. In the 1970s the criteria adopted by a large policy and scientific concensus [28] for extrapolating from the highly uncertain science to human dose–response conclusions were that:

(1) There were plausible but unproved theoretical grounds for using a linear no-threshold dose–effect relationship through zero (i.e. there is no dose–threshold below which there are no effects).

(2) Findings of excess cancers in animals exposed to an agent was "presumptive evidence" of carcinogenicity in humans, and should be decisive, even if there were other studies showing no effect on animals.

(3) Benign tumours are to be counted as damage.

(4) Positive human evidence of excess cancers is not necessary in order to regard an agent as in need of regulation. That is, the resolving power of many epidemiological studies is not sufficient to know whether a null result is a real negative or a no result, nontest. Null results should be taken as nontests.

These criteria were the cornerstone of an interpretive policy of inference rules that effectively lent scientific authority to a *regulatory* policy of pushing industry into investing in improvements with respect to emissions technologies. It was not so much that there was no political cost–benefit calculation, as later critics said [29], but that this calculation was *informal*, and obscured by the apparently scientific, formal rules of inference from a highly uncertain scientific field (uncertain in content *and* relevance).

With the arrival of deregulation objectives as the controlling political forces in the US, new decision rules have been formulated as a proposed government cancer policy, to control the use of science by the different environmental agencies (EPA, OSHA, etc.) [30]. Thus animal studies are not argued to be not relevant on their own; benign tumors are not considered damage; thresholds in dose–response may exist for many agents (a new theory of genotoxic and nongenotoxic mechanisms was even advanced to justify this, though soon abandoned); and a simple reading of the chemical structure of many agents would suffice to evaluate their potential carcinogenicity. These decision rules, explicated as a regulatory *policy*, via science, but not adjudicated within science, had the effect of producing a policy of deregulation, but by apparently scientific inference rules, not via explicit political changes that might have had a harder time being established. What these opposing formulations of science's inference rules show is that there is a significant area in which science and policy are not separable—they organically interpenetrate one another. Thus the idea of "science" as a separate entity making independent inputs to "policy" is misleading for at least some of the most crucial problems in their relationships. The key point is that in both the cases outlined above, important elements of the negotiated judgment of scientists on technical matters were being overformalized so that they could be extracted for external policy argument and legitimation. In reality there are many more scientific judgments that have to be made and that still involve discretion—how does one interpret confounding factors such as infections in highly-bred animal strains? How does one allow for the fact that animal experiments are often set and data selected to produce high effects so as to investigate mechanisms, not to identify dose–effect functions? If the cancer mechanism is a multistage process of somatic cell damage, where different agents can contribute hits, how does one account for the susceptibility to present exposures caused by accumulated damage from previous exposures to altogether different agents? In this specialty alone, according to one expert, there are "at least 50 areas of scientific discretion" [31] (including even the attempt, as with saccharin, to reclassify an agent as something different to have it fall under different legislation that may better accommodate the policy objective). The more important of these informal, internal discretions may be picked out, explicated, and externally controlled *as if* science, in order to achieve a desired conclusion. Equally, however, inference criteria used for purely scientific reasons within science often have intrinsic policy implications, and thus may be political regardless of the motivations that established them.

Even when this manipulation of the informal decision rules of science is not so strong, the general effect of demands for accountability, consistency, etc., has led to elaborate but still essentially ambiguous decision rules, for example, demarcating strongest, sufficient, and suggestive or supporting scientific evidence, as externally controllable triggers for different policy actions [32].

The effect again is to penetrate the science more and more with externally defined and inflexible criteria (e.g. sufficient evidence may be defined with legal cases and criteria in mind, not scientific ones) rather than informally negotiated and evolved criteria within the scientific field. This may well be inevitable; it may even be desirable. My point here is merely to show how easily and extensively the grounds of authority can be confused and to emphasize the dilemma that in important respects there is no science–policy boundary across which information is transferred, but a common field within which conflicting meanings are negotiated.

In fact, on most policy issues the technical uncertainties strictly speaking will far outstrip the capacity of the scientific resources applied to them. Thus demands for accountability in science will always leave science exposed. What is surprising, in the US context for example, is the amount of discretion still left for informal judgment in policy-related sciences despite the feeling that every sliver of judgment is totally documented and tied down. Yet the system suffers a near crisis of credibility already, which further exposures of discretionary, unaccountable judgments only exacerbate.

Thus regulatory authorities are pressed to tackle immense problems such as hazardous waste management or toxic chemicals in short time scales, often written into legal judgments. They must nevertheless be ready to justify every step under the elbaorate scrutiny of legal review. They turn to science, which produces confessedly incomplete, or shoddily complete results, which in turn are shot down as inadequate. Expert judgment is often rife in such studies—they would never be completed without it—but this is almost a social liability, like a guilty secret, in the dominant context of expectation.

For example, in the identification of chemicals to be just tested as possible additions to the lists for the Toxic Substances Control Act (TSCA), a rational priority-ranking method has to be enacted. Each test costs US \$150,000, and the program inevitably is way behind. Thus in 1979 a detailed scoring system for the whole universe of approximately 80,000 chemicals was organized, to meet a six-month deadline imposed by Congress [33]. For all its impressive efforts to be explicit and definitive, the report is larded with honest admissions of expert judgment as determining leaps across large gaps of ignorance and uncertainty. The scoring scheme "incorporated a very significant degree of scientific judgment at every step". Yet however sound and necessary this judgment may have been, one has the feeling that if and when the Inquisition eventually catches up with it, it too will be cut down in a frenzy of external accountability for the decision rules involved. Institutional-ized mistrust is fed by expectations of science that are no longer viable. The process *generates* more and more technical uncertainty rather than less, and offers no help in discriminating which are the ones to worry about and which not.

Conclusions

In this perambulation around several connotations of the present concern about uncertainties, and of Ravetz's idea of robust knowledge, I have tried to show various ways in which uncertainty is a socially mediated thing—where it comes from, what it is used for, and where it ends up, in what shape. This is not to say that technical uncertainties do not exist or are not important. The aim is to establish a framework for understanding which ones are worth our attention as technical problems, which as surrogates for social anxieties or other social problems with which we should deal as such, and which are not worth our attention at all (not *necessarily* because they are unimportant). I therefore tried to show various connections between technical and underlying social uncertainties. The last observation again relates to the key strategic need to establish a new vision of science which manages not to throw the baby out with the relativist bathwater.

In many senses the "new model" sees science as nearly incapable of incorporating genuine uncertainty (as opposed to probabilistic risk) into its normal cognitive apparatus [34]. It depends on entrenched commitments and traditions not unlike other institutions. But in order to make science work as robust public knowledge not only does it need to be revisable as new knowledge emerges, but the policy decisions and commitments it is useful to must be capable of revision too. This is echoed in Ravetz's reference to David Collingridge's Popperian provisionalist epistemology of technological choice [35]. Even if we were to attempt to make policy commitments reversible just in case (and why should this be based only on the chance of new technical knowledge, rather than possible new balances of social values also?), what do we do about those which are not? In any case, where we start from now is not a hypothetically held structure, moved along or changed as knowledge is refined, re-refined, and occasionally overthrown. There is certainly more need to see where policies, including especially technological commitments, could be more reversible. But we should be prepared to face squarely how radical are the implications not only for the received views (and practices perhaps) of science but also for the policy process, and thus for economic and technical structures of power. Then we should ask the next questions of how we can *improve* the human condition, rather than merely have it evolve.

References

1. Ravetz, J. R. (1985) Uncertainty, ignorance, and policy, this volume, Chapter 7.
2. Nowotny, H. (1985) A new branch of science, Inc., this volume, Chapter 6.
3. Polanyi, M. (1958) The tacit component, part II in M. Polanyi *Personal Knowledge* (London, UK: Routledge).
4. Ravetz, J. R. (1973) *Scientific Knowledge and Its Social Problems* (London, UK: Oxford University Press).
5. See, e.g. Oteri, J. S. (1982) Cross-examination of chemicals in drug cases, in S. B. Barnes and D. O. Edge (Eds) *Science in Context* (London, UK: Open University Press); Wynne, B. (1982) Judicial rationality, in B. Wynne *Rationality and Ritual: The Windscale Inquiry and Nuclear Decisions in Britain* (Chalfont St. Giles, UK: British Society for the History of Science); Wynne, B. (1983) *Science and Law as Conflict Resolving Institutions: Formal and Informal Processes in the Construction of Policy Authority*, Working Paper WP-83-116 (Laxenburg, Austria: International Institute for Applied Systems Analysis).

6. Barnes S. B. and Edge, D. O. (Eds) (1982) Science as expertise, Part 5 in *Science in Context* (London, UK: Open University Press); Wynne, B. (1980) Institutional mythologies and dual societies in the management of risk, in H. Kunreuther and E. Ley (Eds) *The Risk Analysis Controversy* (Berlin, FRG: Springer Verlag).

7. Ezrahi, Y. (1980) Science and the problem of authority in democracy, in T. Gyerin (Ed) *Science and Social Structure: A Festschrift for Robert K. Merton*, Vol. 39 of *Transactions of the New York Academy of Sciences*, 43–60.

8. For example Latour, B. and Woolgar, S. (1979) *Laboratory Life: The Social Construction of Scientific Facts* (London, UK: Sage); Barnes and Edge (Eds), op. cit.

9. Gilbert, G. N. and Mulkay, M. J. (1981) Contexts of scientific discourse: social accounting in experimental papers, in K. Knorr *et al.* (Eds) *The Social Process of Scientific Investigation*, Sociology of the Sciences, Yearbook 4 (Dordrecht, The Netherlands: Reidel) 269–294. See also, Gilbert G. N. and Mulkay, M. J. (1983) *Opening Pandora's Box: Sociological Analysis of Scientific Discourse*.

10. Levine, A. G. (1982) *Love Canal: Science, Politics and People* (Lexington, USA: Heath) especially 71–168.

11. Greenberger, M. (1983) *Caught Unawares: The Energy Decade in Retrospect* (Cambridge, USA: Ballinger).

12. Marin, B. (1981) What is 'half-knowledge' sufficient for—and when? *Knowledge: Creation, Diffusion, Utilization*, **3** (1) 43–60, note 47.

13. Wynne B. (1983) *Science and Law as Conflict Resolving Institutions: Formal and Informal Processes in the Construction of Policy Authority*, Working Paper WP-83-116 (Laxenburg, Austria: International Institute for Applied Systems Analysis).

14. See, e.g. Kragg, B. G. (1983) *The Hazardous Waste Industry*, mimeo (Cambridge, USA: Harvard University). Research in the IIASA project on Institutional Settings and Environmental Policies is addressing itself to this problem.

15. Kaufmann, C. G. and Wood, J. (1981) *Portrait of a Poison* (London, UK: Pluto Press).

16. Schelling, T. C. (1983) Climatic change: implications for welfare and policy, in Carbon Dioxide Assessment Committee, *Changing Climate* (Washington, DC, USA: National Academy Press).

17. For a classic critique of the culture of the technological fix, see McDermott, J. (1969) Technology: the opiate of the intellectuals, *New York Review of Books*, **13**, (2). An early explication of the technological fix approach was by Weinberg, A. (1966) Can technology replace social engineering?, *Bulletin of the Atomic Scientists*, **22**, (10).

18. Wynne, B. (1983) *Models, Muddles and Megapolicies: the IIASA Energy Studies Project as an Example of Science for Public Policy*, Working Paper WP-83-127 (Laxenburg, Austria: International Institute for Applied Systems Analysis).

19. Kuhn, T. (1970) *The Structure of Scientific Revolutions*, (Chicago, USA: University of Chicago Press). Mulkay, M. J. (1980) *Science and the Sociology of Knowledge* (London, UK: Allen & Unwin).

20. See, e.g. Gilbert and Mulkay, op.cit. Also Collins, H. J. (1982) Tacit knowledge and scientific networks, in Barnes and Edge (Eds), op.cit.

21. For a discussion, see Pinch, T. The sun set: the presentation of certainty in scientific life, *Social Studies of Science*, **11**, (1) 131–158. Campbell, B. (1983) *Uncertainty in Science: Situational Adjustments*, mimeo of IIASA summer study (Laxenburg, Austria: International Institute for Applied Systems Analysis. For some policy relevant implications, see Thompson, M. and Warburton, M. (1984) *Knowing Where to Hit It: A Conceptual Framework for the Sustainable Development of the Himalayas*, Working Paper WP-84-30 (Laxenburg, Austria: International Institute for Applied Systems Analysis) 33–64.

22. Brickman, R., Jasanoff, S., and Ilgen, T. (1982) *Chemical Regulation and Cancer: A Cross-National Study of Policy and Politics* (Ithaca, USA: Cornell University).

23. Gillespie, B., Eva, D., and Johnston, R. (1979) Carcinogenic risk assessment in the United States and Great Britain: the case of Aldrin/Dieldrin, *Social Studies of Science*, **9**, 265–301.

24. Hutt, P. (1982) *Legal Considerations in Risk Assessment under Federal Regulatory Statutes*, (mimeo) paper to Symposium on Assessing Health Risks from Chemicals (Kansas City: American Chemical Society); Hutt, P. (1983) *Consensus Without Litigation*, paper to Bellagio Conference on International Comparisons in Regulatory Policies for Carcinogens.

25. Kelman, S. (1981) *Regulating Sweden, Regulating America* (Cambridge, USA: MIT Press).
26. A Harwell scientist involved in hazardous waste management, personal communication, March 1983.
27. US National Academy of Sciences (1980) *Committee on the Biological Effects of Ionizing Radiations (BEIR), 3rd Report* (Washington, DC, USA: US National Academy of Sciences).
28. See, e.g. the joint report of the World Health Organization, International Agency for Regulation of Cancer (IARC), International Programme on Chemical Safety, and the Commission of the European Communities (1983) *Approaches to Classifying Chemical Carcinogens According to Mechanism of Action* (Lyons, France: IARC); Nemetz, P. and Vining, A. R. (1980) The biology–pathology interface: theories of pathogenesis, benefit valuation and public policy formation, *Policy Sciences*, **13**, 125–138; Gori, G. B. (1980) The regulation of carcinogenic hazard, *Science*, **208**, 256–261. See also Letters (1983) Carcinogen Policy at the EPA, *Science*, **219**, 794–798, **221**, 810. For the case of formaldehyde, see Perera, F. and Petito, C. (1982) Formaldehyde: a question of cancer policy?, *Science*, **216**, 1285–1291; Ashford, N., Ryan, C., and Caldart, C. (1983) Law and science policy in federal regulation of formaldehyde, *Science*, **222**, 893–900.
29. See, e.g. Morrall, J. F. (1982) Federal regulation of carcinogens, (mimeo) paper for Regulatory Working Group on Science and Technology (US White House Office of Science and Technology Policy, Chairman G. Keyworth). This paper supported the attempt by the Reagan Administration's Task Force on Regulatory Relief to reverse the inference policies laid out by the Carter Administration's Inter-Agency Regulatory Liaison Group.
30. Morrall, *op.cit.*, also Gori, G. B. (1980) The regulation of carcinogenic hazard, *Science*, **208**, 256-261; Ricci, P. F. and Molton, L. S. (1981) Risk and benefit in environmental law, *Science*, **214**, 1096–1100.
31. Wines, M. (1983) Scandals at EPA may have done in Reagan's move to ease cancer controls, *National Journal*, **June 18**, 1264–1269.
32. IARC, op.cit., note 28.
33. Nisbet, I. C. (1979) Ranking chemicals for testing: a priority-setting exercise under the toxic substances control act, Appendix B, *Scoring Chemicals for Health and Ecological Effects Testing* (Rockville, MD, USA: TSCA Inter-Agency Testing Committee, Enviro Control).
34. See notes 5 and 9.
35. Collingridge, D. (1980) *The Social Control of Technology* (London, UK: Frances Pinter).

CHAPTER 9

Science and Socialist Society

FRANTIĔSEK CHARVÁT

A historical review and analysis of the present relationship between science and society testifies to the increasing social character of science and its social conditionality. The quantitative and qualitative development of science not only multiplies the "share of science" in the development of society significantly, but also transforms its social functions. In other words, science evidently participates in social progress to an increasing extent, but it is likewise immediately involved in the threats faced by individual societies, and by the whole of mankind. In spite of extensive scientific efforts in the identification and solution of problems connected with the social application of scientific results, one cannot assert that the problems of utilizing scientific results in the control of social processes belongs to the scientific and, therefore, also to the social problems of the past. While being fully aware of a considerable simplification of the problem, one can say that it appears to be very useful both from the viewpoint of science itself and from that of society to study further and develop such issues as the dynamic social content of science inclusive of its determinants, and the interaction of science as a social institution with other institutions responsible for decision-making processes, etc.

In recent years, many have argued that science has resubstantialized itself from its former position as a pure, objective, and unbiased cognitive activity of individuals into a structured social activity that presupposes not only a certain degree of intellectual ability but also acquired social experience. In this connection, I would like to stress the following hypothesis that is, in my opinion, very natural and therefore very substantial: Science as a social phenomenon absorbs to an increasing extent, in its own determinant features, characteristics that are typical of the society in which it exists. To put it in other terms, society itself, its organization, regularities, and the rules of its development are increasingly decisive in the development of science. The formulation of this hypothesis is, however, too general and, therefore, it

Frantiĕsek Charvát is the Deputy Director of the Institute of Philosophy and Sociology, Czechoslovak Academy of Sciences, Czechoslovakia.

impoverishes the historical and logical extent of the problem to which it refers. It would seem useful, particularly in view of the Forum's and this volume's intentions, to exert a concentrated international effort in the future in order to clarify the actual structure of the development of the relationship between science and society, above all on the theoretical level and, if possible, empirically as well, to create an effective reference point for further deliberations of a more specific type.

It goes without saying that this is a considerably ambitious and scientifically difficult goal. Among others, one should answer such questions as: What are the determinant characteristics of society? Whose intervention in the scope and quality of the relationship of science and society is decisive? What serves as a sufficiently powerful source for explanation of the actual relationship between science and society? If one accepts as a hypothesis that science is congruent with, that science is a social process of a specific type, then one must ask how and by what means of empirical verification can this hypothesis be accepted or rejected. This is not an easy problem. For instance in the modeling of economic development, no one has yet satisfactorily, despite pragmatic efforts succeeded in freeing science from its role as a distinctively latent variable whose efforts can be anticipated only indirectly in terms of the changes of traditional, explicit macroaggregates. In this connection, the following question arises immediately: Is it realistically possible to "squeeze" science as a factor of progress—both in the positive and negative sense of the term—into the deep-rooted schemes and stereotypes of macroeconomic analyses and predictions? It seems to be likely and fully corresponding to our preceding reflections that the meaning and sense of science surpasses the boundaries set by the traditions of contemporary macroeconomic reasoning.

In my opinion, to find an adequate, categorical framework that would enable us to effectively organize and empirically investigate the development of the relationship between science and society is a continuously relevant scientific and social problem. The success and communicability of many solutions to more specific problems, particularly of comparative studies in the sphere under consideration, however, depend substantially on the extent to which the problem of the science–society relationship is addressed.

I believe one of the possible promising ways to approach the problem of the relationship between science and society is to concentrate first on an analysis of the transformation of the determinants in society's social structure into the social structure of science itself. We could then investigate the social structure of the relationship between science and society in the broad sense of the term, involving social relations within the framework of their reproduction; actual social goals, needs, and possibilities; types of decision making activities; etc. I am fully aware that this recommendation may be understood as an overly speculative endeavor. I am, however, firmly convinced that it is of considerable pragmatic significance for solving such concrete problems as, for instance, the description and explication of the processes of implementing scientific findings in social practice, the interaction of the value structures of the communities of policy makers and scientists, the analysis of the usefulness and implementability of scientific products, the evolution of this process over time, etc.

The problem of science and society forms a natural background for the particular theme of science for public policy. In my opinion, however, a broader question cannot be neglected. Just as it is necessary to develop science in the sense of social needs, i.e., public policy, it is also necessary to develop society if the social functions of science are to have a proper place for their realization. In other words, the interaction of science and society is continuously increasing, requiring the concurrence and compatibility of changes in both science and society.

Social Assessment of Scientific Products: Some Experiences in Czechoslovakia

In this chapter, it is possible to present only the briefest description of the planning and control of science in the environment of socialist Czecho-slovakia. It should be stated first that both the formal and informal prestige of science is high, as confirmed by the actual institutional position of science on the one hand and by a great amount of reliable sociological data on the other. However, this does not mean that there are no problems concerning the implementation of scientific findings into social usage. These problems are caused both by the insufficient absorptive ability of managerial economic and social practice and by shortcomings concerning implementation of the products of science themselves.

An important problem regarding the effective interaction of science and socio-economic practice in the natural and technical sciences is that there is often a gap between the final scientific product and a version of it that is necessary for current social application. We can say, with a little exaggeration, that scientists finish their work or, better, they consider it to be finished before the system is ready to absorb it. This gap between the output of science and the requirements for its input into actual practice, whether it be technological developments in production, preservation and cultivation of the living environment, care for the population's health, or the mechanism of social and economic control, virtually defines the limits for further social assessment of scientific findings. For instance, the prognostic studies that were entrusted to the Czechoslovak Academy of Sciences by the Federal Government of the Czechoslovak Socialist Republic were undertaken by teams which addressed the problems of raw materials and energy; agriculture and food production; ecology and public health; transformations of technologies in the engineering industry, electrotechnology, applied chemistry, and transport systems; as well as producing studies of economic and social development as a whole. There appeared significant problems in many cases. These problems resulted from the considerable indeterminateness of the implementability of scientific statements into the actual practice of economic and social life, as well as from the indeterminateness of the economic and social, including ecological, consequences of scientific recommendations. From elementary considerations of the investment needed for the proposed measures, such as certain biotechnological methods, of the financial allocation of ecological consequences and prerequisites, estimates of educational needs, and of social prerequisites and consequences, there appeared considerable differences of opinion as to the "interval of indeterminateness", bounded by two contrasting viewpoints:

(1) Overestimation of and impatience with socioeconomic contributions to the application of scientific findings together with underestimation of the socioeconomic costs of the application of these findings: so-called scientific optimism and socioeconomic naiveté.

(2) Underestimation of and lack of interest in socioeconomic contributions to the application of scientific findings, together with overestimation of the socioeconomic costs of the application of these findings: so-called scientific pessimism and socioeconomic skepticism.

This fact is not at all surprising: similar experiences can be found all over the world. However, it represents an important scientific and practical problem, of a type which should be dealt with both by science itself and by the controlling social practice. We call this type of problem the social assessment of scientific products. In this connection, I would like to mention that it would be insufficient and erroneous to refer the mastering of this problem simply to a new scientific discipline. If, in fact, the overcoming of conflicts, communication difficulties, and other shortcomings in the relationship between science and social order were assigned only to science, there would arise an erroneous, unbalanced solution that would simply push the conflict to a higher level. It would be just as one-sided to refer the problems of social assessment of scientific products only to policymakers. It is more useful to conceive the problems of social assessment of scientific products as being a "hybrid sphere", an interdisciplinary sphere of science and managerial practice, a sphere of creative, common dialogue between the community of scientists and policymakers. In this respect, our experiences fully supported the need for a Forum on "Science for Public Policy", as the first action in the implementation of this dialogue.

In the course of work on the above-mentioned system of selected prognoses in the Czechoslovak Socialist Republic, it happened *via facti*, quite normally, that many such dialogues between policymakers and scientists took place and resulted in some, though not too frequent, shifts of standpoint on both sides. Of course, one cannot presuppose that the social assessment of scientific products, which might still be supplemented by an improvement in the adequacy of the policymakers' attitudes, will be an easy matter. In fact, it is concerned with the first form of interdisciplinarity which surpasses the boundaries of science as a whole.

Moreover, it is clear that not even the scientific aspects of a hybrid procedure of social assessment of scientific products are yet complete, since they involve such fundamental issues as indeterminateness in the means of communication themselves. It is evident that the syntactical, semantic, and, particularly, the pragmatic component of the language and thought of scientists and policymakers possess considerable differences.

I am convinced that the solution of these issues should be taken into consideration in the establishment of follow-up activities within the framework of the research program "Science of Public Policy" organized by IIASA.

Science and the Public: Conception of their Mutual Relation*

The relationship between science and the public or, to put it in more precise terms, science and broad sections of the working people, is one of the major topics of our time. This problem is not a new one; it originated in the very nature of modern science as a specific human activity performed by a relatively small part of the population—the scientific intelligentsia—which differed from the rest of the society in its social status and political influence, the character of its work, and its way of life. Since the times of Descartes and Spinoza, this relationship has been reflected in ideological concepts, both democratic and undemocratic, but past attempts at its explication have always been unsuccessful.

In recent times, this problem has become especially topical and disquieting for a number of scholars, due to the fact that the orientation and application of science have come into direct conflict with living conditions in general, threatening to turn scientific achievements into devices of destruction. This very fact has recently stimulated increasing interest of the public in science, as well as the interest of science in the public, in developed capitalist countries. This interest has resulted in the demand for public control over the development of science, both as regards the social applications of science and the scientific research process itself.

*These comments follow the theoretical legacy of Academician Radovan Richta, who died in June 1983, on the social status of science.

A special tension around the relationship between science and the public is nowadays characteristic of economically developed countries in the West. In socialist countries, this historical problem is posed in different terms. It does not appear in the same form, either, in developing countries.

The new approach of the public to science means that scientific knowledge is beginning to be broadly understood as a fundamentally social cognition and science is beginning to be regarded as a social activity whose relation to society's needs is designed with social intervention and control. The traditional dividing line that has existed throughout the history of modern science today seems to have disappeared, i.e., the line of division between science as a cognitive activity and science as a social institution; between the development of "value-free" science and the sphere of social interests, values, and objectives in which the subject of scientific knowledge is formed; between the professional activity of a scholar and the behavior of people standing outside science. The ideal has ceased to be that of knowledge void of any other values but those in the actual process of cognition; knowledge that would set no other aim but the "production of unbiased information" for an abstract user; knowledge that can penetrate into all spheres but only at the cost of becoming detached from the immediate link to the development of the society and man, thus admitting any use or abuse of its results. The problem of science and the public appears above all as one of the functioning of science as a social system; a problem of the evaluation, control, and application of science according to social criteria, objectives, and needs.

Most analyses of the relationship between science and the public in developed capitalist countries today conclude that the introduction of new relations, led by human needs in the development of science and the concept of the advance of science in the context of broader social processes, gives rise to two questions that must be tackled for a positive solution. On the one hand, there is the problem of understanding the nature of social values and objectives to which science should be directed; on the other hand, there is the problem of shaping the social interests which condition the necessary orientation and applications of science. It becomes clear that even the most thorough description of the forms of mutual interaction of science and the public and of democratic control over the scientific process cannot lead to more profound knowledge if it is not seen as an aspect of the whole issue; if the question of the social aspect of science and of its applications are left aside.

The manner in which the relationship between public and science is presented indicates that social system in which science is separated from the working people, which is a fundamental condition governing the application of science in capitalist society, where "the public" stands, in principle, outside science and science thus becomes an affair of the "scientists' community", a separate elite and "intellectual aristocracy", as it was called by

Max Weber, and regarded as the subject of its own scientific investigation. The limitation of such a starting point inevitably narrows the possibilities of a positive solution.

Today, when the public in the West claims its right to a control over science, when it turns its attention to the social goals of scientific-technological development that have been taken for granted and left to private decision-making until recently, then it expresses the fact that the present development and application of science, typical of the given social system, have reached their limits. At the same time, it also demonstrates the need to go beyond the existing limits of "the public" itself, composed of private individuals helplessly facing the social powers by which present-day science is controlled. This testifies to the growing awareness that the development and application of science in society have a political nature and that a genuine reorientation of science cannot be regarded as a technical problem but, on the contrary, as a problem of broad and consistent democratization of science.

In a socialist society, the problem of historical reconstruction of the relationship between science and the working people assumes different dimensions, corresponding to the different structure of the society as well as to a different conception of science. The relationship assumes the character of a systematically shaped social process and is oriented towards the overcoming of the separation of science from the working people. This orientation is possible mainly because the historical role of the working people has been qualitatively changed in socialist society. The working people have become the decisive factor of social development and, for the first time in history, their activity has become goal-oriented. This is so because the removal of class antagonisms makes it possible to constitute an internally united subject, the entire society, which is capable of linking the process of development and application of science with the process of development and application of social relationships and people, and thus to achieve an essential unity of scientific and social progress on the basis of which the contradictory position of science can be overcome. The formation of a society-wide science is naturally a long-term process involving a number of stages. It can be said that there is a whole complex of socialist transformations, starting with putting all productive forces, including science, at the disposal of the entire society, through the implementation of measures for the general advancement of working people.

In the socialist system, scientific findings function in an entirely different manner to that in capitalist society. Science acts increasingly not only as an external means of knowledge and as a transforming agent of the external world, but simultaneously as an inherent social force in the hands of the working people, incorporated in their historical creativity. It develops its cognitive and transforming functions not only in relation to nature, but also simultaneously influences the formation of the subjective forces of social development. These social objectives themselves can and must, in view of the goal-oriented nature of the socialist process, be formed with the help of science and on the basis of the essential interests of the population that condition the orientation of scientific projects and, in the form of socialist values and objectives, enter the very system of science as a constituent part.

It should be stressed that the coordinated participation of scientists in the process of formulating social objectives to the extent that exists in socialist countries is a completely new phenomenon. It involves not only the work of scientists in bodies of technical experts but also those functions that are connected with both the preparation of related decisions and the responsibility for their implementation. It is not difficult to see the difference in the role of a scientist who provides advice and nonbinding recommendations and a scientist who also participates in collective decisions and their implementation. The fundamental difference in the forms of the relationship between the public, the broad sections of the working people, and science objectively lies in these prerequisites.

While in present-day capitalism this relationship takes the form of workers' struggles to limit and reverse the rationality that science assumes in the service of capital, in socialist society the ever deeper acquisition of science by the working people primarily presumes the development of relationships of the new social structure into better-elaborated and more adequate forms.

Of essential importance in this context is the historical process of deepening social unity and overcoming the differences between the working class, the working people, and the scientific intelligentsia. It goes without saying that in socialism scientific production remains mainly the activity of a specific group of people, the scientific intelligentsia, operating in a relatively independent research system. However, the other aspect of the social division of labor that characterizes capitalism, namely the separation of the working people from science, is gradually disappearing. When there is a purposeful link of science with the working people, when science and technology become an element of people's own activity and development, the growth of science does not involve the transformation of the scientific–technological intelligentsia into a privileged elite. The scientific–technological intelligentsia is then an inseparable component of the working people; its activity is only a part of the general cognitive and transforming activity of society, and its mission consists of developing the intellectual potential of the aggregate social labor force.

Through the system of social relationships, scientists are organically integrated into the whole of society and their position depends on how well science fulfills its social functions and responds to social requirements. In keeping with this principle, voluntary social organizations have been, for instance, established in socialist countries through which the intelligentsia develop broad educational and popular science activities among the working people. The process of deepening the society's social unity makes it possible to systematically expand the immediate contacts of the scientific intelligentsia with the working people in day-to-day efforts to achieve scientific–technological and social progress. Nowadays, the comprehension of the social functions and present-day development of science, as well as the working people's active participation in the application of scientific achievements, are becoming major aspects of the development of science itself. The activation of a variety of forms of practical cooperation of scientists, technicians, and workers, in which scientific activity is integrated with productive labor, has a profound historical sense and is one of the key concepts in the development of socialism.

In socialist countries there exists a whole system of organizations to assist the collaboration of scientists, technicians, and workers. The Czechoslovak Scientific–Technological Association, one of the voluntary organizations associated with the National Front of Czechoslovakia, is an example. Its membership includes more than 420,000 workers in science, technology, and economics, comprising workmen, inventors, and innovators; they operate as special consultants, authors, and executors of scientific–technological solutions, particularly concerning the living and working environments and the technical equipment of services, as well as in the popularization of scientific–technological knowledge. The Society's members work in 14,000 Socialist Labor Teams, in 7000 comprehensive Rationalization Teams that consist of scientists, technicians, and workmen, and in 6000 teams engaged in the solution of specific technical and economic problems. In recent years, they have been submitting over 20,000 innovation suggestions annually.

In socialism, production in this sense, as was predicted by Marx, is the sphere of experimental science. However, this also applies to the whole sphere of controlling social processes. The gradual expansion of scientific activity beyond the limits of science as a professional institution indicates an important trend in the relation of the working masses to science that will be further strengthened with the elaboration of these forms of socialist relationships.

The essence of the new dimensions assumed by science in the socialist society involves the application of science in a substantially broader and simultaneously internally balanced, integrated complex of functions. The public, i.e., the working people, are encountering science that functions in its fullness as a form of social cognition or objective reality, as well as a social productive force. The sociocultural function of science, connected with the formation of a world overview, is developing and science is changing into a theoretical basis for controlling social processes; it is becoming a means of turning historical development into a goal-oriented process of applying the laws of social action.

Historically, the functions of science have been developing unevenly. The capitalist situation, based on the suppression of the working people's subjectivity, has also influenced the social application and the structure of science in the sense that it has restricted its application and development to areas linked to the acquisition of science for the general advancement of the working man. This fact brought about the characteristic disproportion between the relatively extensive application of science in production and its relatively limited function in the sociocultural sphere and in shaping a world overview, as well as the quite inadequate application of science for regulating and controlling social processes in view of the needs of working people. Precisely these socially conditioned disproportions, these uneven and spontaneous relative rates of scientific development and application, not science itself, gave rise to the well-known problems in the relationship between the public and science, and caused distrust of science's significance in solving the fundamental problems of human existence.

Hence an explanation of the fact that science plays a greater role in the life of the working man in socialism than it has played in all preceding societies. Hence also the new relationship of the working people with science. Even empirically it is conspicuously more positive than in capitalism.

In socialist countries, where science develops as part of a goal-oriented control of social processes, orientation today is towards the development and application of science in the overall internally interlinked complex of its functions: scientific procedures concerning the transformation of objective material conditions of the life of people are being anticipated and the ways to implement them are being chosen, while taking into account to what degree they form a part and a mediating link in the development of the society's subjective forces, which in turn stimulate further development and application of science. From this point of view, participation of science is of special importance in drafting long-term prognoses, closely interconnecting the problems of scientific–technological, economic, and social advancement, in order to secure the unity of economic, scientific–technological, and social progress. This task has been successfully accomplished in the Soviet Union, where a long-term Comprehensive Program of Scientific-Technological Development and its socio-economic implications has been drafted, and this is now being started in Czechoslovakia, as well as in other socialist countries.

It is typical of the reflections on "science and the public" made against the background of capitalism, that they take place on the level of investigating the relevance of a variety of partial interests for determining the priorities of scientific development but, in principle, do not raise the question whether, and in what way, these conflicts of interest reflect a genuine interest in the development of the popular masses and an interest in the development of society as a whole. This is connected with the fact that in capitalism the public is not the ruling class and the ruling class is not the public. On the contrary, in socialism where the working people led by the working class are the subject of their own control, there is an essentially different structure and function of the relationships between the working people and science, of democracy and science. This structure relies upon the democratic system of the institutions of socialist society. The working people can, as the subject of control, not only formulate their wishes and requirements to science, but they can also take an active part in determining its future orientation. This is in accordance with the character of present-day science where the choice of decisive fields of research and correct strategies are an organic part of science itself, and are often more difficult than the immediate research process. Experience has shown that in producing the long-term strategy for the development of science, the working people's active participation is most desirable.

The democratization of science, the application of scientific methods to safeguarding social interests and setting social goals, and, last but not least, the growing competence of the working people thus facilitate the solution of one of the most important problems of the relationship between science and democracy—the unity of the scientific procedure in preparing socially important solutions and the democratic procedure in adopting them. What is involved are not formal procedures but a real synthesis of scientific provisions and the democratic, creative initiative of the masses. The characteristic traits of science control in Czechoslovakia include, on the one hand, improvement of the work of specialized organizations and institutions that secure the maximum application of science and draft proposals of long-term fundamental concepts for the solution of various problems concerning scientific control over technological, economic, and social processes and, on the other hand, the application of democratic forms of decision making that secure due respect for the social interests of the people. It can be expected that these forms of uniting both scientific and democratic elements of control will become increasingly rich, along with the progressive build-up of an advanced socialist society.

The development of socialist relations and the advance of the scientific–technological revolution logically lead to a gradual generalization of the elements of scientific activity in the life of the working people. A full creative link between science and the working people will, of course, require systematic efforts for several decades to come. Nevertheless, this profound social process has started developing and it is, no doubt, the need and the hallmark of our epoch.

CHAPTER 10

Lay Participation in Decision-making Involving Science and Technology*

LOREN GRAHAM

In this comparative chapter on the US and the Soviet Union I attempt to answer the question: To what extent in the two countries are lay (nonscientific) opinion and public participation considered normal and necessary in order to resolve policy issues with high scientific or technical content? A preview of my conclusion is the following: Although both the US and the Soviet Union have traditions of lay control over such issues, in recent decades the public involvement has been much greater in the US than in the Soviet Union. In the US during the last ten years there has been much more discussion of this issue than in the Soviet Union; the trend in the US has been toward more and more public participation and lay involvement, including widespread institutionalization of the public role through mixed scientific–lay review committees of different sorts. I am not aware of recent institutional changes in the Soviet Union of this type. At the same time, it must be recognized that many scientists and engineers in the US are worried about the growing influence of the lay public in making technical decisions; some of them no doubt would prefer the type of closed peer group decision-making practiced in the Soviet Union. A great debate is developing on this issue and it is still not clear exactly what pattern of decision-making will prevail in either country.

In both the US and the Soviet Union ultimate authority over scientific institutions and the policymaking process is under lay control. I discuss briefly the forms that these controls take in the two countries, starting with the US.

The United States

In the US the principle of ultimate lay control is expressed in many ways: the boards of trustees of universities, scientific institutes, private founda-

*This essay appeared in an abridged form in the journal *Environment* (Sept. 1984), and is reproduced here by permission.

Loren Graham is a Professor in the Program on Science, Technology, and Society at the Massachusetts Institute of Technology, USA.

tions, and other organizations involved in science are usually composed of individuals whose expertise is in nontechnical areas. The legal and financial controls and responsibilities of most educational and scientfic institutions in the US are in the hands of nonscientists. In the case of public institutions, such as state universities, the state legislatures, subject to an array of political and public pressures, determine the annual budgets. The federal government, which provides heavy financial support to research in the natural sciences and engineering through such agencies as the National Science Foundation, the National Institutes of Health, and the Department of Defense, is dependent on the publicly elected Congress for its appropriations.

This lay control is financial and legal in nature, not usually scientific or intellectual. Lay control is kept distant from the actual conduct of research and normally is not of concern to the individual researcher. It is considered quite inappropriate for boards of trustees to inquire into the research procedures or findings of scientists at their institutions. Governmental bodies funding research, such as the National Science Foundation, are carefully constructed in ways designed to preserve scientific autonomy.

When policymakers turn to the scientific and technical community for advice in making decisions with technical content, the tradition until quite recently (and even yet with regard to the majority of issues involving the natural sciences) has been to make a distinction between the technical and the political or normative aspects of the problem. The technical advisory committees are traditionally composed of scientists and engineers with appropriate specialized knowledge who present actual findings for the use of the policymakers. An important example is the committees of the National Academy of Sciences, a private organization incorporated by the Congress. The National Academy was created in 1863 with the object that it "shall, whenever called upon by any department of the Government, investigate, examine, experiment, and report upon any subject of science or art". In recent years the Academy has produced an average of about 250 reports annually [1].

The typical committee writing a report for the National Academy of Sciences is composed of at least one or two members of the Academy plus other technical specialists with relevant knowledge. The committees normally restrict their investigations to the technical aspects of issues, leaving "value questions" to the policymakers and legislators. This approach is, of course, impossible to observe in the strictest sense, but it retains great influence as a goal. The division of the factual and the normative whenever possible seems sound on several grounds: scientists report on topics on which they are acknowledged authorities; at the same time, the effort to separate facts and values usually protects the National Academy from the storms of controversy that surround political and moral issues. The current President of the

Academy, Frank Press, recently emphasized the effort the Academy normally makes to avoid ethical or political questions by criticizing the authors of a controversial Academy report on marijuana for "stating a judgement so value-laden that it should have been left to the political process" [2].

While the National Academy of Sciences is only one example, it serves as an illustration of the general practice in the US: when policymakers turn to scientific advisory groups it is normal to make, to the degree feasible, this same distinction between the factual and the normative aspects of the problem. The assumption has been that the scientific community should produce technical findings when asked to do so by policymakers, and the policymakers, acting through the normal political process, should decide the issues that are heavily intertwined with politics or ethics.

In recent years, however, important changes have occurred in the US in the practice of involving both lay people and normative questions in evaluating technical issues that affect society. A range of problems has emerged, particularly in the biological and behavioral sciences, in which the distinction between the technical and the normative is very difficult to make, and perhaps even unwise to attempt. In 1976, when David Matthews, Secretary of Health, Education, and Welfare, created an Ethical Advisory Board to help him make decisions about the propriety of scientific research being conducted in the National Institutes of Health, he stipulated that the fourteen-member board should contain a mixture of scientists and nonscientists; according to his directive, no more than seven of the members could be scientists, and no more than four could be biomedical scientists [3]. The others were social and behavioral scientists, specialists in other disciplines, and—most striking—representatives of the general public. Early members of the board included a Catholic priest and a philanthropic leader, and both Protestant and Jewish theologians were invited as consultants.

In 1978 Congress created and in 1979 President Carter appointed the President's Commission for the Study of Ethical Problems in Medicine and Biomedical and Behavioral Research with a mandate to take on ethical problems arising in any federal agency [4]. The Commission has continued its activity since President Reagan's inauguration. Chaired by Morris Abram, a lawyer, only six of the original eleven members of the Commission were natural scientists or physicians. Included among the members were a sociologist, an ethicist, two lawyers, and an economist. Among the subjects studied by the Commission were the definition of death, regulation of medical research involving human subjects, regulation of social science research, the operation of institutional review boards, and the compensation of injured research subjects [5].

One of the activities of the President's Commission was initiated by three major religious organizations whose general secretaries wrote President

Carter expressing concern about genetic engineering [6]. The religious leaders did not think that the government was paying sufficient attention to ethical and religious questions involved in genetic engineering. As a result, the Commission conducted extensive hearings with both biological scientists and representatives of the general public and issued in 1982 a report entitled *Splicing Life: The Social and Ethical Issues of Genetic Engineering with Human Beings* [7]. The President's Commission recommended that research in gene splicing be independent of federal funding and that it be monitored by a widely diverse oversight body that included public representatives.

The principle that lay people should be involved in the evaluation of scientific research that impinges on social and ethical issues is now well established in the US. A mechanism for the formal inclusion of such advice is the Institutional Review Board (IRB), which now exist in hundreds of universities and research institutions. Originally advisory organizations, they have gained more and more power. According to the regulations of the Department of Health and Human Services, research involving human subjects (except for a few exempted categories) cannot be funded by the federal government unless it has been approved by a majority of the members of the local IRB [8]. Furthermore, the regulations state that the membership of the IRBs "should be diverse and include members with nonscientific interests".

These regulations cover the National Institutes of Health (NIH) and the National Institute of Mental Health. No one can receive a grant from the NIH for research involving human subjects, laboratory animals, or recombinant DNA unless he or she has signed statements giving assurance that the research supported by the grant will comply with ethical guidelines drawn up by committees of mixed membership, including both scientists and laypeople [9]. Similar regulations cover the National Science Foundation and other government funders. While Americans often say that politics affects research much more in the Soviet Union than in the US, I am unaware of any procedures in the Soviet Union that, in a formal way, intrude public interests into the heart of scientific research to this degree.

IRBs in the US have gone through a long evolution since the early 1960s, when they first became common [10]. Originally they came out of a consensus that professional scientists should monitor themselves in order to avoid outside control. A study made by the National Institutes of Health in 1968 showed that 73% of the committees' studies were "limited in membership to immediate peer groups" of scientists and physicians [11]. Then in 1969 the US Public Health Service revised its guidelines for IRBs, calling for members with backgrounds not only in the appropriate technical areas, but also with knowledge of "relevant laws, standards of professional practice, and community acceptance" [12]. The phrase "community acceptance" became the door through which public representatives with little or no scientific, or even academic, training entered the committees.

By the 1970s, IRBs commonly included as members not only scientists but administrators, nurses, lawyers, social workers, clergy, and, at least at one hospital, patients [13]. At universities, the committees sometimes included students [14]. Furthermore, a new type of academic specialist—the bioethicist—emerged in the late 1960s and early 1970s, and soon became a standard member of such committees [15]. Many of them had backgrounds either in philosophy or theology.

IRBs have spread very rapidly among American institutions and in the government bureaucracy. Even private physicians and unaffiliated researchers have, in some cases, been required to have their research proposals cleared by IRBs; not belonging to an institution with an existing IRB, they have been asked by their potential funders to obtain opinions about their research plans from IRBs in neighboring institutions. Within the federal government, the IRB model has jumped from the Department of Health and Human Services to other departments, including the Department of Energy [16]. A special publication, entitled *IRB: A Review of Human Subjects Research*, is issued by a leading private bioethics center in an attempt to keep universities, hospitals, and individual research applicants informed of the rapidly changing practices and regulations [17].

A study of the activities in 1978 and 1979 of the IRB at one medium-sized American university—the State University of New York at Albany—illustrates what these organizations actually do [18]. In a one-year period the IRB met 41 times and reviewed 278 proposals, involving approximately 80,000 potential human research subjects. Most of the proposals involved gathering data by questionnaires (60.8%), interviews (33.1%), and psychological tests (23.7%). Over 80% of these proposals were for research financed and sponsored by the University itself; only 13% were related to government contracts and grants, and only 4% were related to private sources. Almost half of the proposals were initiated by student investigators. The IRB cost the University $36,000 during the year, or about $130 per proposal.

The results of the IRB's activities at Albany were not dramatic; of the 278 proposals evaluated during the year, only nine were judged to put their subjects at risk and therefore not approved. Twenty-five proposals were held up, however, until either revisions or additional documentation removed the doubts of members of the IRB.

Biomedical and behavioral research is only one area in the US where the practice of lay involvement in technical decisions has become widespread. Such committees are, for example, important in influencing federal policy on toxic substances [19]. The National Advisory Committee on Occupational Safety and Health (NACOSH) comprises twelve members who include not only experts but also representatives of labor and the general public. In the Environment Protection Agency (EPA), the Administrator's Toxic Substance Advisory Committee (ATSAC) includes, according to its charter, "an appropriate balance" of experts and other interested parties, "including, but not limited to, labor organizations, professional societies and state and local interests" [20]. Environmental impact statements required by law in the US must include evidence of opportunities for public comment.

The spread of lay involvement in technical issues is a source of anxiety to many members of the American scientific community. In this regard, American scientists do not differ that much from Soviet scientists quoted in the last section of this paper. Quite a few molecular biologists, including Nobel laureate James Watson, believe that arousing public concerns about recombinant DNA research at the Asilomar Conference was a mistake that led to unnecessary and inhibitory regulation. Other American scientists are more willing than Watson to acknowledge that some public involvement in such issues is necessary, but fear that a nightmare could be created if the process goes too far. And the American public seems to share the view of the American scientists who want to keep such decisions close to the technical community. Opinion polls show that most American citizens believe that final decisions on technical issues should be left to the experts [21].

At the present time, the predominant opinion among science policy analysts in the US seems to be that some sort of compromise needs to be struck between the principles of expertise and public representation. Harvey Brooks recently pointed toward such a balance when he wrote:

> Citizen commissions, which are analogous to juries, have a fairly good record in dealing with complex technical issues when they have adequate access to experts and when there are ample opportunities for questioning and dialogue. But if such lay decision mechanisms come to be relied on excessively and are used for appeals over the heads of experts every time some interest group fails to get the decision it wants, the right of ultimate appeal to the public will become a sham [22].

In recent years the principle of ethical review by IRB-like committees has spread into the international arena [23]. In 1980 the need for ethical review of research on human subjects was a topic of discussion at the Fourteenth Annual Round Table Conference of the Council for International Organizations of Medical Sciences (CIOMS) in Mexico City. The World Health Organization has proposed international guidelines for ethical review of research projects involving human subjects. These guidelines are much more specific than the earlier statements on the subject contained in the Nuremberg Code, the Declaration of Helsinki, and the Tokyo Amendment. They include the recommendation that "lay representatives and lawyers" be included on the ethical review committees [24].

The argument is often made in the US that when a review board is making ethical decisions about scientific research it should reflect the predominant values of that society. For the US, religious leaders, public representatives, and moral philosophers seem often to be the logical choices for lay membership [25]. We will defer for the moment the question of the analogous choices in the Soviet Union.

The Soviet Union

In the Soviet Union the tradition of public involvement in scientific research is also strong. If one judges by organizational charts and legal charters, the principle of public responsibility may appear to be even stronger than in the US, since there is no private industry in the Soviet Union, no nongovernmental research organizations, and no nongovernmentally sponsored or funded scientific organizations or advisory groups. The Academy of Sciences of the USSR, the Academy of Medical Sciences, the universities, and the industrial research organizations are all ultimately responsible to, and controlled by, the Council of Ministers of the USSR, which, in turn, is legally subordinate to the highest legislative body, the Supreme Soviet. But, as we will see, the reality of the current situation cannot be best seen by looking at organizational charts or laws [26].

The principle of public involvement in Soviet science was one of the main issues of the 1920s and 1930s, when the basic organizational principles of Soviet science emerged [27]. At that time, most leading Soviet scientists had been educated before the Revolution, few of them were members of the Communist Party, and Soviet science had not yet been thoroughly integrated within the Soviet system and ethos. (The first President of the Soviet Academy of Sciences who was a member of the Party was A. N. Nesmeianov, elected in 1951; his successor, M. V. Keldysh, elected in 1961, was not only a member of the Party, but also of its Central Committee; the current President, A. P. Aleksandrov, elected in 1975, is also a member of both the Party and the Central Committee.) Even as late as 1941, less than 5% of the full and corresponding members of the Soviet Academy of Sciences were also members of the Communist Party [28]. In the 1920s and 1930s, the Academy and other scientific organizations were often chastised for being devoted to pure science without sufficient regard for political and economic goals; some critics of the Academy accused it of "caste-like aloofness from the tasks of socialist construction" [29]. In order to correct this situation public organizations were invited to nominate new members of the Academy, scientists willing, as Academician Gubkin put it, to be "not only a representative of science but also a servant of the Soviet Government" [30]. Thus, in the 1920s and 1930s outside, or lay, involvement in Soviet science was strong.

The introduction of new members into the Academy in the 1930s and 1940s who were also members of the Communist Party, the reorganization of the Academy in the early 1930s, and the gradual integration of all Soviet scientific institutions into the Soviet system and ethos resulted in a diminishing of direct public involvement in Soviet science. More and more the scientists were allowed to run their own affairs, especially after the mid-1950s, when ideological intrusions into research markedly decreased. So long as scientists devoted their attention to research and did not get involved in politics they could usually count on the firm support of the Soviet government, a constantly growing budget, and high prestige in Soviet society. By the 1970s the majority of the Academy's administrators—the top officers, the members of the Academy Presidium, the scientific secretaries, the administrators of the divisions, even the laboratory directors—were also members of the Communist Party, people who worked to avoid conflict of interest between science and politics. The President of the Academy was simultaneously a high Party official, a person who was supposed to integrate science and public policy. By wearing several hats, the top scientists in the Academy could argue that the necessity for close outside control had disappeared. By 1982 over 60% of the full members and over 70% of the corresponding members of the Soviet Academy of Sciences were members of the Party [31]. While the Soviet government still had legitimate interests in the finances of the Academy and in setting general priorities, the evaluation of the propriety and quality of individual research projects, including those involving human subjects, was something that could be left to the scientists.

At the same time that the scientific community in the Soviet Union was integrated into the political system, the top governmental and party leaders acquired greater knowledge of science and technology. Scientific and technical education has become for the Soviet leadership what education in the classics was for British civil servants in the nineteenth century and what law and business management have been for recent generations of American leaders. During the last twenty years the majority of the members of the Central Committee and the Politburo of the Communist Party, as well as the members of the Council of Ministers of the USSR, have been men with technical educations [32]. Some people maintain that as a result of the greater technical knowledge of the top Soviet leadership it is less necessary to have a system of technical advisory committees and organizations for the policymakers in the Soviet Union than in the US. It is doubtful, however, that the technical knowledge gained by top Soviet political leaders at the time of their educations, decades before they reach their highest political posts, can still be very fresh or useful. Furthermore, many Americans would argue, as illustrated below, that the advisory committees should present not only technical findings but also represent different interest groups in society.

When the Soviet government wants advice on policy issues with high degrees of scientific content, it usually calls on committees composed entirely of scientists. Soviet scientists, like many American scientists, are usually happy to have it that way. When in 1976 an American delegation of the US-Soviet Working Group on Science Policy visited Moscow, Academician N. G. Basov, a Nobel laureate and member of the Presidium of the Soviet Academy, told the group that "science policy must be made by scientists", clearly implying that lay involvement was not needed [33]. When the Soviet delegation of the same Working Group submitted a paper on science policy in the Soviet Union, they emphasized the predominant "influence of leading scientists" [34]. Discussing the controversial aspects of genetic engineering, Academician A. A. Baev in 1977 cautioned against the inclusion of advice from nonscientists, warning that when a person does not have "adequate competence it is difficult to overcome emotional reactions and to think through peacefully a complicated subject like the role of science in society" [35]. Academician N. M. Zhavoronkov complained to the same American delegation in 1976 that because of public involvement in the discussion of pollution in Lake Baikal, "it was impossible to think calmly about the evidence" because "emotions ran too high" [36]. The Soviet delegation to the Asilomar Conference in California on recombinant DNA in 1975 complained to the American organizers about the presence of invited newspaper reporters at the Conference, maintaining that the discussion of controls over genetic engineering should be restricted to scientific circles [37].

Although I am not aware of all Soviet responses to new issues, like biomedical research, which have involved lay advice in the United States, to the extent that I can determine, nonscientists have been excluded from the biologists' committees. The Chairman of the Interdepartmental Commission for the Rules for Work with Recombinant DNA was Academician Baev, a leading Soviet biologist [38]. I was told in Moscow in January, 1983, that the Commission is made up entirely of natural scientists. The Commission in 1978 drafted rules for recombinant DNA research that are very similar to those used in the US at the same time [39]. Since that time Academician Baev has become Chairman of the Interdepartmental Scientific–Technical Council on Problems of Molecular Biology and Molecular Genetics, a group similar to the earlier one but with broader responsibilities [40]. I have been told that its members are also all natural scientists.

Nonscientists in the Soviet Union have called for their inclusion in the established bodies that make policy about biomedical ethics, so far unsuccessfully. The prominent Soviet philosopher I. T. Frolov has spoken of the necessity for "socioethical and humanistic regulation of science", and has added that the new issues in biomedical ethics present problems that are "radically different from what science and society has known until now" [41]. Frolov is Chairman of the Scientific Council of the Presidium of the Academy of Sciences on Philosophical and Social Problems of Science and Technology, which includes philosophers and historians as well as natural scientists [42]. The functions of Frolov's Council seem to be academic and philosophical rather than directly related to policy, in contrast to Baev's committee [43].

A few attempts have been made in the Soviet Union by groups outside the scientific community—people equivalent to public representatives in the US—to have influence on the debates over biomedical ethics. In the publication *Literary Gazette*, popular among the literary intelligentsia, several articles have expressed anxiety about possible infringements on human dignity by molecular biologists [44]. In 1974 the Orthodox Church entered the debate, just as religious groups in other countries have done [45]. However, in the Soviet Union the theologians met a sharp rebuff. In an article entitled "A Christian View on the Ecological Problem" the editors of the *Journal of the Moscow Patriarchate* agreed with Marxist philosophers who had called for ethical control over the applications of science and asked for inclusion of Christian considerations in the deliberations. The Christian authors wrote, "Science and technology are only a means in the hands of man who can use that means in very different directions. . . . Consequently, ethical control is needed not so much over science itself as over its social organization, over the means of its combination with technology and the economy" [46].

The Marxist philosophers rejected the offer of the priests to participate in the debates, pointing out that the Church maintained that science and technology must be based on nonscientific ethical and religious considerations. The Marxist philosophers maintained, on the contrary, that Marxist ethics are scientific; the philosophers considered themselves scientists just like the biologists, and wanted to be included on the scientific advisory committees. They thought that the priests, however, should be excluded because they are not scientists. The Soviet philosophers said that science should not be controlled from a nonscientific, Christian ethical position, but instead on the basis of a broad, truly scientific framework which included Marxist ethics [47]. But neither the Marxist philosophers nor the priests have been included on the important committees, so far as we can tell.

The Marxist philosophers present a particular problem to the Soviet biologists and biomedical specialists, who still resent the interference of the philosophers during the time of Lysenko's influence, which lasted until 1965. Philosophers in the Soviet Union have such a bad reputation among working biologists that the idea of having both groups together elaborate rules governing research on human subjects seems distasteful to many Soviet biologists [48].

The Differences

An important difference between the Soviet and the American approaches to this problem is that the Soviets seem to believe that the only important factor to include on such advisory committees is competent scientific knowledge, while the Americans have increasingly come to believe that such committees need to include both competent scientific knowledge and representation of the diverse political interests and ethical views of society as a whole. A crucial issue here, then, is the distinction between scientific competence and public representation.

In the West most discussions of biomedical ethics assume that ethics and biology belong to different realms and are different in kind. Ethics deals with values, biology with facts. To confuse the two is to make a "category mistake", to fail to notice, as A. J. Ayer put it, that ethical statements have no cognitive significance [49].

Since most Westerners accept this view, ethics advisory committees in Western countries are usually set up in such a way that two distinctly different strains of thought are represented. The scientists on these boards are supposed to supply the necessary scientific knowledge, while moral philosophers or religious leaders can supply the necessary knowledge of ethics and community standards. In the West, ethics is usually viewed as a set of prevailing principles or a methodology useful for guiding science, but not a part of science. To use a metaphor, the science and technology enterprise is a great ship belonging to the material world, while ethics is a nonmaterial set of beliefs that should guide the ship's rudder.

In the Soviet Union, on the other hand, the official view is that ethics and values are considered no less a subject of scientific study than biology. As A. Ivaniushkin wrote in the *Herald of the Academy of Medical Sciences of the USSR*, Marxists believe that, in principle, values can be submitted to "strict scientific research" [50]. This assertion of what in the West is called the "naturalistic fallacy" places Soviet Marxists in a different position from most of their Western colleagues when they approach problems of biomedical ethics.

A great irony here is that while the Western separation of ethics and science is probably not, in the final analysis, intellectually tenable, this separation has great practical utility. It provides a highly pragmatic approach for overcoming extremely difficult bioethical dilemmas, at least on a temporary basis. When a new development in science raises ethical questions, the common Western approach is to seek a compromise solution between what the new science permits and what defenders of the old values are willing to accept. This sort of temporary solution has been hammered out in the US on a whole range of issues, from birth control, abortion, genetic engineering and fetal research, to the cessation of life-sustaining devices of terminally-ill patients. An absolute position in these debates is often put forth by representatives of fundamentalist religions, which are regarded by most political leaders as one interest group out of many. Physicians, women's rights organizations, and political groups of various orientations often hold clearly contrasting positions, representing sharply different sets of interests.

The typically American middle-line compromise that often emerges is influenced, and even defined, by the extremes. All legislators and government funders in the US know they dare not offend too many of their constituents, even if their positions often seem intellectually primitive. In the US, those who maintain that abortion "violates God's will", or who say that the creation of new life forms by recombinant DNA "is contrary to the laws of Mother Nature", cannot be removed from the debates simply because their arguments seem irrational to many in the scientific community [51]. Their influence depends, in large part, on how many active supporters they can enlist in their cause. Decision makers in the US are often grateful that the spectrum of opinions is so broad and contradictory, because this spread of viewpoints increases their maneuverability, and makes it unnecessary for them to find correct decisions at moments when they do not have the faintest idea what such decisions would be, and even doubt that the term correct is applicable. Most American decision-makers in this situation make compromises, and they are willing to change their minds as public attitudes change. One reason for the inclusion of public representatives on ethical advisory boards and IRBs is to incorporate changing public attitudes at the local level and to remove the necessity for high public officials to take positions on such difficult questions.

Soviet decision-makers do not have the protective cover of strident public debate nor do they have, so far as we can tell, the insulation provided by IRBs and ethical advisory boards. The political and intellectual assumptions of Soviet society hamper the development of these protective mechanisms. On the political level, resolution of issues in public by means of the clash of different interest groups is not a part of Soviet tradition. On the intellectual level, in the Soviet Union arguments on abortion and recombinant DNA such as those voiced by religious fundamentalists in the US are not considered legitimate, since they are based on officially unacceptable philosophical positions—those of religion, mysticism, and dualism. No doubt these viewpoints have supporters in the Soviet Union, perhaps more than we would guess, but they do not figure in the debates, their views cannot be published in the Soviet press, and their arguments cannot be cited as evidence in trying to resolve biomedical dilemmas.

The antipathy of Soviet ethical theorists to compromise based on the clash of interest groups can be seen in the article on "Morality" in the *Large Soviet Encyclopedia*, which states that "communist morality rejects . . . the concept that is characteristic of bourgeois morality—namely, the sacrifice of one moral principle to another (for example, the sacrifice of honesty to advantage, of the interests of one group to the aims of another group, and of conscience to politics). Thus communist morality is the highest form of humanism" [52].

Rather than seeking a compromise in debates over biomedical ethics,

Soviet specialists are expected to find the correct solution, both from the biomedical and the Marxist point of view. Because some problems of biomedical ethics are so inherently complex correct solutions are difficult to find. Who knows in advance the answers to such questions as: Would an attempt to clone human beings be permissible in any circumstances? What are the ethical limitations on medical research on human fetuses? When is it permissible to turn off a life-sustaining device? In conducting psychological research, when is it permissible to deceive the subject? The list of such questions is long, and new ones constantly arise as biomedical and behavioral research possibilities change.

Since Soviet politicians and scientists do not have mechanisms permitting such questions to be resolved through public controversy and interest group conflict, they tend to stay silent on such topics until accepted guidelines and practices have emerged in other countries. Then they often accept those guidelines. No great controversy over recombinant DNA research developed in the Soviet Union in the late 1970s, but eventually biologists there adopted guidelines which were remarkably similar to those in the US, which had been produced only after intensive discussion [53].

One of the reasons that ethical review is less pressing in the Soviet Union than in the US is that the "projects and grants" approach to funding research is much less developed there [54]. In the US, ethical review boards have arisen in the context of the award of grants to scientists in research institutions. With the growth of federal support for research through agencies such as the NSF and the NIH, American scientists became increasingly accountable to Congress and the tax-paying public. As biomedical research grew more controversial, it was inevitable that the responsible federal agencies would wish to protect themselves from criticism. One way to do this was to provide for ethical review of research proposals by committees on which the public was represented.

In the Soviet Union this motive for ethical analysis of research is much weaker. Most scientific research there is supported through block-funding to whole institutions (rather than to principal investigators, as in the US). The system of contracts and grants is much less developed in the Soviet Union, and even when such awards are given, the procedures are different. Each scientific institute in the Soviet Academy of Sciences, for example, submits its budgets for the coming year to the Academy's administrative hierarchy, headed by the Presidium of the Academy; the usual outcome is for the institute to receive an annual incremental increase [55]. Great vacillations in funding are rare, the concept of public accountability is weak, and a formal system of peer review of research applications is not deemed necessary. When one considers these characteristics of Soviet science together with the traditional aversion to public controversy, one can understand why the Soviet Union has still not engaged in the major discussions about biomedical ethics that have become normal in the US, and why they have not developed special institutional mechanisms to handle them.

Nonetheless, it appears likely that pressure for developing some kind of lay involvement in technical decisions in the Soviet Union will grow. The issues on which lay participation seems appropriate are now breaking out of biomedicine and spreading into other areas, such as energy technology. Whether one generates electrical power from nuclear reactors or coal-fired generators, there will be radiation and other harmful environmental effects, hazards of different sorts for the workers in the industry, and other deleterious consequences. Painful decisions involving trade-offs have to be made. Since these decisions involve conflicts or interests, technical knowledge is not enough to ensure good decisions. These decisions are not ones for technical specialists alone, whether they be engineers, economic planners, or political leaders who, years before, earned degrees in technical areas. Ethical issues and political clashes are deeply intertwined with technical problems, and it is not clear that the Soviet Union will be able to keep the debates at a low level indefinitely. We have seen that Soviet authorities are beginning to feel pressure from nonscientific groups who wish to be consulted on technical questions. At the same time, American regulatory authorities are being submitted to a reverse pressure from scientists who believe that the inclusion of lay opinion in technical decision making has gone too far. Several recent polls on attitudes toward nuclear power conducted in the US have shown that the less a person knows about science and technology, the more opposed that person tends to be to nuclear power. These polls have provided ammunition for the critics of lay members of policy committees [56].

At the present time a great difference of opinion exists about the proper way to make policy decisions with high technical content; furthermore, opinion on this issue is split in both the US and the Soviet Union. The prevailing view in the US is, however, still much more strongly in favor of lay participation than in the Soviet Union. Out of such legitimate differences of opinion, international conferences such as those sponsored by IIASA should be able to produce vivid discussion.

References

1. The 250 figure includes all the reports of the Academy System, including the National Academy of Sciences, National Research Council, Institute of Medicine, and National Academy of Engineering. Some of these reports are in letter form. If one counts only those reports of the National Academy of Sciences that are published by the Academy Press, the number would be about 55.
2. Report (1982) Frank Press takes exception to NAS panel recommendations on marijuana, *Science*, **217**, 228–229.
3. See Department of Health, Education, and Welfare (1976) *Charter: Ethical Advisory Board*, approved by David Matthews, Secretary, (Department of Health, Education, and Welfare).

4. Hastings Center (1979) in brief, *Hastings Center Report* (New York, USA: Hastings Center Institute of Society, Ethics and the Life Sciences) October pp 2–3; *ibid* (1980) February, pp 2–3; *ibid* (1981) February p 2.

5. Hastings Center (1981) The Washington scene: President's Commission one year later, *Hastings Center Report* (New York, USA: Hastings Center Institute of Society, Ethics and the Life Sciences) February, p 2.

6. Hastings Center, op. cit., note 5.

7. President's Commission for the Study of Ethical Problems in Medicine and Biomedical and Behavioural Research (1982) *Splicing Life: The Social and Ethical Issues of Genetic Engineering with Human Beings* (Washington, DC, USA: US Government Printing Office).

8. *The Federal Register*, **46** (16) 26 January p 8376.

9. US Department of Health, Education and Welfare, Public Health Service, *Grant Application Forum PHS 398* (OMB No. 68-R0249, Rev. 10; 79), pp 3–4.

10. Nolan, K. A. (1980) The Evolution of IRB Composition: Student Members.

11. Curran, W. J. (1970) Governmental regulation of the use of human subjects in medical research: the approach of two federal agencies, in P. Freund (Ed), *Experimentation with Human Subjects* (New York, USA: George Braziller) pp 442–443.

12. Katz, J. (1972) *Experimentation with Human Beings* (New York, USA: Russell Sage Foundation) p 888.

13. Nolan, op. cit., and Barber, B., Lally, J., *et al.*, the structure and processes of peer group review, in J. Katz (Ed), op. cit., p 902.

14. Nolan, op. cit.

15. Freedman, B. (1981) One philosopher's experience on an ethics committee, *Hastings Center Report*, April, pp 20–22.

16. Institutional Review Board (1981) Department of energy proposes human subjects research regulations, *IRB*, **February**, 10.

17. *IRB* is published by The Hastings Center, Institute of Society, Ethics, and the Life Sciences, 360 Broadway, Hastings-on-Hudson, New York. It began publication in 1979.

18. Cohen J. M. and Hedberg, W. B. (1980) The annual activity of a university IRB, *IRB*, **May** 5–6.

19. Ashford, N. A. (1984) The use of technical information in environmental health and safety regulation: a brief guide to the issues, *Science, Technology, and Human Values*, **9** (Winter) 130.

20. Ashford, op. cit.

21. National Science Board (1980) *Science Indicators 1980* (Washington, DC, USA: National Science Foundation) pp 173–176, referred to in Brooks, H. (1984) The resolution of technically-intensive public policy disputes, *Science, Technology, and Human Values*, **9** (Winter) 39.

22. Brooks, H. (1984) The resolution of technically-intensive public policy disputes, *Science, Technology, and Human Values*, **9** (Winter), 39.

23. Miller, E. (1981) International trends in ethical review of medical research, *IRB*, **October** 9–10.

24. Miller, op. cit., p 9.

25. Cowan, D. H. (1980) IRB review of randomized clinical trials, *IRB*, **November** 2; Ghio, J. M. (1980) What is the role of a public member of an IRB?, *IRB*, **February**, 7.

26. See Aivazian, S. I., Vedeneev, Iu. A., and Supatyeva, O. A. (1980) *Pravovye voprosy upravleniia nauchnymi issledovaniiami* (Moscow, USSR); and Larychev, O. I., Larin, S. I., and Boychenko, V. S. (1978) A system for stimulating the development of fundamental research in the USSR, in Committee for Joint US/USSR Academy Study of Fundamental Science Policy, *Systems for Stimulating the Development of Fundamental Research* (Washington, DC, USA: National Academy of Sciences).

27. Graham, L. R. (1975) The formation of Soviet research institutes: a combination of revolutionary innovation and international borrowing, *Social Studies of Science*, (5) 303–329; Graham, L. R. (1967) *The Soviet Academy of Sciences and the Communist Party 1927-1932* (Princeton, USA: Princeton University Press) Bailes, K. E. (1978) *Technology and Society under Lenin and Stalin: Origins of the Soviet Technical Intelligentsia 1917–1941;* Ivanova, L. V. (1978) *Formirovanie sovetskoi nauchnoi intelligentsii, 1917–1927*, Fediukin, S. A. (1965)

Sovetskaia Vlast' i burzhuaznye spetsialisty (Moscow, USSR); Fediukin, S. A. (1972) *Velikii oktiabr' i intelligentsiia: Iz istorii vovlecheniia staroi intelligentsii v stroitel'stvo sotsializma* (Moscow, USSR); Bastrakova, M. S. (1973) *Stanovlenie sovetskoi sistemy organizatsii nauki (1917–1922)* (Moscow, USSR); (1968) *Organizatsiia nauki v pervye zody sovetskoi vlasti (1917–1925)* Leningrad, USSR).

28. Fortescue, S. (19??) *Party Membership in Soviet Research Institutes*, unpublished paper, p 27.
29. A particularly strong attack of this type was Pletnev, V. (1922) Na ideologicheskom fronte, *Pravda* 27 September.
30. Graham, L. R. (1967) *The Soviet Academy of Sciences and the Communist Party 1927–1932* (Princeton, USA: Princeton University Press) p 80.
31. Fortescue, op. cit., p 23.
32. Bales, K. E. (1980) The technical specialists: social composition and attitudes, in L. L. Lubrano and S. G. Solomon (Eds) *The Social Context of Soviet Science* (Boulder, USA: Westview Press) p 137.
33. US–Soviet Working Group on Science Policy, discussion at the Presidium of the Academy of Sciences, Moscow, 20 September 1976.
34. Larychev, O. I., Larin, S. I., and Boychenko, V. S. (1978) A system for stimulating the development of fundamental research in the USSR, in Committee for Joint US/USSR Academy Study of Fundamental Science Policy, Systems for Stimulating Fundamental Research (Washington, DC, USA: National Academy of Sciences) pp 45–47.
35. Baev, A. A. (1977) Sotsial'nye aspekty geneticheskoi inzhenerii, *Filosofskaia bor'ba idei v sovremennom estestvoznanii*, p 145.
36. US–Soviet Working Group on Science Policy, discussion at the Presidium of the Academy of Sciences, Moscow, 29 September 1976.
37. Goodfield, J. (1977) *Playing God: Genetic Engineering and the Manipulation of Life* (New York, USA: Random House) p 111.
38. Vel'kov, V. V. (1982) Opasny li opyty s rekombinantnymi DNK, *Priroda*, (No. 4), 18–26. Vel'kov was also a member of the Interdepartmental Commission, and he listed Baev as chairman.
39. *Vremennyi pravila bezopasnosti rbot s rekombinantnymi DNK* (1978) Pushchino, USSR. Compare with *NIH Guidelines for Research Involving Recombinant DNA Molecules*, US Department of Health, Education, and Welfare, June 23, 1976, and subsequent revisions listed in *The Federal Register*, **44**, No. 232, 1979; **45**, No. 20, 1980; and **45**, No. 22, 1980. For Soviet discussions of the risks of recombinant DNA research see, in addition to the Vel'kov article listed above, Baev, A. A. (1981) Sovremennaia biologiia kak sotsial'noe iavlenie, *Voprisy filosofii*, No. 3; Uil'iamson, B. (1980) Budushchee gennoi inzhereii, *Mir nauki*, No. 4; and Shirtsov, O. U. (1981) Problema riska pri genno-inzhenernykh issledovaniiakh, *Vestnik akademii meditsinkskikh nauk*, No. 2.
40. *Spravochnik akademii nauk SSSR* (1982) (Moscow, USSR).
41. Frolov, I. T. (1981) Nauka-tsennosti-gumanizm, *Voprosy filosofii*, No. 3, 30; see also Frolov I. T. (1979) *Perspektivy cheloveka* (Moscow, USSR) Frolov, I. T. (1980) *Odialektiki i etike biologicheskogo poznaniia* (Moscow, USSR) and Iudin B. G. (1980) Etika nauchnogo issledovaniia, *Priroda*, No. 10, 1980.
42. This council was formed in February, 1980; the four sections are headed by B. M. Kedrov, S. R. Mikulinskii, B. F. Lomov, and E. K. Fedorov. See Ob osnovnykh napravleniiakh deiatel'nosti novogo nauchnogo soveta, *Voprosy filosofii* No. 10, 1980.
43. Frolov, I. T. (1981) Nauka-tsennosti-gumanizm, *Voprosy filosofii*, No. 3, 27–41.
44. See, for example, Dyban, A. (1978) Schastilivyi zapret prirody, *Literaturnaia gazeta*, August 23. For a Soviet author who is rather horrified by the whole idea of genetic engineering, see Shiskin, A. F. (1979) *Chelovecheskaia priorda i nravstvennosti* (Moscow, USSR) who comments on p 223 of his book that "progressive scholars of the whole world are experiencing alarm in connection with the dangers which can be brought by 'gene engineering' ".
45. Khristianskii vzgliad na ekologicheskuiu problemu, *Zhurnal moskovskoi patriarkhii*, No. 4, 1974, 35–39.
46. Note 45 and Solov'ev, E. Iu. *Voprosy filosofii*, No. 8, p 105.
47. Solov'ev, op. cit.

48. See Joravsky, D. (1970) *The Lysenko Affair* (Cambridge, USA: Harvard University Press; Medvedev, Z. (1969) *The Rise and Fall of T.D. Lysenko* (New York, USA: Columbia University Press) Graham, L. R. (1972) *Science and Philosophy in the Soviet Union* (New York, USA: Alfred Knopf) and Graham, L. R. (April 1982) When ideology and controversy collide: the case of Soviet science, *The Hastings Center Report*, **12** (2), 26–32.

49. The influence of this particular view on American teaching about ethics is discussed in Sloan, D. (1980) The teaching of ethics in the American undergraduate curriculum, 1876–1976, in D. Callahan and S. Bok (Eds) *Ethics Teaching in Higher Education* (New York, USA: Plenum Press) pp 1–57.

50. Ivaniushkin, A. Ia. (1977) K voprosu o sushchnosti meditsinskoi deontologii, *Vestnik Akademii meditsinskikh nauk SSSR*, No. 4, 48–55.

51. For examples of the seriousness with which such objections have to be taken by ethics advisory committees, see *Testimony on In Vitro Fertilization*, submitted to Ethics Advisory Board, HEW. The EAB traveled around the US and listened to testimony from all who wished to appear, thus encountering people representing widely diverse viewpoints.

52. *Great Soviet Encyclopedia* (1977) Volume XVI (New York, USA: Macmillan) p 549.

53. See note 39 above.

54. See the discussion in Gustafson, T. (1980) Why doesn't Soviet science do better than it does?, in L. L. Lubrano and S. G. Solomon (Eds) *The Social Context of Soviet Science* (Boulder, USA: Westview Press) pp 31–67.

55. US–Soviet Working Group on Science Policy, discussions in Moscow, September, 1976.

56. Cohen, R. L. and Lichter, S. R. (1983) Nuclear power: the decision makers speak, *Regulation*, **March/April**, 32–37.

CHAPTER 11

The Role of International Research Institutions

HARVEY BROOKS

Introduction

From the perspective of most scientists, science for public policy means how science can be used to teach policymakers to make the most rational choices among alternative policies so as to further the common good. In this perspective the most rational course of action would ideally emerge in a compelling fashion from the proper marshalling of the relevant "facts". The difficulties of implementing this rational policy in the real world are seen as problems for the policymaker or the administrator, not the analyst or researcher. If the world is embarked on a self-destructive course, the demonstration and clear explanation of this should suffice to convince key decisionmakers of the folly of their ways and to lead them to change the undesirable course of events. To induce national governments to reduce SO_2 emissions from their power plants, for example, it should suffice to project convincingly the cumulative destructive effects of these emissions on the environment of their own or nearby countries. While there is no question that accurate and convincing forecasts of the consequences of pursuing various policies helps decisionmakers to justify to themselves and defend to their constituencies choices among alternatives which may be more rational from the standpoint of some conception of the common good, such information is seldom conclusive and may even be irrelevant from the standpoint of most of the stakeholders. Any one decisionmaker controls only a few of the many parameters that affect the net outcome of a policy change. Many individual actors with different concerns on their agendas have to be induced to agree on actions which may have adverse consequences for other goals which may be of greater importance to them or to the constituencies to which they consider themselves most accountable. This is why we see people who, when out of power, advocate policies in accord with what scientists or policy analysts consider rational, take quite different positions when they are in power and are under pressure to take into account quite a different mix of interests and perspectives than when they had the luxury of being able to maximize a single objective function.

145

In short, the application of science in the real world must be seen more as part of an enlightened negotiation process to which science is a contributor than as a transfer of certified knowledge to decisionmakers for them to implement.

Distributional Consequences of the Application of Knowledge

A common ideal for the application of science in our contemporary world has been encapsulated by William Evan in the claim that the "rationality of pursuing power through the pursuit of national interests will have to be replaced with the rationality of pursuing science and applying scientific knowledge on behalf of the human species" [1]. This could form as good a motto as any to express the ideals and purposes which lay behind the creation of IIASA, and make it especially attractive as a place to work. The difficulty, though, is that there is almost no application of science to the real world that is completely neutral in its distributional effects among nations or individuals, i.e. which benefits or injures everybody equally. Indeed a typical application of knowledge may be one which benefits a great many people a little, but has substantial adverse consequences for a few. Large industrial or energy facilities provide a good example, and as they increase in scale, the disjunction between risks or costs and benefits tends to increase. Thus the notion of "benefit to the human species" is, in practice, constrained by notions of equity or justice in the distribution of benefits and costs among individual members or subgroups of the species such as nations, classes, regions, corporations, institutions, professions, or associations of like minded individuals. Even when there is almost universal agreement on the benefits of certain policies or actions, there is little agreement on how the costs or risks of taking these actions should be shared among the people affected. If the existing state of knowledge were capable of providing a confident prediction of the consequences of particular policies or actions, including their incidence on various groups, "objective" knowledge would still be incapable of providing a basis for arriving at a consensus concerning which consequences were most desirable or acceptable.

Local vs. Global Problems

Although distributional considerations are especially difficult to deal with in the solution of global problems because of the lack of established political forums for the adjudication or resolution of issues where conflicting national sovereignties are involved, the distributional problem can equally frustrate the resolution of issues in a much more localized context. This has been graphically described by Michael O'Hare and his collaborators in their study of the politics of facility siting [2]. Their study illustrates how a situation can develop in which a number of interests, each striving to maximize somewhat different goals, can arrive at a final result which is worse than any one of them would have been willing to settle for initially, while achieving the goals of none of them. There seems to be an interesting analogy here with the bargaining among sovereign states on such issues as arms limitation or trade restrictions. O'Hare *et al.* point to the "consistency with which parties in siting disputes act rationally and effectively to serve their interests as they perceive them" while, at the same time, there are few instances in which "the opponents who generate the individual failures favor the aggregate result" [3]. It becomes a decision process which exhibits the classical "tragedy of the commons" dilemma [4].

One of the best examples is the siting of hazardous waste facilities, where the contending parties almost always agree that some form of well-managed and monitored site is in everybody's best interest, but nobody wants it in their vicinity. The end result is that no proper disposal facility is implemented and hence everybody is exposed to the hazard of temporary storage or illegal dumping, as well as eventually having to share in the much increased cost of future cleanup.

Such a description seems strikingly reminiscent of negotiations to limit the deployment of new weapons systems, where each side strives to preserve a temporary advantage provided by a new weapon even when it should be entirely clear to all parties that everybody's security will be greatly reduced once the new weapons system has been deployed by two nations or, worse, many. O'Hare *et al.* go on to point out that a prime source of breakdown of negotiations in the hazardous waste example arises "because the social, political, and economic structures by which information is made available obstruct its efficient use or generation" [5]. What this critique amounts to is that too much thinking has been concentrated on improving the rationality of the choice of policy (e.g. selection of the best site by some objective scientific criteria) and too little on the details of implementation of the policy once chosen. For it is in the process of implementation that the distributional effects become apparent, and the political opposition of the various stakeholders becomes mobilized. This has its counterpart in Brickman's choice of strategies between improved knowledge generation in the expectation that deeper knowledge will overcome political controversy and "developing institutions and procedures to further consensus when science is inadequate or irrelevant".

This seems to be one of the key factors also in the interaction between international scientific institutions and national decisionmakers. In practice, the information they transfer to national decisionmakers is usually not in a form that addresses the most immediate action requirements of these decisionmakers. Not enough attention is paid to understanding why the rational solution is hard to implement and in devising strategies to reinforce the interest of decisionmakers in choosing the rational solution. Any policy, no matter how demonstrably beneficial to the more inclusive community, adversely affects some subgroups within that community. These adverse effects are often much larger on a *per capita* basis for the groups affected than are the more diffuse benefits, also when measured on a *per capita* basis. The ability to mobilize political opposition or support for a policy is probably more related to the *per capita* impact of that policy on each affected group than to its aggregate impact. This makes it clearer why the resultant of many groups each pursuing its own interests or goals through political or judicial processes is an outcome which is irrational from a more detached and comprehensive standpoint. O'Hare *et al.* remark that the "difference in *per capita* stakes has the utmost importance for the design of a siting process in which efficient outcomes can be expected" [6] since . . . "although the total benefits at stake may be larger for the diffuse beneficiaries, local opponents will be more motivated to take action because of their higher *per capita* stake in the outcome" [7].

The applicability of these considerations to the acid rain problem as it has been posed to the political process both in Europe and North America seems self-evident. Either the preservation of the *status quo* or most proposed remedies generate large *per capita* costs for some subgroups, who are thereby mobilized to block solutions. Basically, it is this fact that has produced an impasse in both Europe and North America. In both regions the most serious and visible impacts are confined to relatively few locations, and are highly variable geographically. Similarly, the costs of reducing emissions from the sources of pollution vary radically among sources and frequently fall most heavily on those least able to bear them.

The tendency towards stalemate may be aggravated by doctrinaire insistence on the "polluter pays" principle. There are rational economic arguments for this principle in that if polluting institutions are compelled to pay the costs of avoiding pollution, the costs will be passed along to their customers in the form of higher prices for their products or services, and this will tend to reduce both the level and the rate of growth of the activity which is the source of the damage. There are, of course, also arguments of fairness or justice which argue for some form of equitable sharing of the costs of mitigating pollution among all polluters, and not imposing these costs on a public which does not necessarily benefit from the activity in question. However, this is a long run argument that does not take into account the political problems of implementation. If the objective of good policy is to achieve its benefits to the general public as rapidly and economically as possible, there are strong arguments for distributing the cost of implementation more widely than might be required by strict adherence to the polluter pays principle, i.e. by strict economic rationality, or the view that the guilty should pay for their sins. In particular, the sharing of costs between polluters and the beneficiaries of reduced pollution might be more effective as an initial strategy by virtue of the fact that the sudden high *per capita* costs to a few polluters are phased in more gradually, while the *per capita* costs to beneficiaries, representing a much larger group, are relatively minor.

In the North American case most of the sulfur loading from the Canadian side comes from about six point sources associated with nonferrous smelting operations. The cost of reducing emissions from these sources is relatively small. On the American side a large part of the sulfur loading comes from older coal-fired power plants which were "grandfathered" under the provisions of the Clean Air Act because of the high cost of retrofit compared to inclusion of scrubbers on new plants. While an optimal policy might be to phase out these old plants as soon as possible on the grounds that the seriousness of the acid rain problem is great enough to justify either requiring that they be retrofitted with scrubbers, be shut down immediately, or replaced with new plants if that is uneconomic. But one of the most economically depressed regions of the country is being asked to bear large costs for the benefit of other regions of the United States and the citizens of another country. One could thus also argue that society as a whole, or possibly the downwind beneficiaries of sulfur emission reduction, should be prepared to pay at least the difference in cost per kwh of retrofitting old coal plants vs. establishing controls on new sources. In the present North American debate other options are also being considered, such as a countrywide electricity surtax which would be used to subsidize emission reductions at the most critical or expensive-to-retrofit plants. Another suggestion is the setting of an overall emission ceiling for a region, leaving the allocation of emission reductions among sources to emission permits which can be traded or marketed among sources so as to achieve the required aggregate reduction at the least net cost to the region as a whole.

Similar strategies might be followed in northern Europe, with the possibility of trading emission ceilings among countries as well as among individual sources. Victim nations might even be given the option of buying and retiring emission permits from polluting countries or source organizations in order to accelerate their realization of the benefits of emission reductions. The detailed study of the implications of such strategies could become an essential part of the agenda of international research institutions assessing the problem of acid rain. Merely trying to quantify the benefits of emission reduction and then leaving implementation to a separate political negotiation may not be an adequate research agenda. IIASA has in fact initiated this type of study with respect to hazardous waste siting, where similar considerations may apply.

In all these cases the issue of fairness and equity among affected interests greatly complicates the discussion of solutions. The most rational or efficient allocation of pollution abatement among the sources of pollution may frequently violate people's feelings about what is fair. Many people feel that there is something morally reprehensible or irresponsible about causing pollution, and that those responsible should not be allowed to escape punishment for their sins even if, in fact, the costs are ultimately borne by the consumers of their products or services, who could be regarded almost as much innocent bystanders as the victims of pollution themselves. On the other hand, the few polluting sources that might have to bear inordinately high costs compared with most plants in a uniform percentage rollback of emissions may also feel unfairly singled out for punishment for an activity undertaken in good faith for the benefit of society long before air pollution was a major public concern.

Knowledge and Power

Knowledge may be cultivated for different purposes. Ideally it is often thought of as divorced from the exercise of political power, but if it is at all applied, or just potentially applicable, its generation is inevitably affected by the nature of the institutions which apply it and by its ultimate use. It is thus, implicitly or explicitly, cultivated to support some kind of exercise of power. The agenda for applied research, and even the form in which research results are analyzed or interpreted is thus influenced by the purpose for which the knowledge is expected to be used, as Ravetz has emphasized elsewhere in this volume.

The power to be exercised may be mainly national power, for example, in direct support of military power, or to enhance the national "image" and thereby the political influence of the nation through the demonstration of scientific or technological prowess, as in the space programs of the United States and the Soviet Union or between the United States and Europe in certain fields of "big science" such as high-energy physics or radioastronomy. To the extent that the cultivation of technical knowledge supports national military or economic power against other nations it may be viewed as violating the universalistic norms of science; nevertheless, nationalistic aims have become deeply embedded in the practice and institutions of scientific and technological research, and have, indeed, been a main driving force for constructive technological progress in the past. This can be expected to change only slowly.

Knowledge may also be cultivated for the support of the exercise of power at the national level for purposes which are, at least in initial intent, humanitarian and universal. Such is the case, for example, with research in support of environmental, health, and safety regulation, designed to protect society from the possible adverse effects of technology. Despite the fact that this use of knowledge is in principle more compatible with the universalistic norms of science, the exercise of power which it supports inevitably confronts the differing interests and goals of particular groups, and may appear to many to be just as much of an abuse of science as its use for nationalistic aims. Knowledge in support of regulation is especially crucial in the American political system, where the strong emphasis on "due process" in administrative law means that all regulations are subject to challenge in the courts by the interests affected. Regulators, to withstand this challenge, must be able to show that their decisions are adequately grounded in scientific evidence. The character of the evidence required for regulations to withstand challenge in the courts has a major influence on the agenda of research related to the environmental, health, and safety effects of technological activities [8]. Because of this, science is, perhaps, a more important source of the legitimacy of political authority in the American system than in any of the other western industrial democracies [9].

Global Problems

Many have argued that the "absence of an infrastructure of scientific and technological research institutions with a mandate to study global problems" results in a "failure to integrate knowledge with power on behalf of global society" [10]. Those arguing this point also maintain that such a scientific infrastructure may be a prerequisite for the emergence of a matching sociopolitical infrastructure that is capable of carrying such knowledge into application without the risk of neutralization by claims of national sovereignty.

Despite the political polarization that has plagued some of the UN agencies in recent years, these specialized bodies have been among the most successful in the UN system, in part because their grounding in applied science gives them a legitimacy that other international bodies lack. Although they do not carry on much original generation of new knowledge, they have succeeded in integrating existing knowledge and understanding in certain fields of global significance, such as food, health, and environment, and also in translating such knowledge into beneficial action. Often this part of their work gets less attention from the media than the more dramatic ideological confrontations.

On the other hand, attempts to apply knowledge without adequate understanding of the potential effects of such application on various national or subnational interests may be totally frustrated for political reasons. The record on acid rain, stratospheric ozone, transboundary waterway pollution, and radioactive waste management has been mixed at best. The record on radioactive fallout from atmospheric nuclear testing and on marine pollution from petroleum has been somewhat better.

By and large, past attempts to use international scientific networks to influence national political decisions have had limited success because of insufficient sensitivity to the problems of implementation arising out of national or subnational constituency interests. It is not that knowledge itself should be altered by the interests involved, but rather that in delineating the consequences of policy, analysis must spell out not only the aggregate benefits but also the costs or risks to particular stakeholders. Otherwise these are likely to become an unanticipated focal point for national opposition. Policy research should pursue the implications of the implementation of recommended policies in much greater depth than has been traditional, particularly in international institutions. It should attempt to identify in advance the likely points of resistance by identifying affected interests and devising implementation strategies that may forestall or mitigate opposition through compensation and other devices. Such an approach recognizes that all policy implementation involves a negotiation, whether implicit or explicit, among affected interests, and part of the goal of analysis should be to illuminate and facilitate this negotiation process. One powerful way of doing this may be to persuade stakeholders that their interests are different from what they had thought.

The Virtues of Hypocrisy

Kenneth Boulding, in a very provocative lecture given at IIASA [11], has extolled the virtues of hypocrisy in inducing nations to introduce reforms that align their practices more fully with their professed ideals. Boulding's idea may apply especially to the universalistic ideals of science. Despite the fact that most science and technology today have been, to a large extent, coopted by national rather than more inclusive human interests, the universalistic vision exercises a powerful countervailing attraction not only on scientists themselves, but also on political leaders more generally. The latter feel compelled to pay at least minimum lip service to this universalistic ideal in their public pronouncements, and over time this can exert subtle pressures to bring reality more in conformity with their public professions. Thus, pretense of a non-existent reality always contains the latent possibility of something more in the long run.

Constraints at the Interface Between Science and Politics

Evan has suggested that the "most visible barrier . . . to increasing the influence of International Scientific and Professional Associations (ISPA's) on international policymaking . . . is the economic and political dependence of scientists and technologists on their governments and employers" [12]. He argues for much larger independent sources of finance for "transnational policy-related studies and for the wide dissemination and popularization of the results of such studies". While this is certainly important, it may not be the biggest barrier to increasing the role of scientific analysis and insights in the management of human affairs. The failure to find effective modes of interaction between policymakers and knowledge producers is equally, if not more, important. Furthermore, the conventional wisdom among most scientists that the failure of politicians and decisionmakers to listen to scientists is the source of the problem is a dangerous oversimplification. The failure of communication is two-sided; neither the politicians nor the scientists are prepared to understand the constraints under which the other operates. The blame may lie especially on the side of scientists or analysts who belittle the constraints of the politicians and managers and do not address the problems of implementation outlined above. Evan goes on to say that "if any segment of society can possibly contribute to transcending the 'ideals of the tribe' it is the community of scientists, engineers, and professionals whose work brings them into recurrent contact with colleagues the world over" [13]. In this respect institutions such as IIASA provide an ideal setting for the realization of the benefits of that "recurrent contact" among colleagues because it encourages much more sustained interaction and actual collaboration than the usual international meetings, conferences, laboratory visits, correspondence, and "invisible colleges". These networks are important, but they cannot provide the intensity of interaction necessary to work problems through comprehensively and in detail, and especially to overcome the culture-bound differences in perspective which particularly plague applications of science.

Such institutions can probably contribute most to the solution of global problems, problems which are inherently international, interlinked with each other (such as food and energy), and multidimensional [14]. The biggest limitation in the contribution that science and analysis can make to the solution of global problems lies in the distributional dimensions of such solutions.

Problems of balancing the total supply and demand for resources such as energy and food, for example, are almost surely soluble by means of science and technology, even for considerably higher population levels than are now contemplated in most projections of a steady state world [15]. What is not soluble by technical means alone is the distribution of these resources among nations and groups, or their compatibility with conflicting views among different groups of what is a desirable quality of life. However, analysis should be capable of generating a consensus on the most probable distributional consequences of various policies, thus narrowing the political focus on choice among consequences rather than hopelessly entangled political *cum* technical arguments. What appeared initially as an irreconcilable technical disagreement can frequently be reduced to a difference in perceived interest, or to an argument over the sharing of risks or costs. Furthermore, science and analysis can often uncover policies where mutual gains are possible, replacing what was originally seen by politicians and administrators as a zero-sum game by a positive-sum one, but this usually requires a much more accurate identification of the true interests of the stakeholders, which can be facilitated by good science and analysis. Research can thus broaden the agenda of policy options while narrowing the specific areas of conflicting interest or goals. The experience of IIASA seems to show that even global issues that are inherently political can be partially depoliticized and analyzed dispassionately, given the right environment. This environment must be carefully designed to enhance the universalistic ideals of science, including Merton's four norms of "universalism, organized skepticism, disinterestedness, and communality"[16].

Global vs. National Stewardship of Resources

One of the major areas of conflict in the world arises over the control and management of natural resources, both renewable and non-renewable. In one sense this is no different from the environmental issues already discussed, because a clean environment can be regarded as a finite natural resource in its own right. However, there is a long societal tradition of national sovereignty over natural resources which does not apply in the same measure to the environment. That the environment belongs to the global "commons" is much more accepted than that resources in the ground or on the land should. On the other hand, the whole international community has a stake in the wise management of all the world's resources because of the "spillover effects" in other countries arising from the mismanagement of resources in one country [17]. For example, the felling of forests on the steep hillslopes of Nepal causes flooding in India and Bangladesh, and affects the supply of hydropower in those countries. Pricing and production of oil and gas in various regions that control large resources of these can have profound economic affects around the world. The genetic resource base for many important cash crops on which particular countries depend may lie in other countries; 40 percent of the world's coffee crop, for example, is said to depend upon germ plasm found only in the forests of Ethiopia [18].

Not only does each sovereign nation have a responsibility to safeguard key resources under its control for the benefit of mankind as well as its own future, but the rest of the world has a reciprocal responsibility to provide whatever support lies within its capability to help other nations in managing their resources wisely. As in many other instances, the problem of wise management of resources may come into collision with concepts of fairness and equal sacrifice mentioned earlier. What is generally acknowledged to be in the collective interest of all may nevertheless fail of implementation because of disagreements over what constitutes a fair method of sharing benefits and costs. The claim of sovereignty over resources tends to be taken as implying a principal obligation on the part of the sovereign nation, but this nation in turn feels it unfair that it should have to bear the full cost of reducing spillover effects from the exploitation of its own resources that mainly affect other nations. Frequently interdependence among nations on the use of resources is not appreciated or understood by the actual people who exploit the resources. The farmers of Nepal are too remote to understand the problems their activities create downstream, and, by themselves, do not command the means necessary to change their actions for the benefit of their neighbors.

The summoning of the political will necessary to insure exercise of the reciprocal responsibilities among nations and groups within nations for the husbanding of key resources depends on wide diffusion of understanding of the consequences of various actions and policies, and this in turn depends on convincing scientific information, which, however, is a necessary but not a sufficient condition for arriving at a consensus among all those whose behavior affects ultimate outcomes. The reason it is not sufficient is that no scientific information can deal completely with the sharing problem. The most that scientific information by itself can hope to achieve is to help identify the magnitude of the stakes involved in *not* arriving at an accommodation in relation to the sharing of the burdens of constructive action. International research institutions should have a comparative advantage in developing and certifying scientific information and analysis which will have credibility among the wide variety of commercial, industrial, regional, and national bodies that must act, and in persuading them that it is their ultimate self-interest to cooperate in maintaining the natural resource/environmental base which in the last analysis sustains all economic activity.

Commentary: *John Gibbons*

The following are some brief remarks on the need for science-for-public-policy research, both nationally and internationally. They are in part based on impressions formed at IIASA, but I have also drawn upon my experience as Director of the Office of Technology Assessment (OTA) of the U.S. Congress.

My experience at OTA, bolstered by dialogues with colleagues from many different countries with very diverse forms of government and in different states of economic development, has taught me that each nation needs the equivalent of an OTA process. By process I mean the distillation, from many diverse sources and points of view, of technical (scientific and other) judgment about issues of policy relevance. As was brought out at the Forum, in olden days the political community appealed to the Church as a source of

John Gibbons is Director of the U.S. Office of Technology Assessment, Washington, D.C.

legitimization, but today it appeals to "scientists" and other "experts." Such analyses need to be carried out in close — but not too close — proximity to the center of the decision process (OTA is a convenient, but important, 10 minute walk from the U.S. Capitol Building!).

At the same time, there is an increasing imperative to bolster such national analysis centers with international centers, shielded from bureaucratization and politization. Such international centers (there need be only a very few) can serve to amplify the effectiveness of domestic centers in extraordinarily important ways, one of which is to further the understanding of the remarkable impact of cultural, geographical, and historical differences on the perceptions of analysts and their approaches to analysis, as well as on those of the decisionmakers.

While political decisions and decisionmakers usually depend heavily upon informal personal anecdotes and necessarily biased inputs, that is not necessarily the best process. Surely it is better to at least inject into that process some channels for nonpartisan, digested information derived from constructive criticism provided by diverse experts and stakeholders. In the West the involvement of "nontechnical" people in that process seems much more vigorous than in Europe or the USSR. Perhaps one reason for that difference is the fact that technically trained people have traditionally held more high political offices in Europe and the USSR than in British or American governments.

In a world that can be characterized as increasingly unstable, largely due to the continuing "advances" of the technological revolution, it is essential that analysts of different nations receive firsthand knowledge of how problems are viewed and attacked in different cultures. The emergence of issues such as global atmosphere alterations should remind us that an institution like IIASA, if it didn't already exist, would now need to be established. Nations not only have much to learn from each other, but face an increasing number of common interests. If we can learn, through cooperative ventures like IIASA, how to work together on civil issues (examining problems such as the environment and conservation of resources), perhaps we can move more effectively toward stopping the monstrous march of military armaments.

The reality that reaching mutinational accord on socio-technical issues is complex, in comparison with reaching effective consensus within a given country, is a vital lesson. IIASA provides a unique setting for people who have been successful at the national level to contribute to the resolution of international issues, while providing a good return on the investment to the individual nations involved. In doing so, of course, the work can be very helpful within the individual nations. For example, the IIASA study of the impacts of acid rain in Europe provides important information not only for those nations, individually and collectively, but also for the United States. Some problem areas that could be usefully addressed by IIASA include:

testing and screening methods and procedures of international interest (e.g., pharmaceuticals, chemicals); disposal of nuclear waste; implications of advances in biotechnology, neurobiology; the conservation and substitution of energy and materials; and the potential future role of computers in multilingual communication.

There are at least three complementary views of work at IIASA that should be kept in mind: First, IIASA is a shared international analytical resource, performing critical review, synthesis, and interpretation of information on explicitly recognized issues of current interest. IIASA can be particularly valuable when the issues being analyzed are of direct national interest, but where national decisions have multinational or international implications. Such issues include the case of energy and other resources, and use of the "commons" of air and water. Second, IIASA can also be viewed as a shared resource for exploration, investigation, and monitoring of selected long-range emerging issues, i.e., serving as foresight and "as an early warning" mechanism. Nations have considerable interest in common problems, but they are not always prepared to commit resources to carry out independent analyses. By pooling resources into an organization like IIASA, every participant can have access to the deliberations of a very capable analysis group. Third, for its participants and sponsors, IIASA offers a unique environment and opportunity to gain international perspective (political, cultural, and methodological). This can be particularly helpful in assuring that analysis at the national level takes full advantage of international efforts, and that the analysis is properly scoped.

A final value of IIASA is the environment it provides for extended dialogue and exchange of ideas between analysts from different nations — an especially important feature to improve mutual understanding between the capitalist and centrally-planned countries.

Commentary: *Giandomenico Majone*

The chapter by Professor Harvey Brooks is so rich in insights and suggestions as to invite, more than comments, reflections and further developments of some of the important issues he raises. In this chapter I would like to add something to his discussion about the universalistic ideal of science, its legitimating function, and the role of international research institutions in realizing that ideal.

Giandomenico Majone is a research scholar at IIASA and Professor at the John F. Kennedy School of Government, Harvard University, USA.

Some Preliminary Distinctions

I begin my argument by introducing several distinctions that are only implicit in Brooks's chapter. In the present context, science can be, and has been, used in two rather different meanings:

(1) As a collective noun for all the research results that have been tested, and accepted into the body of *scientific knowledge*.

(2) As the *social process* by which those results have been produced and validated. I speak of a *social* process because the production and validation of scientific results take place in specialized social institutions such as universities, academies, professions, laboratories, scientific journals, and the like.

The notion of the universality of science also includes two distinct, though related, meanings. The first refers to the *general validity* (in time and space) of certain scientific statements, for instance, the conservation principles of physics or the laws of genetics. In its second meaning, universality is to be understood as *consensus of rational opinion*. John Ziman exemplifies this second meaning of universality when he argues that among all human activities science is unique in striving for, and insisting on, the broadest possible consensus of (informed) opinion[19].

These different meanings of science and universality match in a natural way, as shown in Fig. 11.1.

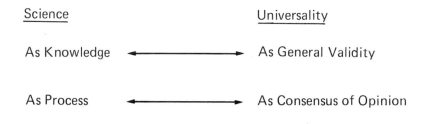

FIG. 11.1

Another distinction also plays a role in the following argument. Scientific disciplines may be classified in terms of two dimensions corresponding to their level of maturity or their abstract or applied character, as shown in Fig. 11.2.

In quadrant I, we find such disciplines as mathematics, physics, or theoretical biology; in II, most social sciences; in III, social technologies and much of regulatory science; in IV, most physical technologies.

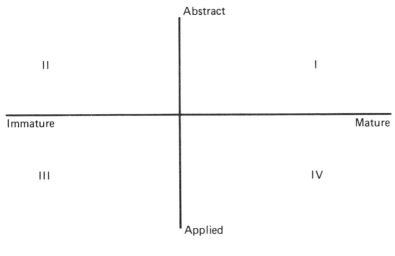

F<small>IG</small>. 11.2

Mature Sciences as a Special Case

The first step in my argument is that, while the universality of science has a powerful ideological and normative appeal, only a handful of scientific disciplines, relatively speaking, actually satisfy Brooks's universalistic norms. In our diagram, these disciplines are clustered in the first quadrant; they are intellectually mature *and* (more or less) abstract. Precisely because of this dual characteristic, they produce knowledge that is accepted as being generally valid, and also use methods and processes that are generally acknowledged as being appropriate to the nature of their objects of inquiry. The case of immature disciplines is quite different, especially if their immaturity is combined with an orientation toward practical problem solving[20]. Immaturity means that powerful generalizations are lacking and that there is, therefore, little consensus about results. At best, consensus may be claimed for the methods used, and this explains why immature disciplines (both in the natural and in the social sciences) tend to adopt mathematical and experimental methods developed by the older, more successful sciences. But a practical orientation is a serious obstacle on the road toward universality (of methods, if not of results). The closer a discipline is to practical problems, the greater the influence of local priorities, traditions, and styles of research. For example, the methods used in setting environmental, health, and safety standards vary considerably from country to country. These variations are due to differences in biological and regulatory philosophies, in levels of economic development, and even in experimental methodologies. Thus, European standard setters tend to rely less on epidemiological evidence than their American colleagues, and Soviet toxicologists emphasize nervous system reactions rather than the physiological responses used in the West[21].

Cosmopolitans and Locals in Science

Hence, scientific workers seem to fall into two classes: the cosmopolitans and the locals, to use the terminology of Alvin Gouldner[22]. Cosmopolitans are likely to adopt an international reference-group orientation, while locals tend to have a national or subnational (e.g. an organizational) reference group orientation. The difference begins to appear at the level of graduate education. Students in the more mature and abstract fields of science learn to think of themselves as members of a worldwide research community, while their colleagues in applied and less mature fields are much more exposed to the influence of local schools and traditions. For example, European textbooks and teaching methods in statistics vary much more across various countries (down to the level of notation) than textbooks and teaching methods in mathematics. As a consequence, statistical practice also exhibits a great deal of national variation. A certain amount of internationalization in teaching and practice has been achieved only in the last two decades, as a consequence of an increasing acceptance of what used to be called the Anglo–American school of statistics with its basic probabilistic paradigm. Similar trends are noticeable in several other areas, such as microeconomics and numerical mathematics. Younger professors, often trained abroad, have played a crucial role in such developments.

The trend toward cosmopolitanism in science has its negative aspects involving as it does a loss of cultural traditions and intellectual variety. For the present argument, however, it is more important to point out some of the consequences of localism. First, the phenomenon of localism helps to explain why the academic and scientific incentive system does not favor those disciplines and skills that are most directly policy relevant. The big prizes go to cosmopolitan science (theoretical physics, mathematical economics, or clinical medicine, for example) rather than to "local" disciplines such as public health or urban planning. Safety experts, it has been often said, do not get Nobel prizes, nor do applied toxicologists, standard setters, and all other practioners of regulatory science.

Second, localism reduces communication among groups of scientific workers engaged in similar tasks, and impedes the efficient transfer of research results. Toxicological testing is a good example of how national traditions, conditions, and ideologies affect problem formulation, empirical methodologies and regulatory conclusions[23].

A third consequence of localism in science is that local experts tend to be more submissive to the institutional and hierarchical structures in which they operate than cosmopolitan experts, who can appeal to the standards and criteria of an international body of scientific peers. This is an important reason, I submit, for the general lack of legitimacy of regulatory science which Harvey Brooks notes and deplores in his chapter.

The Professionalization of Regulatory Science

As a further consequence of localism, the practitioners of immature and applied disciplines tend to be loosely organized in associations that are considered, at best, quasi-professional since they do not quite share the prestige and influence of the established learned or academic professions. Professionalization is a complex process which has recently received a good deal of attention by sociologists[24]. A key step in that process is the achievement of cognitive exclusiveness—the recognition of being uniquely qualified to deal with some well defined range of problems—which, in turn, depends on the creation of a coherent cognitive basis and a certain standardization of tasks and skills. In my opinion, international research organizations can play an extremely important role in encouraging and assisting the process of achieving full professionalism of regulatory science, thus helping to realize the universalistic ideal also in this domain.

The example of the business or management schools is relevant in this context. Such schools have succeeded in transforming an important group of traditionally local functions, such as accounting, financial management, or production engineering—in which one's colleagues and superiors in the organization used to be the main reference group—along more professional and cosmopolitan lines. The result has been a greater level of sophistication and, especially, greater mobility across departments, organizations, and even internationally. More recently, graduate schools of public policy have attempted to achieve analogous results in the field of public management.

In regulatory science, greater sophistication and standardization of methods and problem-solving skills are badly needed. The emerging professions or quasi-professions in this field are vitally important, but because they are so close to actual problems they are always exposed to the risks of localism. Hence, means must be found to help them in developing greater intellectual depth and a broader international orientation. International scientific institutions could play a crucial role here, perhaps analogous to the role of business schools in the business community. Of course, this requires more than providing a meeting place for recurrent contacts among practitioners of regulatory science. The development of a coherent cognitive basis and adequate quality standards requires a critical examination of the logical foundations of the various branches of regulatory science, combined with a sophisticated understanding of the dynamics of policy making. On this basis it should then be possible to design suitable curricula for an international body of practitioners of regulatory science.

References

1. Evan, William M. Chapter 1. Some Dilemmas of Knowledge and Power: An Introduction, in W. M. Evan (ed), *Knowledge and Power in a Global Society* Sage Publications, Beverly Hills, 1981, p. 7.
2. O'Hare, M., Bacow, L. and Sanderson, D. *Facility Siting and Public Opposition*, Van Nostrand Reinhold Company, New York, 1983, especially p. 2.
3. Ibid.
4. Hardin, G. The tragedy of the Commons, *Science*, **162** (Dec. 13, 1957), pp. 1243–8. Cf. especially the following: "Ruin is the destination toward which all men rush, each pursuing his own best interest in a society that believes in the freedom of the commons."
5. O'Hare *et al.*, op. cit., p. 3.
6. O'Hare *et al.*, ibid., p. 31.
7. Ibid., p. 69.
8. Harter, Philip J. negotiating regulations: a cure for malaise, *The Georgetown Law Journal*, **71**, no. 1 (Oct. 1982), pp. 11–118.
9. Price Don K. *The Scientific Estate*, Harvard University Press, Cambridge, MA., 1965.
10. Ibid., p. 13.
11. Boulding, Kenneth E. National defense through stable peace, *Options* 1983/3, International Institute for Applied Systems Analysis, Laxenburg, Austria 1983, pp. 10–13.
12. Evan, op. cit., p. 22.
13. Evan, op. cit., p. 23.
14. Levien, Roger. Global problems: the role of international science and technology organizations, in J. Gvishiani (ed), *Science, Technology and Global Problems*, Pergamon Press, Oxford, England, 1979, p. 46.
15. Cf., for example, Marchetti, C. *On 10^{12}: A Check on Earth Carrying Capacity for Man*, Research Report RR 78–7, International Institute for Applied Systems Analysis, Laxenburg, Austria (May 1978).
16. Merton, Robert K. *Social Theory and Social Structure*, Macmillan, New York, 1957.
17. Myers, Norman and Dorothy. How the global community can respond to international environmental problems, *Ambio*, **12**, no. 1, pp. 20–26, 1983.
18. Ibid., p. 20.
19. Ziman, J. (1968) *Public Knowledge* (Cambridge, UK: Cambridge University Press).
20. Ravetz, J. R. (1973) *Scientific Knowledge and its Social Problems* (Hardmondsworth, UK: Penguin Books) for the best discussion of immature fields of inquiry.
21. Majone, G. (1983) *The Logic of Standard-Setting: A Comparative Perspective, Research Report 83–15* (Laxenburg, Austria: International Institute for Applied Systems Analysis).
22. Gouldner, A. W. (1957–58) Cosmopolitans and locals: toward an analysis of latent social roles, I and II, *Administrative Science Quarterly*, 281–306 and 444–480.
23. Majone, *op. cit.*
24. See, for example, Sarfatti-Larson, M. (1976) *The Rise of Professionalism* (Berkeley, USA: University of California Press) and Starr, P. (1982) *The Social Transformation of American Medicine* (New York, USA: Basic Books).

CHAPTER 12

A History of the Acid Rain Issue

GREGORY S. WETSTONE

In the past several years, acid rain has grown from a relatively obscure concern—regarded as serious by a narrow group of specialized scientists—to one of the most prominent environmental problems of our time. To the casual observer this transformation may seem to have taken place overnight. In fact, the problem was first identified more than a century ago. But it did not begin to evolve as a public issue until the early 1970s, when Scandinavian countries discovered that fish in their aquatic systems were dying over widespread areas and so resolved to bring acid rain to the attention of the international community.

The issue raises unprecedented challenges. As a long-range air pollution problem, it defies traditional approaches to air-quality control, which were designed mainly to grapple with health problems caused by high pollution concentrations relatively near the source.

As an international issue, acid rain presents a difficult test case. Most industrialized nations have formally endorsed the proposition that states have an obligation to control pollution causing damage to a foreign environment. But past international pollution problems have involved specific pollution sources near the boundary or pollution in a clearly defined watershed, while damages from acid rain are the aggregate result of the sulfur dioxide and nitrogen emissions of an entire region. Never before has the international community been forced to contend in such a major way with the conflict between each state's sovereign right to formulate its own energy and environmental policies, and the sovereign rights of other states to be free of environmental damage from foreign pollution.

Disturbingly, there are good reasons to believe that acid rain is but the first of a new second generation of pollution problems, caused not by pockets of high pollution levels, but by an aggregate assault on our ecosystems until

Gregory Wetstone is Director of the Air and Water Program of the Environmental Law Institute, Washington, DC, USA.

their tolerance to man-made pollution is exceeded. Other examples include the pollution of the oceans and the atmospheric build-up of carbon dioxide. In response to today's acid rain problem, we are setting a precedent for efforts in coming decades to deal with these other more sweeping ecological problems. Hopefully, we are also learning valuable lessons.

This chapter traces the development of the acid rain issue in Europe and North America, examining how scientists, national governments, and multinational organizations have combined to propel the problem to international prominence. Particular attention is devoted to scientific information and the forms in which it has been translated into pressures that have influenced national governments and the international community. Insights gained in more than a decade of efforts to come to grips with the acid rain issue that might be productively applied to other second generation pollution problems, especially the atmospheric build-up of carbon dioxide, are then discussed.

The European Experience

Historical Beginnings

Scientific understanding of air pollution and acid rain was pioneered in Britain. In 1661, British scientist John Evelyn wrote of the hazards of sulfur pollution in his book *Fumifugium* [1]. Some two hundred years later, British researcher Angus Smith first described the acid rain phenomenon in his remarkable book *Air and Water: The Beginnings of a Chemical Climatology* [2]. In this 1872 work, Smith provided detailed documentation of acid rain as an urban problem in the City of Manchester and briefly discussed damage to vegetation, fabrics, and building structures.

Finally, it was in Britain that Eville Gorham, now Professor of Ecology at the University of Minnesota, USA, published a series of papers, beginning in 1955, that brought acid rain to the attention of the modern scientific community and first associated the phenomenon with distant, as opposed to local, air pollution [3]. He correlated precipitation acidity in the rural English Lake District with air pollution from fossil fuel combustion in distant industrial areas. And, with his colleague John Macbereth, Dr Gorham first associated acid precipitation with aquatic impacts, relating the loss of alkalinity in lakes and the heightened acidity of bog waters to acids in rainfall.

Dr Gorham's finding, that aquatic systems can be altered by air pollution from distant sources, received little immediate attention in the scientific community. Also, these results had little, if any, influence on the deliberations of policy makers when several of the world's industrialized nations worked to establish the foundations for governmental air-pollution control policies in the ensuing decade. The significance of Gorham's work, and its policy implications, was recognized only after the widespread acidification of lakes was discovered in Scandinavia in the late 1960s.

The Issue is Born in Scandinavia

It was Svante Oden, a soil scientist with the Agricultural College in Uppsala, who first integrated information from a variety of disciplines and concluded that Scandinavian rivers were becoming increasingly acidic as a result of sulfur emissions from central Europe and Britain. Oden combined data generated by Euope's first systematic effort to monitor precipitation chemistry, initiated in the 1940s in Sweden by soil scientist Hans Egner, with data from a Scandinavian network measuring surface water chemistry that Oden had begun in 1961. The implications of his conclusions were ominous. Oden found that acid precipitation from distant industrial emissions was acidifying fresh water ecosystems, leaching toxic metals from soils into surface waters, and leading to dramatic declines in fish populations. His findings were published in the respected Stockholm newspaper *Dagens Nyheter* [4], and in the scientific journal *Ecology Committee Bulletin* [5].

Dr. Oden's conclusions met with skepticism in much of the scientific community, even within Sweden. Dr Ellis Cowling, who worked with Oden for several years in Europe, has described the furor that resulted in the several disciplines of the scientific community that Oden's work crossed:

> Suddenly, limnological, agricultural, and atmospheric scientists began to argue and debate with each other about Oden's unconventional ideas and his general theory of atmospheric influences. Multidisciplinary discussions and international conferences ensued all over Europe and around the world as scientist after scientist was inspired (or provoked) into designing experimental tests to prove or disprove Oden's ideas [6].

The Swedish government was unconvinced and, in fact, declined to continue funding Oden's research. Without research support, Oden devoted his energies for the next few years mainly to lecturing in Sweden, elsewhere in Europe, and in North America.

The press was less unbelieving. In 1968 and 1969 the Swedish media erupted with detailed reports of Oden's research. The populace was warned that an alarming ecological calamity was occurring in Scandinavia. Public education on the acid rain issue had begun in Europe.

By 1971 public pressure in Sweden, fueled by media reports, and increasing scientific acceptance of Oden's findings, led the Swedish government to adopt a different stance. Officials deciding upon the subject of a paper to be submitted by Sweden at the UN Conference on the Human

Environment, scheduled for the next year in Stockholm, became interested in preparing a case study on the environmental aspects of sulfur pollution.

With Oden's assistance, Dr Bert Bolin, a Professor of Meteorology at the University of Stockholm, penned the historic Swedish *Case Study on the Environmental Impact of Sulfur in Air and Precipitation* [7]. The study—a basic text on the effects of sulfur emissions—contributed to unqualified acceptance of Oden's thesis in Sweden and Norway. Its presentation at the 1972 Stockholm Conference heralded the arrival of the acid rain issue in the international community. While the report initially met with considerable skepticism, it began the slow process of gaining international recognition of Scandinavia's transboundary pollution problem.

Only Norway was prepared to immediately accept the findings of the Swedish case study. The study reinforced concern partly attributable to reports of decreasing pH values in the nation's rivers and lakes over the past several years. Moreover, a 1971 study by the Norwegian Institute for Water Research, concluding that fish populations in southern Norway had declined dramatically in the 1950s and 1960s, was taken very seriously by government officials.

The International Campaign Begins

The 1972 Conference on the Human Environment marked the onset of a new level of environmental consciousness among national governments. It was at this gathering that the UN Environment Program (UNEP), a global center for the study and discussion of world environmental problems, was created. In addition, the Conference fathered the adoption of a UN Declaration on the Human Environment, intended to provide a foundation for the eventual establishment of a structure of international environmental law. The Declaration's Principle 21 remains today the most important single enunciation of the responsibility of nations to assure that their actions do not cause damage to a foreign environment.

> States have, in accordance with the Charter of the United Nations and the principles of international law, the sovereign right to exploit their own resources pursuant to their own environmental policies, and *the responsibility to ensure that activities within their jurisdiction or control do not cause damage to the environment of other states or of areas beyond the limits of national jurisdiction* (emphasis added) [8].

In the years since the 1972 Conference, Norway and Sweden have worked to translate this laudable, but vague, principle into specific action to cope with Scandinavia's transboundary air pollution problem. As concern grew in both nations, the two governments joined in an effort to enhance scientific understanding of the problem, and promote an international response. Sponsoring research efforts, hosting international conferences, and promoting remedial action in multilateral organizations, the two nations have orchestrated a patient but determined international campaign.

This effort began in 1972 when Norway embarked on the largest multidisciplinary research project in the nation's history—an eight-year, sixteen million US dollar effort to determine the effects of acid precipitation on forests and fish. The SNSF Project, as it came to be known, was undertaken through the cooperative investigations of more that 150 scientists and 12 Norwegian research institutions. The Project culminated in March of 1980, with a major scientific conference in Sandefjord, Norway. The final SNSF Report documented extensive damages to Scandinavia's fresh water aquatic systems. It found that fish populations had been eliminated in more than half of the lakes of southern Norway. The key question of whether forests might be seriously damaged was left open.

Taking the Issue to International Organizations

In seeking to forge a cooperative solution to international air pollution problems, Sweden, Norway and other aggrieved nations have looked mainly to negotiations and technical studies conducted through key international organizations. In the roughly ten years of concerted international activity in this area, the leadership role has been passed between the Organisation for Economic Cooperation and Development (OEDC), the European Economic Community (the Community), and the Economic Commission for Europe (ECE), a regional organization established under the auspices of the UN. Each has helped to move the international community toward the evolution of a cooperative response to the acid rain problem.

The UN played an important early role through its sponsorship of the Conference on the Human Environment where, as discussed earlier, it was agreed that nations have a responsibility to control pollution damaging a neighboring country's environment. In the years immediately following the 1972 Stockholm Conference, the Paris-based Organisation for Economic Cooperation and Development worked to provide the technical foundation necessary to apply the Stockholm Declaration's principles to Europe's transboundary sulfur pollution problem.

The OECD Study of Long-Range Air Pollution

Since the early 1970s, the OECD, which includes the countries of Western Europe and North America as well as Japan, Australia, and New Zealand, has been a leading center for study and discussion of international environmental issues. It was the OECD's ground-breaking research and monitoring work that made many national and international policy makers aware for the first time of the extent and importance of transboundary air pollution in Europe.

In April of 1972 the OECD Council which includes representatives from each member state, inaugurated a Cooperative Technical Program to Measure the Long-Range Transport of Air Pollutants, in which 11 European nations participated (Austria, Belgium, Denmark, Finland, France, FRG, The Netherlands, Norway, Sweden, Switzerland, and the UK). Measurements from aircraft sampling and a network of 76 ground-level stations were reported monthly to the Norwegian Institute for Air Research, which coordinated data collection and analysis. Using 1974 data, the program estimated the domestic and foreign contributions to each participating country's sulfur deposition with special attention to acid precipitation. The measurements and findings of the OECD Program on the Long-Range Transport of Air Pollutants were first published in 1977 and revised and expanded in a second edition in 1979 [9].

The OECD's findings offered the first independent verification of Scandinavian charges that imported air pollution was the primary source of sulfuric air pollution in Sweden and Norway. The study affirmed that a substantial portion of Europe's sulfur emissions are transported long distances (hundreds of kilometers) and deposited within the borders of downwind countries. Countries were classified as either net exporters or net importers. In five of the eleven participating countries, more than half of the total deposition of sulfur was estimated to come from foreign sources. The OECD staff concluded that the problem of multinational pollution should be addressed "by actions undertaken at the national level and integrated internationally . . . so as to achieve the most efficient and equitable use of . . . the European 'airshed' ".

The study findings were not whole-heartedly embraced by all of the participating nations. The OECD made clear that, owing mainly to uncertainties surrounding emission data and dispersion models, the program's findings were only accurate to within plus or minus 50%. Nations shown to be large pollution exporters, noting this caveat and other studies demonstrating that changes in wind and weather patterns could substantially alter the transboundary contributions of emitting countries, questioned the reliability of the OECD conclusions. Nevertheless, for the first time national policy makers throughout Western Europe had been alerted to the magnitude of transboundary pollution flow on their continent.

Early National Responses

By the late 1970s, many countries had long believed that transboundary air pollution was an important concern. But until the OECD study, the problem was perceived mainly as a local one. Now it was clear to Finland, Denmark, and The Netherlands, which were already sympathetic to Sweden and Norway's concerns, that they too were importing tremendous quantities of sulfur pollution. Although they did not approach the issue with the same urgency, these nations supported Swedish and Norwegian efforts to prompt international action. But until recently, they did so more for the sake of Scandinavian unity than for environmental benefits within their own borders.

Austria and Switzerland were also shown to be on the receiving end of a great deal of foreign pollution, more, in fact, than they produced themselves. But prior to 1982 these countries remained unconvinced by the OECD study and other scientific information, and unreceptive to Scandinavia's calls for international action.

Major pollution exporting nations were also not convinced. According to the OECD study, the UK is the largest single contributor to acid deposition in Norway, even larger than Norway itself, as well as the largest *external* contributor to acid deposition in Sweden. In the early 1970s, British officials denied that their sulfur dioxide (SO_2) emissions might be carried across the North Sea to Scandinavia, although studies demonstrating that dust from sand storms in the Sahara Desert could be blown thousands of miles were widely accepted. As support for their view, the UK cited shipboard monitoring results indicating that sulfur pollution levels decreased as a ship left Britain and headed across the North Sea, and increased again as it approached the land mass of Scandinavia. Sweden and Norway, they contended, were responsible for their own problem. But the shipboard readings proved to have been influenced by the neutralizing effect of sea spray. In the mid-1970s aerial monitoring efforts clearly demonstrated that parcels of high sulfur concentration in air masses could indeed cross the North Sea. The 1976 Conference of the SNSF Project in Telemark, Norway, was an early turning point in the international acid rain debate because there British officials conceded that sulfur dioxide emissions from the UK could indeed reach Sweden and Norway [10]. However, the UK remained unconvinced of the severity of the aquatic impacts in Scandinavia, the causative role of acid rain, and the responsibility of the UK for controlling its emissions for Scandinavia's benefit.

Officials of the FRG held a similar view. This nation is the third largest SO_2 producer in Western Europe and, according to the OECD, an important contributor to Scandinavia's acidification problem. As the 1980's began, FRG officials were satisfied that their moderately stringent pollution control policies were more than sufficient, and were unconcerned about transboundary pollution problems. Elsewhere in Western Europe, Belgium, France, and Italy showed little interest in Scandinavia's acid rain problem.

The Problem Reaches North America

North Americans had the benefit of Scandinavia's experience and scientific data, as well as Sweden's 1972 case study to the Conference on the Human Environment which warned that "a similar situation might exist in regions of Eastern Canada and the Northeast United States." Yet, acid rain did not emerge as an important issue in North America until nearly 1980, many years after it had developed in Europe. In part this was a reflection of the fact that damages to North American ecosystems, although potentially severe, have not been comparable to those in the lakes of Scandinavia and the forests of central Europe. Additionally, scientific awareness of the acid rain problem in North America has been hampered due to the absence of continuous records of longterm trends in precipitation chemistry analogous to those in Europe.

North American concern over acid rain began in Eastern Canada. The studies of University of Toronto zoologist Harold Harvey and his graduate student Richard Beamish provided the first documentation of aquatic impacts from acid pollution in North America. In 1972 they published the results of a five-year survey of 150 lakes in Ontario's Killarney region, "Acidification of the LaCloche Mountain Lakes" [11], in a Canadian fisheries journal. In the first report of lake acidification in Canada, they concluded that 33 of the surveyed water bodies were "critically acidified". The authors identified air pollution as the most likely cause and, drawing on the Scandinavian experience, warned of a potentially much more sweeping problem. For the next several years these findings went largely unnoticed, although Dr Harvey attempted through a series of lectures to bring them to the attention of the public and the federal and provincial government.

Dr Gene Likens and his colleagues at Cornell University in the state of New York had been monitoring precipitation chemistry in areas of New England for many years, but decided to analyze hydrogen ion data, the indicator of acidity, only after speaking with Svante Oden in Sweden in 1970. In a seminal 1972 paper Likens *et al.* first discussed the regional distribution of acidic precipitation in North America and its significance for aquatic and terrestrial ecosystems [12]. Two years later Dr Likens and colleague Charles Cogbill authored a major article providing pH isopleth maps which indicated that precipitation acidity in the Eastern US increased dramatically in the 17-year span between 1955–6 and 1972–3 [13].

Lake acidification was first reported in the US in 1976 when Dr Carl Schofield of Cornell University published survey results in the international journal *Ambio* showing dramatic declines in fish populations associated with the acidification of lakes in the Adirondack Mountains of New York State [14]. These studies, combined with important international conferences such as the International Limnological Congress in Winnipeg, Manitoba, in 1974, and the First International Symposium on Acid Precipitation and Forest

Ecosystems sponsored by the US Forest Service in Columbus, Ohio, in 1975, led to a growing scientific awareness of the acid precipitation phenomenon and its effects in North America in the mid-1970s.

These early studies and meetings were given little attention in the popular media in North America. Similarly, Scandinavia's lake acidifications had not been widely reported. The public and most US and Canadian government officials remained largely unaware of the acid rain problem.

Serious concern developed first in Canada. The issue's profile in that country was dramatically enhanced in 1977 when Canadian Environment Minister Romeo LaBlanc branded acid rain an "environmental time bomb" in a speech to air pollution experts in Toronto [15]. As the first government official to sound the warning, LaBlanc prompted a new level of media attention to the issue in Canada. But press interest and public concern did not solidify until 1979.

In October of that year the first joint US–Canada scientific assessment on acid rain was released. US–Canada governmental discussions had begun in 1978 as a result of an initiative from the US Congress, which was concerned about the impact of emissions from a Canadian power plant on the nearby Boundary Waters Canoe Area in northern Minnesota. Canada successfully expanded the discussion to encompass the range of important transborder pollution problems. In 1978 the two governments established a "bilateral research consultation group" to coordinate research efforts on long-range air pollution transport. US officials saw air pollution as exclusively a health problem and entered the effort extremely skeptical of Canadian concern over ecological impacts. However, in the discussion and exchange of scientific data that followed, a consensus emerged that generally endorsed the Canadian viewpoint.

The 1979 preliminary report of the joint research group documented acid damage to lakes, confirmed the possibility of crop and forest damages, and suggested possible health impacts from toxic metals leached free by acid rains and washed into drinking water [16]. In the US, the report's publication markedly raised government awareness, but received little media attention. In Canada, the press seized upon the bilateral research group report as a credible confirmation of earlier reports of a severe threat to Canada's environment. Former Canadian Environment Minister John Fraser added to the furor the same year with projections that more than 48,000 lakes in the Province of Ontario would be threatened by acidification over the next 20 years if current emission levels were not reduced. Attention in Canada was focused on the problem as never before.

Another major milestone in 1979 was the Action Seminar on Acid Precipitation (ASAP), a conference convened by a coalition of citizens groups in Toronto. More than 800 persons attended as Canada's Environment Minister, the Environment Minister of the Province of Ontario, a US

Congressman, and experts from a variety of disciplines offered presentations. At that meeting the seeds were sown for an extensive citizen's campaign in the US and Canada to educate the public and prompt government action.

Public pressure for government action to better control emission of acid-forming sulfur dioxide was building rapidly in Canada. But government officials in Canada, noting that the US was responsible for roughly half of the sulfur pollution deposited in Canada's most sensitive areas, sought a cooperative program including a commitment for SO_2 abatement action from the US [17].

A concerted campaign was begun to encourage US cooperation. Environment Canada, the federal ministry, directed a sweeping public information effort including the preparation and distribution of literature on acid rain [18], extensive speaking engagements by high Canadian officials, and even the dissemination of "stop acid rain" buttons and bumper stickers. A separate, nongovernmental effort to inform the public and policy makers in the US was undertaken by the Canadian Coalition on Acid Rain, an alliance of over a million Canadians including tourist outfitters, fishing tackle industry representatives, native peoples, cottagers, and environmental and conservation organizations [19].

The level of concern in the US continuously lagged far behind that in Canada. But government interest increased rapidly under the strong environmental leadership of President Carter. In 1979 the US Environmental Protection Agency (EPA) published a special report characterizing in detail the extent and potential severity of the impacts of acid deposition [20]. That same year, President Carter identified acid rain as one of the two most serious environmental problems associated with the continued use of fossil fuels, and inaugurated a ten-year Federal Acid Rain Research Program that was later given congressional sanction. These developments provided some grounds for optimism as informal discussions between the US Department of State and the Canadian Department of External Affairs got under way.

Cooperative US–Canada Activity

US–Canada discussions began in 1978, and in 1979 the governments signed an informal accord. The Joint Statement on Transboundary Air Quality expressed the "common determination to reduce or prevent transboundary air pollution which injures health or property" [21]. The Joint Statement was followed a year later by the more specific Memorandum of Intent Concerning Transboundary Air Pollution (MOI), which once again was not a binding formal agreement [22]. In that document the governments, after a brief discussion of the gravity of the problem, declared that the best means to protect the environment from the effects of transboundary air pollution is through the achievement of necessary reductions in pollutant loadings" and that "this common problem requires cooperative action by both countries." Toward this end the US and Canada pledged to continue efforts to develop an agreement, and agreed to establish joint technical and scientific "work groups" to assist in the preparations for and conduct of negotiations. (The fate of the joint scientific efforts set in motion by this agreement is discussed below).

Formal Negotiations

After nearly two years of preliminary talks, formal US–Canada negotiations over an air quality accord began in the autumn of 1981. Four meetings have been held to date. At the third meeting in February of 1982, the Canadian team offered for the first time a proposed treaty formulation. The Canadian proposal, a 30-page draft modeled on the US–Canada Great Lakes Water Quality Agreements, called for a 50% reduction in SO_2 emissions from eastern Canada and a parallel rollback in the US. This emission reduction level was derived from limits for wet sulfate loading arrived at in early drafts of the MOI work group reports. The proposed 50% cutback was formally rejected by the US in June of 1982 at the fourth negotiating session. Although informal talks continued, the formal negotiating sessions ground to a halt.

Joint Scientific Efforts and International Politics

While US–Canada negotiations and domestic debates over acid rain control proceeded, the joint scientific work groups established under the MOI worked toward the development of a shared data base. Working groups were formed to investigate emission trends, atmospheric chemistry, environmental impacts, and control strategies. The efforts of the work group moved forward rapidly in the months immediately following the August 1980 signing of the MOI. But in the summer of 1981, the US withdrew support for the joint investigation of alternative emission control scenarios, declaring instead that each nation should conduct that assessment unilaterally. Despite a number of serious setbacks, the working groups in the remaining areas managed to produce major reports summarizing scientific knowledge in each of the areas listed above.

The joint reports reflect a consensus on a number of important matters. The existence of severe acidification damage to aquatic systems in areas of Eastern Canada and Northeastern US is affirmed in the report on impacts. Additionally, the atmospheric modeling work group evaluated eight distinct models of long-range air pollution transport in Eastern North America. While the exact estimations of the modeling techniques differ, all attribute a significant portion of deposited sulfur compounds in Northeast US and Southeast Canada to SO_2 emissions originating in the Midwestern US.

Although there was a consensus on the reports themselves, independent US and Canadian conclusions differed on several key points. Probably the most important area of disagreement concerned the establishment of a threshold level of pollutant deposition, below which an unacceptable level of environmental damage would not occur. In the early phases of the work group efforts, the two nations agreed to a threshold value of 20 kilograms of wet sulfate per hectare per year. Canada continued to support this figure. However, the US eventually concluded that adequate information did not yet exist to support the establishment of a threshold level.

The work group reports seek to summarize a complex and rapidly evolving body of science. It had been anticipated that they would undergo some form of scientific peer review. Presumably this step would be conducted jointly. When the US National Academy of Sciences (NAS) combined with the Royal Scientific Society of Canada (RSC) to form the Joint Scientific Committee on Acid Precipitation, the first international cooperative review ever undertaken by either scientific organization, most participants and observers expected this group to undertake the peer reviews. But the involvement of the joint NAS/RSC committee was opposed by the US, reportedly because of official unhappiness with an earlier, separate NAS report recommending emission reductions to minimize environmental damages associated with acid rain [23]. Despite Canadian requests for a joint peer review, the US insisted on unilateral efforts and selected the White House Office of Science and Technology Policy (OSTP) to oversee its side of the task. The Royal Scientific Society of Canada was selected to undertake Canada's effort.

The Canadian peer review report, entitled *Acid Deposition in North America*, was released in May of 1983 [24]. It was conducted under the chairmanship of Kenneth Hare of Trinity College, Toronto. The RSC Committee concluded that the work group documents represented an accurate and reasonably comprehensive up-to-date evaluation of current information concerning transboundary air pollution. Despite admitted technical limitations in the joint work group efforts, the committee concluded that the reports provided an adequate basis to support an emission control strategy. On the key point of how much emission reduction is appropriate, the committee quoted the joint work group report:

> There have been no reported chemical or biological effects for regions currently receiving loadings of sulfate in precipitation at less than 20 kilograms per hectare per year. Evidence of chemical change exists for some waters in regions currently estimated or measured to be receiving 20–30 kilograms per hectare per year.

Based on this statement, the RSC Committee concluded that the environmental target of 20 kilograms per hectare per year suggested in the Canadian

MOI summary was appropriate. Commenting on the disagreement over this matter in the work group reports, the Committee reported that it could "not reconcile" the US conclusion that the agreed-upon text does not support the establishment of a threshold level.

The US peer review committee was chaired by Professor William Nierenberg, Director of the Scripps Institute for Oceanography in La Jolla, California. To the surprise of most onlookers, the Nierenberg Committee proved eager to go on record in support of the MOI documents and in favor of acid rain control. In June of 1983, the month following the release of the Canadian report, the Nierenberg committee issued a press release with interim findings. The preliminary statement concluded that "The incomplete present scientific knowledge sometimes prevents the kinds of certainty that scientists would prefer, but there are many indicators which taken collectively lead us to our finding that the phenomenon of acid deposition is real and constitutes a problem for which solutions should be sought." The committee recommended that "additional steps should be taken now which will result in meaningful reductions in the emissions of sulfur compounds into the atmosphere."

It is perhaps ironic that the independent scientists selected by the White House Office of Science and Technology Policy offered in many ways a less critical review of the MOI documents than might have been expected from the original joint NAS/RSC Committee, where members were more intimately familiar with the work group documents and their faults. Observers concerned about the fate of joint scientific efforts could see in this development an affirmation of the value of such cooperative endeavors. Although one government might lose interest in the joint studies, and even seek to obstruct them, the integrity of participating scientists could, in the end, preserve the credibility of the exercise.

The US Position

The findings of the Nierenberg committee are an important addition to a series of scientific and policy reports suggesting the need for a new acid rain control program in the US. In its 1981 report to Congress, the National Commission on Air Quality (NCAQ), an influential organization created to assess the impact and effectiveness of the US Clean Air Act, recommended that "Congress should require a significant reduction by 1990 in the current level of SO_2 emissions in the Eastern United States" [25].

That same year the US National Academy of Sciences, in a report on the ecological consequences of fossil fuel combustion that reportedly led to considerable friction between the Academy and the Administration of President Ronald Reagan, resoundingly affirmed the need for acid rain abatement programs.

Although claims have been made that direct evidence linking power plant emissions to the production of acid rain is inconclusive . . . we find the circumstantial evidence for their role overwhelming.

Though necessarily incomplete in many respects, the information synthesized by the Committee renders a rather unfavorable picture of the consequences of the current fossil fuel burning practices. It is the Committee's opinion, based on the evidence we have examined, that the picture is disturbing enough to merit prompt tightening of restrictions on atmospheric emissions from fossil fuels and other large sources, such as metal smelters and cement manufacture. Strong measures are necessary if we are to prevent further degradation of natural ecosystems, which together support life on this planet [26].

This report was widely reported in the popular media. But it had no perceptible impact on policy making in the US, at either the EPA or within the Administration. Since taking office, the position of the Reagan Administration has been, and remains, that while acid rain may present serious problems there are too many scientific aspects of the problem that are not well enough understood to justify the establishment of new control programs.

In the summer of 1983, the interim findings of the Nierenberg committee contributed to increasing pressure on the Administration to adopt a more aggressive stance toward control of acid rain precursors. Only days later, the National Academy of Sciences added significantly to this pressure with the release of a second NAS report on acid deposition. On a key issue of controversy in the US, the relationship of emission levels to deposition levels, the NAS report concluded that reductions in sulfur dioxide emissions would lead to a roughly proportionate reduction in the deposition of sulfur pollution [27]. Like the Nierenberg report, the NAS report attracted considerable media attention and fueled public pressure for government action.

Under pressure from the environmental community and the New England states, President Reagan announced that a new acid rain policy would be one of the top priorities for the new EPA Administrator, William Ruckelshaus, in March of 1983 [28].

Acid rain's status as a Reagan Administration priority, however, proved to be extremely brief. Ruckelshaus's recommendation for a limited control program was hotly debated with the President's Cabinet Council on Natural Resources, and ultimately defeated by opposition from OMB and other agencies. In January of 1985, Ruckelshaus left the EPA. His successor, Lee Thomas, has been a vocal opponent of Congressional acid rain control proposals [29].

The major focus of recent acid rain policy efforts by the Reagan Administration has concerned the activities of the "special envoys" on acid rain appointed by the United States and Canada as an outgrowth of the March 1985 "Shamrock Summit" between President Reagan and Canadian Prime Minister Brian Mulroney. In March of 1986 the two leaders formally embraced a Joint Report prepared by the Special Envoys [30].

The envoy's report includes encouraging language endorsing the scientific basis for acid rain control. The report specifically acknowledges that acid rain is a serious environmental problem, that man-made emissions of sulfur and nitrogen compounds are the major causes of acid deposition, that emissions transported long distances through the atmosphere are contributing to the acidification of sensitive areas, and that acid deposition threatens surface waters, man-made materials, and, potentially, forests.

Such conclusions represent a major departure from prior Reagan Administration statements regarding the science surrounding acid rain. However, this dramatic shift was accompanied by no real change in policy.

The Envoys Report does not recommend or endorse immediate control action. Instead the report's central recommendations call for the United States to embark upon a $5 billion program for research into new technologies for burning coal more cleanly. However, it quickly became clear that the United States did not intend to follow through on this pledge. In testimony presented to a United States House of Representatives Subcommittee only two months after the official adoption of the Envoy's Report, Energy Department Secretary John Herrington testified that the United States did not intend to devote such a large sum to clean coal technology research [31].

Taken as a whole, the Joint Envoys exercise was a major disappointment. If anything, the effort to promote emission reductions has been set back. While United States policies and emission rates remain unchanged, Canada, for its part, has been neutralized as an advocate for tougher pollution control in the United States. Moreover, through its agreement to a joint report that calls only for research, Canada has provided additional credibility to continued U.S. opposition to national and international acid rain control efforts.

The ECE Convention on Transboundary Air Pollution

Efforts on a wider scale to reconcile the divergent national viewpoints on transboundary air pollution in Europe and North America began in the late 1970s when the focal point for multilateral discussion of the international pollution issue in Europe shifted to the UN Economic Commission for Europe (ECE).

The Beginnings of an Air Accord

The opportunity for an international agreement on transboundary air pollution was not the result of increasing recognition that a serious environmental problem had been scientifically documented, which could be dealt with only by multinational action. The unlikely seed of international action was a statement by President Leonid Brezhnev of the Soviet Union at the 1975 East–West meeting of the Conference on Security and Cooperation in Europe in Helsinki, Finland [32]. There Brezhnev challenged his fellow conferees to reach multilateral solutions on three pressing problems affecting all of Europe: energy, transport and the environment.

Of Brezhnev's three agenda items, environment was by far the most innocuous. But Swedish and Norwegian officials, concerned over the evidence of severe transboundary pollution impacts in Scandinavia, saw in Brezhnev's Helsinki speech an opportunity for international discussion, negotiation, and perhaps even progress toward resolution of their acidification problem.

Having decided to seize upon the Brezhnev initiative, Scandinavian diplomats concluded that the most suitable forum was the ECE. Comprised of 34 countries from Eastern Europe, Western Europe, and North America, the ECE is housed in the old Palais des Nations in Geneva, Switzerland. The ECE Secretariat already had an environment unit and had sponsored a declaration in 1969 calling for SO_2 emission reductions.

Negotiations

The ECE Secretariat accepted its new mission with alacrity. Serious negotiations got under way in 1977 and efforts to reconcile the various governmental positions began. Although scientific information played an important role, the discussions did not turn on a critical evaluation of the available data. International politics and the domestic economic repercussions of action or inaction were the key factors in the debate.

Delegates from Sweden and Norway, supported strongly by Canada, pressed for a tough agreement that, even if not enforceable, would at least call on signatories to hold the line against further SO_2 increases (the standstill clause) and begin to abate SO_2 pollution levels by fixed, across-the-board percentages (the rollback clause). The Nordic proposal, as it came to be known, made special provision for countries that had already put strict control and abatement measures into effect (The Netherlands) and also for countries at a relatively early stage of industrial development (Ireland).

It soon became apparent that the leaders in resistance to the Nordic proposal were the large polluters of Western Europe, especially the FRG and UK. The FRG was skeptical of the whole enterprise, and especially so of any attempt to empower the ECE Secretariat to make enquiries regarding SO_2 emissions in signatory nations. The UK was equally reluctant. British scientists called for more research to firmly establish responsibility for long-range pollution. The UK position regarding the terms of a new agreement was clear. Broad, general statements of policy and even of means to achieve the policy were fine, as long as no positive obligations were imposed or assumed.

As negotiations proceeded at the ECE through 1978, the UK and FRG positions began to harden, especially against the standstill and rollback provisions of the Nordic proposal. Since the European Community had competence in the area of international environmental controls, the Community spoke with a single voice in ECE deliberations. As two of the Community's most influential members, the UK and FRG had little difficulty in making their views Community views, even though some member states—notably The Netherlands and Denmark—might have liked to accept the Nordic plan.

The US position was ambiguous. The US sought to support as many friends as possible: the Scandinavians, the European Community, and the ECE Secretariat. In the course of negotiations, the US delegation tried unsuccessfully to promote the establishment of an ambient air quality standard for sulfur dioxide. The proposal was resisted, especially by the Community countries, because scientists could not agree on what constituted a safe level of SO_2 or even how to measure air quality. The US also helped to mediate between the Community and the Scandinavian contingents, although it was no more ready than the Community to accept standstill or rollback of emissions.

In January 1979, the ECE optimistically scheduled a high-level meeting of member states for November of that year, at which it was hoped that an agreement would be presented and signed. The ECE Commission, comprising representatives from each of the member states, was scheduled to meet in the early spring to fix the terms of a multinational agreement.

The UK eventually agreed to go along with the Convention, in the belief that their plans for an increased reliance on nuclear power to generate electricity would bring about a net reduction in sulfur emissions. Accordingly, they could adhere to the terms of the Convention without changing their energy or pollution control policies.

The FRG successfully resisted the standstill and rollback positions of the Nordic proposal, and managed to require that the words "economically feasible" be added to the Nordic provision that the "best available technology" be used to reduce sulfur emissions. Even so, the FRG was uncomfortable with the proposed agreement, and was concerned that the proposed coordinating function of the ECE Secretariat could give the Secretariat authority to intervene in the internal (pollution control) affairs of

Science for Public Policy

member states. Such interference would be interpreted as a "loss of sovereignty". This concern is often a major obstacle to cooperative international action in the environmental area, even where there is a relatively clear consensus on key scientific issues.

Three diplomatic maneuvers were undertaken to gain the concurrence of the FRG. During the first half of 1979, France was the president-country of the ECE, a role that rotates every year among the member states. France's Community representatives, determined that if the proposed ECE agreements were to fail the Community must not be responsible, put pressure on the FRG to join in the accord. Simultaneously, the Norwegian Foreign Minister contacted his counterpart in the FRG while the Swedish Prime Minister contacted Helmut Schmidt, the Chancellor of the FRG, urging them most strenuously to support the prospective agreement. These appeals apparently brought the FRG around.

Once the Community was unanimous in its support of the draft Convention, it was assumed that the agreement would have a smooth sailing. Since the original initiative for the Convention cane from Brezhnev, it was expected that Eastern European countries would be willing to take part in the Convention.

But the Eastern European countries resisted the Community's claim to represent its member states in negotiating the agreement and declined to be a signatory of the agreement. The meeting of the ECE Commission came to an abrupt halt over this issue in April 1979—supposedly suspending all further work on the Convention. The Convention was nearly aborted as a result of this seemingly extraneous dispute. However, a compromise amendment to Article 14 of the Convention was eventually agreed upon. It entitled regional economic organizations to sign the Convention if, and only if, they had been granted authority to act internationally on behalf of their constituent states. Thus the status of the Community as a signatory was acknowledged, and the last obstacle to an agreement was removed.

The Provisions of the Convention

The Convention established important avenues of international cooperation in monitoring and research activities, and put in place a valuable structure to assemble information on national emissions, as well as pollution control and energy policies. The accord also imposed "notice and consultation" requirements, applying to national policy changes likely to have "significant" impact on levels of transboundary sulfur pollution [33].

But it did little to move beyond the Declaration of the 1972 Stockholm Conference in defining national responsibilities to control transboundary pollution, or to compensate for the damage it causes. Nations were allowed ample room to continue with the energy and pollution control policies of their preference. Signatory states pledged only to "endeavour to limit and, as far as possible, gradually reduce and prevent air pollution" [34].

The Convention designated an Interim Executive Body (IEB) to coordinate implementation under the aegis of the ECE Secretariat. The IEB's agenda was to inaugurate a multilateral research program, gather country-by-country information on policies and strategies for sulfur control, and set in motion machinery for consultation among signatory states. The IEB has since recommended the adoption of "clear goals for sulfur emission reduction", and is now directing research activities including the monitoring of the concentration and deposition of air pollutants, air pollution impacts, control technologies, and cost–benefit analyses of various emission–reduction programs.

But the ECE Secretariat has extremely limited resources. Its environment unit has only seven staff members, whose responsibilities include a whole range of environmental protection matters besides transboundary air pollution. Hence, its capacity to productively absorb the scientific research findings accumulated by the Interim Executive Body is limited.

The Convention's Significance

For the most part, the Convention was a symbolic victory. The notice and consultation provisions will come into play rarely—only when a nation unilaterally reaches the unlikely conclusion that a planned action will cause a "significant" increase in transboundary pollution. No numerical goals, timetables, abatement requirements, or enforcement provisions were included.

But the Agreement did further efforts to control transboundary pollution in several respects. One of its most important virtues is that for the first time the nations of Eastern Europe joined Western countries in an environmental agreement. Eastern and Western European countries agreed to cooperate in setting up air quality and precipitation monitoring stations, and in pooling the data gathered from these stations through the ECE Secretariat.

The ECE Convention also strengthened the key European pollution data gathering network, the cooperative Programme for Monitoring and Evaluation of Long-range Transmission of Air Pollutants in Europe (EMEP) of the ECE. EMEP is designed to provide scientists and governments with information on the transport and deposition of transboundary air pollutants. It is implemented in cooperation with the Geneva-based World Meteorological Organization (WMO), which has the nearly impossible task of attempting to assure uniformity among the various national monitoring efforts. During the first phase of its activity, the EMEP collected emission data and monitored SO_2 levels in 20 countries of Eastern and Western Europe. In

1981, the first EMEP estimates of transboundary sulfur deposition were released [35]. Building upon the OECD's earlier transboundary pollution flow figures, the EMEP sulfur deposition estimates are now generally accepted as the most accurate available. Nations opposed to Scandinavian pleas for cooperative control of SO_2 now ground their opposition to international control efforts on other contentions. They seldom dispute the existence or magnitude of transboundary flow in Europe.

Perhaps the most important result of the Convention was the impact it had on other cooperative efforts. The consensus on the severity of the problem and the commitment to pursue abatement of SO_2 played an important role in facilitating enactment of the Community-wide ambient standard for SO_2 (discussed below). By making national governments more conscious of transboundary pollution concerns, the Convention enhanced prospects for future cooperative abatement efforts, and demonstrated how one international organization can propel another toward effective action.

The European Economic Community

Comprised of the ten nations of the European Common Market, the Community wields a level of authority unparalleled among multilateral organizations in Europe. While other organizations can promote international actions by undertaking technical studies or eliciting national commitments to general principles of environmental responsibility, only the Community has the authority to establish pollution control directives binding upon member states. However, since the approval of Western Europe's largest polluters—the UK, FRG, France, and Italy—is required before a proposed directive can become Community policy, stringent pollution abatement requirements are not easily imposed. Nevertheless, the Community has prompted important innovations in pollution control in Europe, requiring the establishment of national programs to control fuel sulfur content and ambient air quality—approaches new to most Community countries.

The Community relies on a unique, independent entity, the Commission, to play a key role in the development, initiation, and implementation of Community policies. The Commission is composed of 14 members—two each from the Community's largest member states, UK, France, Italy, and the FRG; and one each from the remaining countries—Belgium, Denmark, Greece, Ireland, Luxembourg, and The Netherlands. It is supported by a staff of 9000 international civil servants with headquarters in Brussels, Belgium. Commission members act collegially in the joint community interest rather than as representatives of their respective national governments.

The Commission is the Community's mechanism to link policy with scientific information. Based on its assessment of economic and political constraints and its evaluation of scientific information, such as that developed by the World Health Organization (WHO) and the OECD, the Commission develops directives and proposes them to the Council of Ministers, where representatives from member states convey their governments' approval or disapproval. The Council must unanimously endorse a proposed directive for it to become Community policy.

The Commission's environment staff has proven remarkably adept at developing meaningful, though not especially rigorous, environmental directives and securing the necessary endorsement of the Council of Ministers, despite substantial opposition. Among the more than 40 environmental directives successfully initiated by the Commission are important pronouncements establishing Community-wide limits on new car emissions, gas–oil (light fuel oil) sulfur content, and ambient levels of sulfur dioxide and particulates.

The 1980 Directive on SO$_2$ and Suspended Pariculates

In 1976 a proposed directive establishing an ambient SO$_2$ standard of 120 micrograms per cubic meter ($\mu g/m^3$) (taken as a yearly median figure of daily averages) was submitted to the Community by the Commission. The proposal was based in part on 1979 health criteria document of the WHO for that pollutant. Although the standard itself was rather modest (roughly half as stringent as the WHO recommended), the notion of a Community-wide ambient limit marked a major change. Among Community members, only the FRG already had a national ambient standard for sulfur dioxide. The proposed directive, part of a package including a standard for suspended particulates as well, evoked resistance from several member states, including France, Ireland, the FRG, and the UK.

The requirement for unanimous endorsement of the SO$_2$ directive seemed impossible to meet, until 1979 when the ECE Convention on Transboundary Air Pollution supplied the Community's environment staff with leverage to bring reluctant nations on board. Having accepted the principle of international cooperation in the ECE agreement and officially noted the severity of the SO$_2$ pollution problem, nations found it more difficult to oppose the Community's SO$_2$ directive. Hence, the activities of one international organization made the actions of another possible.

The Directive's Provisions and Impact

The SO$_2$ directive is a complex instrument containing 16 articles and 5 annexes. An annual limit value (for health protection) of 80–120 micrograms per cubic meter ($\mu g/m^3$) and a nonbinding annual guide value (for environmental protection) of 40–60 $\mu g/m^3$ were established. Nations were directed to put in place measures necessary to achieve compliance with limit values by April 1983 (33 months after the directive's enactment). But a generous grace period of ten years is allowed for areas exceeding the standard on this date. The directive also provides for consultation when the ambient standards "are or might be exceeded following significant pollution which originates or may have originated in another Member State" [36].

In terms of emission reductions, the Community's SO_2 directive will have little impact. The vast majority of the Community's land areas are already in compliance. Action will be required in some heavily industrialized areas, including parts of the FRG, France, the UK, Belgium, and Italy. But member states have until 1993 to achieve compliance. In some cases the normally scheduled retirement of older power plants and their replacement by nuclear plants or more efficient, new, fossil-fuel fired facilities will suffice. In the remaining areas, modest shifts to lower sulfur fuels may be necessary. Alternatively, nations may resort to a wider dispersion.

The program is not specifically geared toward control of transboundary pollution or environmental acidification. In fact, to the extent that tall smokestacks are constructed to achieve compliance with the ambient standard, an increase in long-range transport of pollutants and transboundary flow could result. The Council has unofficially sought to encourage member states to use emission reductions rather than dispersion to achieve the required ambient levels. However, this thought is not formally included in any of the directive's provisions.

The directive was a major achievement despite its limitations. Unlike the ECE Convention, it imposed numerical limits on atmospheric pollution concentrations and timetables for their achievement—although lenient ones. It promoted fundamental changes in the approach toward air pollution control in the eight member states that previously had no national ambient standards. These countries must now establish measurement regimes consistent with those treated in the directive's annex, and some form of national oversight mechanism to assure that the standard is attained in heavily polluted areas. For countries where air pollution control has been treated as purely a local prerogative, this represents a major departure from past practice. Community nations will now be better prepared to respond to scientific information on long-range pollution problems, at least with respect to their institutional structure for monitoring and pollution control.

Finally, the directive established important precedents. All of Western Europe is to achieve some minimal air quality level, and that level will be determined by the Community. Having established its authority for air quality control in Western Europe, the Community is looking to extend its reach to ambient regulation for other pollutants, and to problems such as acid rain.

The Third Action Program

In November of 1981, the Community released its draft Third Action Program on the Environment, outlining its plans for environmental initiatives in the years 1982 to 1986. Although the objectives are outlined only in very vague terms—for sound political reasons—the Community's draft action plan reflects an increasingly broad perception of its role in the formation of Western Europe's environmental policies. In fact, the Commission now appears to see an important role for the Community in following through on the technical studies, statements of scientific consensus, and formal agreements on transboundary pollution produced by the OECD and the ECE. The Third Action Program announces the Community's intention to devise a policy that "will stabilize and thereafter gradually reduce total emissions by establishing emission standards"—standards that would actually mandate specific levels of control for particular types of sources—"where necessary" to reduce total emissions at "large, fixed sources with high stacks which distribute pollution over a wide radius." The draft Action Plan states that "this action will form part of the Commission's contribution to the effort to resolve the acid rain and transboundary pollution problem."

The 1982 Stockholm Conference

Signatories to the 1979 ECE Convention met again in June of 1982 at the Stockholm Conference on Acidification of the Environment. Convened by the Swedish government on the occasion of the tenth anniversary of the 1972 UN Conference on the Human Environment, the meeting was another step in continuing Scandinavian efforts to preserve momentum towards international abatement action. Although almost three years had elapsed since the 1979 Convention, the agreement had neither formally entered into force (lacking the requisite 24 ratifications), nor yielded important actions under the unanimously endorsed resolution of the ECE to implement the obligations of the accord provisionally, pending its official ratification.

At the Conference, scientists from participating countries reported on new research and debated the terms of a consensus report in three days of expert meetings. National and international representatives presented formal addresses expressing their concern and reviewing their nation's progress in controlling pollution. Closed negotiating sessions were conducted where a nonbinding Conference statement was hammered out, including recommendations for implementation and improvement of the Convention. Finally, the way was cleared for receiving the last national ratifications necessary to formally bring the Convention into force.

As an effort to shepherd the development of an international consensus on scientific information concerning transboundary sulfur pollution, the meeting was a model of success. At the expert mettings, over one hundred of the leading scientists, engineers, and pollution control officials from 20 nations gathered to produce a detailed summary of the current state-of-the-art knowledge of the scientific, technical, and policy issues surrounding the acidification problem. The conclusions of the expert meetings offered considerable support for Sweden, Norway, Canada, and other nations arguing that enough is already known about the nature and effects of acid rain to justify remedial action. Specifically, the experts concluded that:

(1) Man-made sulfur and nitrogen emissions are primarily responsible for acid deposition.
(2) A decrease in emissions over a large industrialized region would lead to an "approximately proportionate" decrease in acid deposition.
(3) Any reduction in acid deposition "will bring a positive improvement" in aquatic ecosystems under stress.
(4) Sensitive Canadian lakes in Ontario and Quebec are "based on the Scandinavian experience . . . expected to undergo acidification in the next several decades.
(5) Sulfur dioxide can cause "physiological and biochemical changes of significance to [forest] growth" at concentrations lower than previously thought possible without necessarily developing visible damage.
(6) ". . . tree growth may be decreased in association with annual mean SO_2 concentrations as small as 25–50 micrograms per cubic meter $(\mu g/m^3)$." These concentrations prevail over large parts of Europe.
(7) "Recently reported forest damage in an estimated one million hectares of Central Europe seems to be related to the direct effects of gaseous pollutants and soil impoverishment, and toxicity arising from large amounts of wet and dry deposition."

The Conference's nonbinding final statement, which required unanimous approval, was also supportive of the states most concerned about transboundary pollution. It concluded that:

> The acidification problem is serious and, even if deposition remains stable, deterioration of soil and water will continue and may increase unless additional control measures are implemented and existing control policies are strengthened [37].

In addition, it mandated adoption of a "concerted international control program" through the auspices of the ECE. The ECE signatories had never before been able to agree, even in principle, that international abatement programs should be incorporated into the ECE Convention.

It was at this meeting that the FRG, concerned by recent reports of widespread pollution-induced forest damages within its borders, abandoned its opposition to international control efforts and became the first major industrial national—and major polluter—to join the Scandinavian cause.

The Swedish hosts considered the Stockholm Conference a success, if only because a sufficient number of ratifications were assured to bring the 1979 Convention into force by early 1983. Additionally, the affirmation of scientific evidence regarding the causes and potential severity of acidification impacts emerging from the expert meetings strengthened prospects for the eventual establishment of multilateral abatement programs in Europe. However, subsequent events, in particular the formal gathering of the ECE executive body one year later, have made it clear that nonbinding declarations and statements of scientific consensus are sometimes of little utility in efforts to assemble a concrete international response to transboundary problems.

The First Session of the ECE Convention Executive Body

Having at last secured the required ratifications from 24 signatory nations, the ECE member states met once again, 7–10 June 1983, in Geneva, in the first session of the Convention's Executive Body. Attention focused quickly on the crucial issues surrounding the development of emission reduction programs for SO_2. Two major proposals for implementation of the Convention's provisions concerning abatement of sulfur dioxide air pollution were offered. Sweden, Norway, and Finland proposed that member states agree to each embark on a program to reduce SO_2 emissions to 30% of the 1980 levels by 1993.

Driven by concern over pollution impacts on the forests of central Europe, Austria, Switzerland, and the FRG endorsed the Scandinavian plan and proposed that, in addition, the ECE nations adopt a limit of 0.3% weight on the sulfur content of light fuel and diesel oil. They also proposed that an inventory of nitrogen oxides emission-control technologies be undertaken with an eye toward application of such measures. The proposal is noteworthy not only because of the stringency of the control steps that it calls for, but also because the FRG because the FRG broke ranks with the EEC.

In discussions at the official meeting, delegations stressed the importance of pollution due to sulfur emissions as a major environmental problem, and welcomed the entry into force of the Convention as a basis for taking action. The growing damage to ecosystems in a number of member countries was "noted with concern", and many delegations emphasized the importance of taking immediate action to reduce sulfur emissions. This concern was manifested in support of the 30% rollback proposal by Switzerland, Austria, the FRG, Canada, Denmark, Sweden, Norway, and Finland. The Soviet Union did not endorse the program but did commit itself to reducing its transboundary flux 25% to 35%.

Despite the cry for stronger controls under the ECE, it quickly became clear that neither of the abatement proposals was likely to be adopted. There was a powerful, although quiet, opposition which included the US, France, the UK, the Soviet Union, and the countries of Eastern Europe. Delegates from victim countries quickly lowered their sights, and the conferees settled down to the drafting of a joint conference statement. The final result was a one-page decision paper containing only qualified commitments to take abatement action where feasible.

Although scientific statements agreed to at the 1982 Stockholm Conference's expert meetings justified much stronger action, the attendees in 1983 at this meeting agreed only that the contracting parties need to further develop emission reduction programs before the third session of the Executive Body in 1986. Surprisingly, the US—alone among the participants—refused to join in the consensus on the decision paper, in deference to the continuing US national debate over acid rain control.

The Geneva meeting marked some interesting developments on the evolution of the international debate over acid rain. With the emergence of the forestry issue (discussed below), an influential block of central European nations joined the Scandinavian campaign. Yet, Geneva demonstrated that even a formal consensus on key scientific issues, like that which emerged from the expert meetings of the 1982 Stockholm Conference, may have little impact. The failure of the US, formerly a world leader in environmental responsibility, to endorse the document underscored the difficulty of forging the consensus needed to produce a meaningful program for the control of transboundary air pollution.

Growing Damages and Changing National Policies

Although neither the ECE Convention nor the Community's ambient standard specifically requires emission reductions, energy and pollution control policies have changed considerably in the past several years in those countries experiencing the most severe impacts. Sweden, which has seen 18,000 of its lakes acidified, has reduced its SO_2 emissions by more than 40% over the past decade, and plans to reduce pollution levels by an additional 50% by 1993 in accordance with the Scandinavian proposal to the ECE. Norway's emissions are already among the lowest in Europe, but that nation too plans to reduce its SO_2 emissions by an additional 50% over the next decade. Canada has also vowed to reduce its SO_2 emissions by 50% by 1994.

But other nations, not experiencing severe aquatic impacts or possessing extensive, vulnerable lake areas, had not altered their energy or environmental policies. This picture, and more generally the international debate on acid rain, was dramatically altered in the early 1980s when a new and potentially more serious form of ecological damage was associated with the release of acid-forming emissions. Severe damages to forests in widespread areas of central Europe and parts of North America were attributed to emissions of sulfur dioxide and other pollutants.

The most startling change occurred in the FRG. Throughout the 1970s policymakers in the FRG were sanguine about the nation's moderately stringent air pollution control policies, and largely unconcerned about international air pollution. However, in the 1980s the nation awakened to mounting evidence that there is something seriously wrong in its forests. Researchers found that stands of fir and spruce trees, especially those in high altitude areas, were suffering from a serious, but poorly understood, malady. The most common manifestation is a symptom known as crown die-back, where leaves and needles at the tree top turn yellow, then brown, and ultimately drop off. In many areas the problem has progressed to include thinning of branches over the entire tree, and even large-scale forest destruction. Now the nation is looking apprehensively at its substantial domestic SO_2 sources and at the large international contribution to the FRG's pollution problem.

Awareness of the FRG's forestry problems began as a result of the work of Dr Bernd Ulrich of Göttingen University. Since 1966 he has been studying the beech and spruce forests on the FRG's Solling Plateau, where crown die-back is now prelevant. Dr Ulrich hypothesized that trees are suffering as a result of pollution-induced changes in the forest soils. Acids from rainfall and dry sulfur deposition are leaching important plant nutrients, such as calcium and potassium, from the soils, making them unavailable to trees. In addition, potentially toxic metals, such as aluminium, are chemically liberated from harmless soil compounds, such as aluminium silicate. Dr Ulrich has theorized that these two effects interact to produce tree damage. In 1979 Ulrich summarized his research findings in a major report to the Deutsche Forschungsgemeinschaft, the nation's scientific research agency, *The Deposition of Air Pollutants and Their Effects on the Wooded Ecosystems in Solling* [38].

For the next two years Ulrich's findings went largely unnoticed, as had the findings of others, such as Dr Wilhelm Knobe who had been reporting serious forestry damage in the state of North Rhine–Westphalia since 1968. As of the fall of 1981 the government remained unconvinced by Ulrich's research, and the public remained unaware of the problem.

But in November of 1981 a dramatic cover story in the popular weekly magazine *Der Spiegel* caught the public's attention and thrust the issue into national prominence. Several special television programs, discussing Ulrich's conclusions and other relevant research in great detail, followed. Acid rain and forest death became a major subject of public concern and media attention.

As in other nations, the government's first response to an independent researcher's alarming reports of an ongoing ecological catastrophe was to convene an official committee to evaluate the threat. Amidst increasing media attention, a 40-member committee of experts from the federal government and the scientific community concluded in the fall of 1982 that fully 560,000 hectares, some 7.8% of the FRG's forest area, had been damaged [39]. The nation's four most important tree species—Norway Spruce, White Fir, Scotch Pine, and Beech—were all reported to have shown signs of vulnerability.

Not surprisingly, the discovery of so severe a problem in the forests, which comprise 25% of the FRG's land area and which have been zealously protected and appreciated for generations, had a profound effect. The nation's domestic and international environmental policies changed quickly and dramatically.

For three years the government had been desultorily considering the adoption of new regulations to govern emissions from large fossil-fuel fired power plants. In 1982 things suddenly began to move very quickly. Four drafts of the regulations were proposed and revised in the spring and summer of that year. A stringent standard requiring for the first time that heavily polluting, older power plants install expensive control technology or cease operation was promulgated at last in the summer of 1983. The government projects that the new program will reduce aggregate SO_2 emissions in the FRG by 50% before 1993. Control programs were also introduced at the state level in the industrialized state of North Rhine-Westphalia, where 16 of the largest power plants agreed to reduce aggregate SO_2 emissions by 15% by 1987. National concern has also been translated into a greatly expanded research effort.

On the international level, the FRG has, as mentioned earlier, made a complete about-face from its position at the time the 1979 ECE Convention was negotiated. It now strongly supports the establishment of an international program to guide the control of SO_2 pollution throughout Europe, and has endorsed the adoption of SO_2 emission reduction programs throughout the EEC.

The FRG's rapid shift to an aggressively pro-control international posture and a domestic pollution control program second only to Japan's in its stringency has been propelled by a series of increasingly dire government assessments of forest damages. The 1983 government survey estimated that 34% of the nations trees had been damaged by air pollution, nearly a four-fold increase from the 1982 figure [40]. More recent surveys in 1984 and 1985 found pollution-induced damage in greater that 50% of the nation's trees. [41].

A number of other nation's have also been afflicted by forest damages. The most seriously impacted countries include Switzerland, Austria, France,

Poland, Czechoslovakia and the GDR. Several of these governments have embarked on SO_2 control regimes of their own in the past several years. France and Austria have joined Canada and the Scandinavian nations in putting in place a program to reduce their SO_2 emissions by 50%, while Switzerland and Czechoslovakia have adopted programs to achieve a 30% reduction. (The Czechoslovakian program, like those put in place in the Soviet Union and other eastern European countries, actually calls for a 30% reduction in transboundary flow, rather than a reduction in total national emissions).

Development of the Issue: Lessons for Future Problems

The development of the acid rain issue, both within nations and internationally, offers some useful insights regarding what it takes to move governments to respond to new environmental problems. Government responses to scientific information in this instance offer a valuable indication of society's ability to come to grips with future threats to our ecosystems, such as a global climate change associated with the build-up of carbon dioxide in our atmosphere.

As the preceding pages describe, nations have been moved to respond to the acid rain problem by a number of forces, including scientific information in several forms. Original research findings, media coverage, government scientific reports, technical studies by multilateral organizations, internation-lands would have liked to support a stronger ECE Convention in 1979, but were discouraged from doing so by their partners in the European Community, especially the UK and the FRG.

Cooperative multilateral action has proved discouragingly difficult to achieve. Not surprisingly, the reluctance of nations to undertake obligations requiring that they yield some degree of national sovereignty has been an important obstacle. Another predictable problem has been the difficulty of forging an international consensus on key scientific issues, such as the appropriate threshold levels to which control programs should be targeted.

These difficulties are exacerbated by the fact that, to date, most nations do not attach great importance to initiatives that deal with multinational environmental problems, even when neighboring nations see them as very pressing. Cooperative efforts in the environmental area are fragile and often subject to major setbacks, owing to seemingly irrelevant considerations. A dispute over recognition of the GDR kept the Soviet Union and the countries of Eastern Europe from participating in the 1972 Stockholm Conference and becoming part of the landmark 1972 UN Declaration on the Human Environment. The 1979 ECE Convention enjoyed a fortuitous advantage as a pawn in East-West relations at a time when Leonid Brezhnev was seeking an area for cooperative activity. But the agreement was almost scuttled in a dispute over the European Community's status as a signatory.

Taken as a whole, our experiences with acid rain do not bode well for efforts to deal with other second-generation pollution problems. Even where serious impacts have already occurred, strong public pressure was needed before governments would seriously consider scientific information suggesting that policies must be changed to protect the nation's ecosystems. Remedial action to deal with acid rain is still under development in some nations suffering damage, such as the US, where the issue is the subject of fractious debate. In most cases, countries not suffering damages have not altered their policies, although most now recognize the problem.

The problems such as the atmospheric build-up of CO_2 are likely to have irreversible global consequences before their impacts can actually be measured and, perhaps, public concern can be mobilized. If nations are to deal successfully with such concerns, a better structure must be devised for bringing relevant scientific information to the attention of national policy makers and the general public and encouraging a response before damages are evident.

Another important and somewhat obvious lesson to emerge from the acid rain issue is that the influence of scientific information on national governments is determined in part by internatioanl politics. A cooperative effort to respond to global problems, such as the CO_2 build-up, would be greatly facilitated if leading nations from the range of social and economic al accords, and straightforward international politics, have all played a part. Generally speaking, the influence of scientific data has been a function of its institutional origins; of whether it is independent research, the product of a government committee, or the result of an international effort. The level of media interest, the extent of public concern, and external factors, such as economics and international politics, played a key role in determining how governments responded to research data.

In those nations experiencing serious environmental damage, the problem was detected, officially acknowledged, and responded to via surprisingly similar chains of events. The findings of individual scientists, in themselves, counted for little. Initial reports of damages from researchers such as Oden in Sweden; Harvey, Beamish, and Schofield in North America; Ulrich in the FRG; and a host of other scientific pioneers who never attained such prominence, were ignored by policymakers. In each case public concern, fueled by media reports, was needed to prompt a government reaction. The first government step in each instance was to undertake an official evaluation of the problem. The reports resulting from these government studies, including, for example, the 1972 Swedish study of sulfur emissions and the 1982 government study of air pollution impacts on forests in the FRG, have been the single most influential bodies of information. In the cases of Sweden and the FRG, these reports, and the public pressure they generated, provided a major impetus for changes in national policies.

But official government reports were given little credence outside of the nation sponsoring their preparation. Possible exceptions may apply to other countries faced with similar environmental problems. Hence, Norway readily accepted the conclusions of Sweden's case study while the UK and the FRG did not.

Nations not experiencing serious domestic impacts have proved difficult to reach with scientific information on international pollution. International technical studies, such as the OECD study of transboundary pollution flow in Europe, proved valuable as a means of broadening international recognition of multilateral problems. However, nations were unwilling to enact policy changes on the basis of such studies without independent confirmation from domestic scientists.

The one force that has prompted action from countries not suffering damages within their borders is international politics. Denmark, Finland, and The Netherlands joined the Swedish and Norwegian campaign for international action mainly to preserve Nordic unity. Similarly, the nations of Eastern Europe—who may have damages, but have not admitted their severity—took part in the ECE accord mainly because the agreement was an outgrowth of Chairman Brezhnev's call for international cooperation in environmental protection. Political pressures between nations can also work against the development of cooperative action. Denmark and The Nether-philosophies and stages of economic development moved as quickly as possible to set an example. Credible commitments to principles of environmental responsibility, such as Principle 21 of the Stockholm Declaration on the Human Environment, would provide an excellent start.

References

1. Evelyn, J. (1661) *Fumifugium* (London, UK: Bedel and Collins).
2. Smith, R. A. (1872) *Air and Rain: The Beginnings of a Chemical Climatology* (London, UK: Longmans, Green).
3. Gorham. E. (1958) *Quarterly Journal of the Royal Meteorological Society*, **84**, 274–276, 247; *Philosophical Transactions of the Royal Society of London: Series B*, **1958**, 247–178; Cowling, E. (1982) Acid Precipitation in historical perspective, *Environmental Science and Technology*, **16**, 111A (hereafter cited as "Historical Perspective").
4. Oden, S. (1967) *Dagens Nyheter* 24 October.
5. Oden, S. (1968) The acidification of air and precipitation and its consequences in the natural environment, in *Ecology Committee Bulletin No. 1*, (Stockholm, Sweden: Swedish National Science Research Council); translation by Consultants, Ltd, Arlington, Virginia, USA.
6. Cowling, E. (1982) Acid precipitation in historical perspective, *Environmental Science and Technology*, **16**, 115A.
7. Bolin, *et al.* (1972) *Sweden's Case Study for the United Nations Conference on the Human Environment: Air Pollution Across National Boundaries*, (Stockholm, Sweden: Norstadt and Sons).

8. Declaration of the UN Conference on the Human Environment. (1973) *Report of the UN Conference on the Human Environment, Stockholm, Sweden, June 5–16, 1972* (New York, USA: United Nations) pp 3–5.

9. Organisation for Economic Cooperation and Development (1977) *The OECD Programme on Long-Range Transport of Air Pollutants* (Paris, France: OECD).

10. Author's interview with Ellis Cowling, 11 October 1983.

11. Beamish, R. J. and Harvey, H. H. (1972) Acidification of the LaCloche Mountain Lakes, *Journal of the Fisheries Research Board of Canada*, **29**, 1131–1143.

12. Likens, G. E., Bormann, F. H. and Johnson, N. M. (1972) *Environment*, **14**, 33–40.

13. Cogbill, C. V. and Likens, G. E. (1974) *Water Resources Research*, **10**, 1133–1137.

14. Schofield, C. L. (1976) *Ambio*, 228–230.

15. Howard, R. and Perley, M. (1980) *Acid Rain: The North American Forecast* (Ontario, Canada: House of Anansi Press Limited) p 155 (hereafter cited as *Acid Rain: The North American Forecast*).

16. The Research Consultation Group has published two comprehensive assessments of the air pollution problem: The Research Consultation Group (1979) *The Long Range Transport of Air Pollutants Problem in North America: A Preliminary Overview* (Washington, DC, USA: Canadian Embassy, Public Affairs Division) and The Research Consultation Group (1980) *Second Report of the US/Canada Research Consultation Group on the Long-Range Transport of Air Pollutants* (Washington, DC, USA: Canadian Embassy, Public Affairs Division).

17. See Howard and Perley op. cit.

18. Ontario Ministry of the Environment (1980) *The Case Against the Rain: A Report on Acidic Precipitation and Ontario Programs for Remedial Action* (Toronto, Canada: Ontario Ministry of the Environment); and Environment Canada How many more Lakes have to die? *Canada Today*, **February** 1981.

19. Hurley, A. (Executive Coordinator, Canadian Coalition on Acid Rain, Testimony before the Senate Committee on Environment and Public Works (1981) *Clean Air Act Oversight (Field Hearings), 98th Congress, 1st Session, Augusta, Maine 97-H12, Part 6, 14 April 1981* (Washington, DC, USA: US Government Printing Office) pp 40, 124.

20. Environmental Protection Agency, Office of Research and Development (1979) *Acid Rain Research Summary* (Washington, DC, USA: EPA 600/8-79-028).

21. Joint Statement on Transboundary Air Quality by the Government of Canada and the Government of the United States of America, 26 July 1979, in Gregory S. Wetstone (1982) *Final Report—Long Range Air Pollution Across National Boundaries: Recourses in Law and Policy*, A US/Canada Case Study for the Congressional Office of Technology Assessment (Washington, DC, USA: OTA) Appendix I.

22. Memorandum of Intent Between the Government of the United States of America and the Government of Canada Concerning Transboundary Air Pollution, *Common Boundary/Common Problems*, American Bar Association, Appendix B, **March** 1981.

23. Reinhold, R. (1982) Acid rain issue creates stress between administration and science academy, *New York Times*, 8 June Cl. The report referred to is: National Academy of Sciences (1981) *Atmosphere – Biosphere Interactions: Toward a Better Understanding of the Ecological Consequences of Fossil Fuel Combustion*, Committee of the Atmosphere and the Biosphere, Board of Agriculture and Renewable Resources, Commission on Natural Resources (Washington, DC, USA: National Academy Press) (hereafter cited as *Atmosphere–Biosphere Interactions*).

24. Hare, K. (Chairman Royal Society of Canada, Committee on Acid Deposition) (1983) *Acid Deposition in North America* (Toronto, Canada: Royal Society of Canada).

25. National Commission on Air Quality (1981) *Report of National Commission on Air Quality: To Breathe Clean Air* (Washington, DC, USA: NCAQ) pp 2.2–20.

26. National Academy of Sciences (1981) *Atmosphere – Biosphere Interactions: Toward a Better Understanding of the Ecological Consequences of Fossil Fuel Combustion* (Washington, DC, USA: National Academy Press).

27. National Academy of Sciences (1983) *Acid Deposition: Atmospheric Processes in Eastern North America: A Review of Current Scientific Understanding* (Washington, DC, USA: National Academy Press).

28. Confirmation Hearings of William D. Ruckelshaus to position of Administrator of US Environmental Protection Agency, 16 May 1983.

29. See, e.g., Statement of Lee Thomas before the U.S. House of Representatives, Subcommittee on Health and the Environment, Hearing on H.R. 4567, the Acid Deposition Control Act of 1986, April 28, 1986.

30. Lewis, Drew and Davis, William, *Joint Report of the Special Envoys on Acid Rain* (Jan. 1986).

31. Statement of John Herrington before the U.S. House of Representatives, Subcommittee on Health and the Environment, Hearing on H.R. 4567, the Acid Deposition Control Act of 1986, April 28, 1986.

32. The 1979 Convention on Transboundary Air Pollution, UN/ECE/GE 79-42960, reprinted (1980) *Environmental Law and Policy*, **6**, 37–40 (hereafter cited as 1979 Convention on Transboundary Air Pollution).

33. This discussion draws primarily on interviews with: A. Bishop, Director, ECE Environment Division, Geneva, Switzerland, 17 April and 16 November 1979; J. Stanovnik, Secretary General, ECE, Geneva, Switzerland, 15 November 1979; U. Zito, Director, International Affairs Section of the Environment Department, European Economic Community, 25 April 1979; and Konrad Von Moltke, Director, Institute for European Environment and Society, Bonn, Federal Republic of Germany, 21 March 1980.

34. 1979 Convention on Transboundary Air Pollution, op. cit., Articles 5 and 8. For a discussion of international consultation, see Kiss, A. (1976) *Survey of Current Developments in International Environmental Law*, Chapter III, (International Union for the Conservation of Nature, Policy and Law Serial).

35. 1979 Convention on Transboundary Air Pollution, op. cit., Article 2.

36. *Council of European Communities on Air Quality Limit Values and Guide Values for Sulphur Dioxide and Suspended Particulates* (1980) 80/779/EEC-OJ L 229, amended by 81/887/EEC.

37. Swedish Ministry of Agriculture (1982) *The 1982 Stockholm Conference on Acidification of the Environment, June 28–30, 1982* (Stockholm, Sweden: Departementens Reprocentral) p 31.

38. Ulrich, B., Mayer, R., and Khanna, P. K. (1979) *Deposition of Air Pollutants and Their Effects on the Wooded Ecosystems in Solling*, report to the Deutsche Forschungsgemeinschaft, Vol. 58. (Göttingen, FRG: University of Göttingen).

39. The Ministry of Food, Agriculture and Forestry (1982) *Forest Damage Due to Air Pollution; The Situation in the Federal Republic of Germany* (Bonn, FRG: The Ministry of Food, Agriculture and Forestry).

40. Federal Ministry of Food, Agriculture and Forestry, *1983 Forest Damage Survey* (Bonn, FRG, 1984).

41. Federal Ministry of Food, Agriculture and Forestry, *1984 Forest Damage Survey* (Bonn, FRG, 1985). The 1985 assessment placed the damage figure at 55%, Federal Ministry of Food, Agriculture and Forestry, *1985 Forest Damage Survey* (Bonn, FRG, 1986).

CHAPTER 13

The CO$_2$ Challenge

CHESTER L. COOPER

This chapter explores in a necessarily brief, admittedly even sketchy, compass how questions involving complex technical content and having enormous transnational ramifications are addressed at national and international policy levels. Such issues embrace many fields, ranging from the economic to the strategic. Although this discussion focuses on two environmental matters, the conclusions can be generalized to include a wide range of problems. Acid rain is referred to as an example of how scientists and policymakers have engaged with regard to one major environmental issue, but the primary focus is placed on CO$_2$-induced climate change as a problem still hovering over the science-for-policy process.

An important, if not always explicit, theme of much that follows is the inadequacy of the science-for-policy process to deal with seminal environmental challenges. This is woefully apparent in national policy systems; it is even more so when issues must be addressed at regional and international levels. Thus, while there may seem to be a comfortable period of time still available to plan for and cope with the economic, social, and ecological traumata of CO$_2$ induced climate change, the institutional arrangements that would be required to deal with its causes and effects are at present grossly inadequate. Responsible members of both the scientific and policymaking communities would be remiss if they did not factor this consideration into their calculations of the time available to deal with the CO$_2$ question at policy levels.

The Setting

Experts and Laymen

Despite the growing proliferation, specialization, and sophistication of natural and social scientists and of the tools they employ, many grave and

Chester Cooper is Resident Consultant at Resources for the Future, Washington, D.C. He is a former Special Advisor to the Director of IIASA and Assistant Director of the Institute for Energy Analysis, Oak Ridge Associated Universities, USA. He has served on the staff of the US National Security Council from 1963 to 1966 and in the State Department from 1966 to 1969.

worrisome technical and social problems still elude solution, even compre-hension. There is a host of reasons why this is so, not the least of which is the still imperfect state of many investigative and analytical arts and the still primitive techniques for detecting and understanding linkages among individual complex problems.

We are concerned here, however, not only with research and analysis, but also with planning and prescription. This involves a more intricate set of considerations: we must examine the community of policy advisers, planners, and officials as well as the community of technicians and scientists. The former requires an array of more general, yet well-honed, talents to govern modern societies, to grapple with competing demands for scarce resources, and to balance short-term imperatives with long-term goals; the latter needs specialized technical skills to investigate the cause and effect of complex natural and man-made perturbations and trends.

Whenever it addresses matters within its own competence, each of these communities is composed of experts; when it confronts the concerns of the other, each is composed of laymen; communication within each is easier than between them. But the effectiveness of communication and interaction between the two influences the quality of public policy on technical issues. Typically—and regardless of a society's political ideology or institutional structure—communication–interaction has been imperfect. This has resulted in groping and coping, quick fixes, and the pervasive sense of fatalism that frequently characterize national and international decision making on complex technical issues.

The Confrontation of Science and Policy

In many fields of research (primarily in the basic sciences), scientists can proceed with little or no prospect of interacting with policymakers. But in others (and, in the past several decades, ecology ranks high among these), confrontation between the two communities is, sooner or later, inevitable.

Such confrontation can occur through planned, thoughtful exchanges among scientists, science advisors, and officials; or as a result of public pressure, based on real or unfounded concern; or from some combination of scientific findings–media attention–public clamor. Most often the confronta-tion is initiated by the scientists through a warning: unless steps are taken to deal with the cause of a specified problem or to counteract its effects, undesirable, even dangerous, consequences could ensue. But if such a warning is to be effective, it must be sounded clearly and understandably to a responsible audience—that is, directly to the policymakers, or indirectly to them through influential elements of the public.

Ideally, a warning process would take the following course:

(1) Experts present their findings to concerned policymakers, probably initially in meetings with policy advisors. The findings are accompanied by the range of uncertainty, the degree of urgency and risk involved, the recommended steps to arrest or reverse the danger, and the time scale in which ameliorative action can be effectively taken.

(2) When (or if) the policy community is satisfied that the experts' findings are valid and compelling, two alternative courses are available:

    (i) Policymakers can decide to take *no action*, or to *postpone action* (which, in the event, may turn out to be the same as taking no action).

    (ii) They can decide to *take action*. At this point the issue moves from confrontation into the policy process.

Unless the experts' finding and/or warning is acknowledged and responded to by the policymakers, (even by a conscious decision to ignore it), the issue has not entered the policy process.

The Policy Process

Many factors, some having no direct relationship to the matter at stake, determine whether or not policy makers choose to confront, let alone to resolve, an issue. And so, before examining specific cases in terms of their science-for-policy implications, it may be helpful to explore some broad considerations likely to affect the nature of policymakers' responses.

Despite the size and scope of most modern policy systems, their carrying capacity at any time is sharply constrained. Yesterday's major issues tend to fade away in the face of today's more urgent, more dramatic concerns.* However well organized and staffed a senior policy maker may be, and whatever his or her adrenaline level, each day is nonetheless finite and each crisis list is dynamic and frequently invaded by unforeseeable events. Every policy agenda, consequently, consists of only a relatively few items at a given moment—whether it is addressed in the White House, the Elysée, Number Ten Downing Street, the Kremlin, or elsewhere.

A myriad of national and international events in constant motion determines whether a particular issue at a particular time is actively addressed by top policymakers, reduced to a watching brief, or shelved altogether. But other less dynamic considerations are also in play. Thus, certain matters (environmental issues, for example) may receive serious policy attention if the overall economy is in a healthy state, but be postponed

---

*What has happened to the "crisis" in urban mass transportation which seized US policymakers only a short time ago?

or ignored if the economy is depressed. The relative state of domestic or international stability and, particularly in democracies, the intensity of public concern (however irrational such concern may be) also weigh heavily in a conscious or subconscious decision to address, postpone, or ignore a particular issue.

The following propositions (by no means a comprehensive list) illustrate the general point:

(1) A rich society—national, regional, or global—is more likely to consider costly policy initiatives in response to experts' findings (warnings) than a poor one.

(2) The fewer profound problems (war, plague, famine, economic stagnation) they face at a particular time, the more receptive and resilient national and world leaders are when confronted by an additional problem.

(3) A stable society is likely to address difficult policy options more readily and more thoughtfully than an unstable one.

(4) Societies characterized by an aging population tend to be especially vulnerable to environmental perturbations and social adjustments. But a younger population is likely to place a higher value on future benefits than an older one.

(5) There is a sensitive negative relationship between the prospect for leadership change and the timing of policy initiatives that carry heavy political or economic costs.

(6) To the extent that experts' findings are unpalatable (e.g. implying costly remedial measures), officials are less likely to tolerate uncertainty in the findings.

(7) Policymakers are more likely to address emerging new complex problems if there is popular consensus on national economic and social goals. Under circumstances in which public discussion of public policy is characterized by shrill, polarized debate, national leaderships are less likely to embark on new, cost-laden initiatives.

These are but a few examples of considerations well outside the compass of a particular issue which could profoundly influence how, or even whether, an issue is addressed and resolved. It is within the context of such overall influences which pull and tug at national and international policy systems that profound environmental challenges—in particular, acid rain and CO_2-induced climate change—are addressed below.

The Case of Acid Rain

The evolution of acid rain policy—a matter now demanding national and international attention—provides insights into the interaction of scientists and policymakers and the interplay of scientific, political, and economic considerations. This important, contemporary science-for-public-policy issue is dealt with in Gregory Wetstone's historical case-study in this volume [1]. The experience illuminated in the Wetstone chapter reflects many of the awkward, untidy, and stressful problems that occur at the nexus between the scientist and policymaker when environmental, economic, and political interests clash.

Can the acid rain issue contribute to an understanding of how other transnational, man-made, serious environmental problems should be addressed? Can science–policy lessons be drawn from the acid rain experience that will be relevant to other major environmental concerns not yet on national and international policy agendas? [2]. Can useful prescriptions, or even relevant cautionary notes, be derived to improve the overall science-for-public-policy process?

The answer to these questions is yes—but an equivocal and conditional yes. After all, politicians and policymakers have no dearth of lessons available on virtually every important issue, but few governments have long or accurate institutional memories.

Having said this, it may still be instructive to examine whether and how policy experience with the acid rain problem might provide guidance to scientists and policymakers confronting another grave, transnational environmental threat. The problem of CO_2-induced climate change is a good case in point: it is on the global horizon rather than on the doorstep, although the remoteness of the horizon and, therefore, the appropriate sense of urgency is by no means clear. Unlike the case of acid rain, there may still be time to make thoughtful policy choices and develop effective policy responses.

It will be useful, then, to summarize some key features of the acid rain policy experience. The time scale between early scientific concern (Eville Gorham's research in Britain in the late 1950s) and actual evidence of the effect of acid rain (Svante Oden's findings in Sweden in the late 1960s) was only a decade [3]. Yet, it was not until very late in the day that acid rain was inscribed on the political agendas of countries primarily affected, to say nothing of countries that were principal exporters of acid rain. And, for both victims and exporters, the issue became politicized only after massive intervention by the media.

The matter of time scale arises in another connection: in the acid rain experience, the typical dilemma of reconciling the long-term view (decades, even centuries) of scientists with the short-term perspective (years, at most a decade or two) of politicians and government officials barely intruded. This was because the period between the scientists' warning and the obvious need for a policy response was telescoped to the point where the two communities had a common sense of operational urgency. Thus, in the case of acid rain the usual mismatch in time perspectives held by scientists and politicans was absent, simplifying the problem for the two disparate communities. The time-scale factor for CO_2-induced climate change takes on an entirely different complexion.

In the case of acid rain, ordinary knowledge (gained through actual observation of the effects) dramatically buttressed the warnings of the scientific community. This obviously made the task of policymakers much easier as they confronted the need for costly economic and political corrective action.

The concept of uncertainty, addressed in J. R. Ravetz's [4] and Brian Wynne's [5] chapters, has clearly been a significant factor in the evolution of acid rain policy. In contrast to some of the central questions of uncertainty that pervade the CO_2 issue, important *effects* of acid rain are already dramatically evident. But there still may be some questions as to the *cause*—or at least the full cause.*

Unlike most air pollution problems that have seized the attention of policy-makers and environmental interest groups until now, the acid rain problem cannot be resolved by local or even national regulatory and administrative action. The transport of acid rain over large distances, the variability of the direction of movement, and the difficulty of ascertaining specific sources of acid rain production require multinational approaches to regulation and control.†

Moreover, problems of regional economic and political trade-offs continue to pose difficulties for those who must set policies and standards: should the consumers of electricity in Ohio pay higher charges to save the fish and forests of Vermont or Canada? Should the German steel industry suffer competitive disadvantages to save Swedish forests? Although regional and international considerations also play an important economic and political role in the overall CO_2 question, they involve even more difficult choices than in the case of acid rain.

As a starting point, at least, the acid rain experience may hold many beguiling, possibly important, lessons for policymakers when CO_2-induced climate change does appear on policy agendas. But there are critical differences that warrant care and discrimination in using the acid rain policy experience as a prologue to CO_2-climate policy.

---

*This is particularly the case in the US where additional research as to causes is being undertaken.

†A previous problem that policy analysts and policy makers can draw on here is the case of pollution management for large, international waterways.

The Carbon Dioxide Question

Uncertainty Abounds

The enormous worldwide increase in the use of coal, oil, and natural gas during the past century has caused an acceleration in the rate of atmospheric accumulation of CO$_2$. This is a matter of considerable concern in the scientific community; research into all aspects of the question is proceeding in North America, Europe, and the Soviet Union. Although many uncertainties remain, a few dolorous generalizations now seem warranted:

(1) CO$_2$ loading of the atmosphere is a global problem; no one country can, by itself, undertake a course of action that will significantly mitigate it.

(2) Increasing atmospheric accumulations of CO$_2$ will, at some point, lead to irreversible changes in the global climate. These climate effects will take the form of significant annual mean temperature increases and consequential shifts in global precipitation patterns.

(3) Complicating and exacerbating the CO$_2$ effect in the atmosphere is the impact of certain other trace gases associated with human activities.

(4) Even if there were concerted international action to constrain the use of fossil fuels (especially coal, the principal offender), it would seem that the CO$_2$ problem can only be postponed for a matter of decades, not solved. CO$_2$-induced climate change, in short, may already be an intractable problem.

Unlike acid rain, the *causes* of CO$_2$ atmospheric accumulation have been reasonably well established, but the *ecological effects* of such an accumulation and, in particular, the *climate change* effects that can be expected are much less clear. In short, "the 'why' of the CO$_2$ question is beginning to be understood; the 'so what?' remains elusive" [6]. And the "so what?" is the question that especially concerns observers and practitioners of the public policy process.

The Scientist–Policymaker Confrontation

Until the autumn of 1983, the CO$_2$ problem, in the US at least, had not yet become politicized. Except for a few congressional hearings and a few references in the media, it remained aloof from political or policy attention and from public concern. Indeed, only in the past decade has the issue become a matter of serious scientific research and analysis. But, in mid-October, 1983, two separate investigations were simultaneously completed and widely publicized [7].

Inadvertently and unwittingly, the responsible institutions—the US Environmental Protection Agency (EPA) and the US National Academy of Sciences (NAS)—provided IIASA's Forum on Science for Public Policy with a dramatic case study. Each institution examined the same issue, CO_2-induced climate change. The public policy thrust of each report, however, was substantially different: the EPA called for a robust public policy response within the next few years [8], while the NAS concluded that the need for, indeed the appropriateness of, a public policy response was still decades away [9].

Overnight, the CO_2 issue became a matter of American media concern and public bewilderment. But unlike the case of acid rain, where widespread publicity caused the issue to have a high priority for policy attention, the CO_2 question did not quickly invade the public policy agenda. As we shall see, the science policy establishment was obviously anxious that it should not do so.

The present purpose is not to delve into the technical merits of either the EPA or the NAS reports.* Rather, using the reports as fortuitous case studies, we shall seek some insights into the science-for-public-policy process and identify some questions for further examination.

It should be noted that the two reports were undertaken for different purposes. The EPA study is the more policy-oriented document and "aims to shed light on the [CO_2] debate by evaluating the usefulness of various strategies for slowing or limiting a global warming . . ." [10]. The NAS report, on the other hand, was "a sustained attempt to achieve assessment of the CO_2 issue" [11].

To a policy establishment already pressed by calls for costly initiatives to deal with acid rain and other environmental issues, the EPA warning of impending danger and its thinly veiled call for early government action would obviously be uncongenial. Moreover, the acknowledged uncertainty that surrounds the timing and the extent of global warming made the EPA's conclusions and recommendations vulnerable to real or cosmetic requirements for a higher degree of certainty on the part of scientists and of prudence on the part of policymakers.

George Keyworth, the President's science advisor, virtually dismissed the EPA findings, referring to them as "unwarranted and unnecessarily alarmist . . . Contrary to a recent report issued by a branch of the Environmental Protection Agency, there is no evidence to indicate that the gradual rise in carbon dioxide in the air would have environmental effects pronounced enough to require near term corrective actions." He then cited the NAS report and noted that the Academy scientists "emphasized that at this time there are no actions recommended other than continued research on this issue". Although both reports are replete with uncertainty, Keyworth's

*Only one chapter in the NAS report dealt with policy issues. This is addressed below.

statement has the EPA report "speculating" and the NAS report "indicating" [12].

Is Keyworth's reaction unique to a particular administration or even to a particular country? A case can be made that the science advisor was acting as a surrogate for policymakers and advisors everywhere who are faced with many other urgent environmental issues (including acid rain) involving costly policy responses—to say nothing of pressing economic, energy, and national security concerns. It would be a rare official who would not be tempted to support a body of experts advocating a stance of caution, not panic and recommending more research in the face of large uncertainties, as opposed to another group (even one with more official status) calling for an early policy response.

In the end, Dr. Keyworth's reaction was consistent with two observations about policy systems in general:

(1) Policy establishments (no less than individuals) tend to postpone decisions involving high costs until the last possible moment (sometimes, wittingly or not, until unfavorable trends are irreversible).
(2) Policy establishments (again, like individuals) tend to seek a high degree of certainty with regard to experts' findings (warnings) involving high-cost responses. But, in cases where experts suggest low-cost solutions or no need for a policy response, a much lower level of certainty will probably be tolerated by policymakers.

The CO₂ Doubling Scenario

It has become a standard analytical technique in the CO_2 research community, largely because of modeling and statistical convenience, to use a doubling of CO_2 in the atmosphere* as the benchmark for assessing climate change and other effects. Most of the estimates with regard to global temperature increase and the time scale involved stem from models and forecasts of CO_2 doubling.

There is considerable consensus among scientists that a doubling of CO_2 in the atmosphere will produce an increase in the global mean annual temperature in the range of 1.5° to 4°C. A relatively high probability is assigned to an increase in the neighborhood of 2.5° to 3°C. There is also general agreement that an increase in global mean temperature of this magnitude will bring about major shifts in global precipitation patterns. The accompanying effects on agriculture, fisheries, human health, economic productivity, resource (including water) availability, and even geopolitics could produce Wagnerian challenges for virtually every society on the globe.

*Doubling means a CO_2 content of 540 parts per million compared to the 270 parts per million at the beginning of the Industrial Revolution, about a century and half ago.

Many factors (some, perhaps, not yet identified) will influence the timing of a CO_2 doubling, but the single most important one is the future consumption of energy from fossil fuels. Obviously, a precise year, or even a particular decade, cannot be predicted. The NAS assessment, which addresses CO_2-induced climate change in terms of the conventional doubling device, presents a probability distribution indicating a 50% chance of a CO_2 doubling in the period 2050–2100 [13]. This finding and its implication of a seminal global climate change sometime in the latter half of the next century is consistent with other investigations that have been based on CO_2 doubling.

The use of CO_2 doubling as a benchmark should be regarded with caution by observers and analysts of the science-for-public policy process. It is an analytical contrivance, rather than a policy tool. Calculations of temperature rise that flow from a CO_2 doubling and estimates of the time when this will occur are scientifically illuminating, but do not necessarily have great policy significance. In fact, quite the reverse: the time period (75 to 100 years hence) spewed out by computers on the basis of the CO_2 doubling approach may be dangerously seductive; weary policymakers, already grappling with overflowing agendas, will be all too ready to pass the CO_2 issue on to future generations of public officials.

The 2° Scenario

Although projections of temperature change and its timing are commonly based on the CO_2 doubling approach, this is not the only way the CO_2 issue can be addressed either from an analytical or from a policy perspective. The EPA report, for example, eschewed the doubling device in favor of measuring various policy choices in terms of the "number of years a particular [fuel mix] option delays a temperature rise of 2°C" [14]. On the basis of this approach, the EPA found that a worrisome amount of global warming could occur well before the NAS forecast. "In the mid-range baseline [of the EPA CO_2/climate model] a 2° warming is reached around 2040" [15].

The difference between the NAS and the EPA estimates of the time when a significant global warming will occur represents only an instant in geological terms and only a brief moment in historical perspective. For policymakers, however, it is sufficiently distant that they can relax in the knowledge that complicated planning and disagreeable decisions will not have to be undertaken during their professional lifespans.

But CO_2 policy concerns cannot be dismissed so readily. The global warming and precipitation associated with CO_2 will be incremental: the world will not awaken one morning in, say, 2068, to discover that the day has suddenly become hotter and wetter or drier, or the frequency of crop failure has suddenly and significantly changed for the better or worse.

If it is true (and the scientific community holds it to be true) that (a) CO_2 atmospheric loading is inexorably increasing year by year and (b) increasing atmospheric CO_2 will be accompanied by a global warming, then the decade of the 1990s is likely to be warmer than the decade of the 1980s (leaving aside perturbations caused by volcanic dust, etc., etc.). But how much warmer—enough to affect human health, delicate ecological balances, vegetation, and agriculture? And will the human and ecological costs of small climate change be offset by advantages accruing, say, from increased agricultural yields due to enhanced CO_2? Answers (or at least informed guesses) to such questions should be at least as relevant to CO_2-climate policy concerns as the timing and implications of a CO_2 doubling.

The 1° Scenario

It is not beyond the bounds of reason, nor inconsistent with some current scientific investigations, to pose a somewhat different scenario—one that might call for policy responses in the short-term future. Suppose, for example, the experts concentrate, not on the timing and climate implications of a *doubling of atmospheric CO₂* (as did the NAS), nor even on the *options that could be brought to bear to delay a 2° global warming* (as did the EPA), but, rather, on the timing and implications of a *1°C temperature rise* as a consequence of atmospheric increases in both CO_2 and trace gases [16].

Harassed policy makers can be excused if they tend (or wish) to regard a 1°C increase in global warming as a trivial, possibly even transitory, event—one not requiring the expenditure of their limited time and of scarce national resources. But, as scientists should be quick to remind them, the matter is deserving of more attention; at issue here is a *mean* global increase; temperature increases significantly higher than 1°C, with attendant changes in precipitation patterns, will occur in latitudes north and south of the equator.

A mean global increase of 1°C could well be accompanied by nontrivial consequences, especially with regard to climate-sensitive, localized sectors of national economies. Martin Perry has shown that even small changes in average temperature could lead to large increases in the frequency of adverse or beneficial effects on crops, especially in areas where farming is only marginally profitable. For example, in certain sections of Scotland, a 0.5°C decrease in temperature could lead to a doubling in the probability of crop failures and a *sixfold* increase in the probability of two successive failures. Another study estimates that a 1°C temperature increase could shift the corn belt area of the US by over 100 kilometers northward [17]. Thus, a seemingly insignificant average temperature change could have very real consequences in terms of an increase in the frequency of such low-probability events as droughts, crop failures, and floods. It could also pose serious health hazards;

the heat-related death toll in the American Midwest during the summer heat wave of 1983 or in the Southeast in the summer of 1986.

There is, of course, another side to the picture. A modest warming in the far northern latitudes could carry some advantages for such countries as Canada, China, and the Soviet Union; resources in their Arctic regions would become more accessible and more easily exploitable. But each of these countries covers a vast land mass and each relies heavily on agriculture as well as on mining. The advantages of an irreversible warming effect in Canada's Far North, in Manchuria, or in Siberia may not necessarily offset problems caused by temperature and rainfall changes in Saskatchewan, in southwest China, or in the Ukraine.

In essence, the 1° scenario could pose to this generation of policy makers grave questions that are comfortably swept aside or unwittingly masked by the use of the standard CO_2 doubling device. While this does not necessarily imply the need for immediate and perhaps precipitate action, it does suggest that the time available before the CO_2 issue intrudes on national and international policy agendas may be much shorter than has been assumed.

The Policy Dilemma

What options are available? Theoretically, at least, there are three obvious choices: *to prevent* CO_2-induced climate change; *to delay* it in the hope that a future generation of scientists will develop ways to prevent or reverse it; or *to adjust and adapt* to it.

Both the EPA and the NAS studies suggest that it is already too late to choose any policy option other than adjustment and adaptation. Although the EPA examines several possibilities for reducing CO_2 emissions by cutting back on the international reliance on fossil fuel, especially coal, its conclusion is pessimistic: "Of the various energy policies designed to slow the rate of atmospheric warming over the next century . . . only two have been demonstrated to effectively delay the timing of a 2° rise in temperature. Both include a ban on the use of coal which becomes fully effective in 2000" [18].

The NAS, for its part, is more cautious, but no more optimistic: "Even very forceful policies adopted soon with regard to energy and land use are unlikely to prevent some modifications of climate as a result of human activities" [19].

In the only section of the NAS report that specifically addressed policy issues, Thomas Schelling elaborates this point:

> . . . it is unlikely in the foreseeable future that national govern-
> ments will embark on serious programs to reduce further their
> dependence on fossil fuels to protect the Earth's climate against
> change . . . any single nation that imposes on its consumers the cost

of further fuel resrictions shares the benefits globally and bears the costs internally. For only the very largest fuel-consuming nations, probably for only the Soviet Union and the United States, might it be in the national interest unilaterally to suppress further the use of fossil fuels in the interest of mitigating climate change. And even that trade-off is certain to look unpersuasive to consumers paying fuel prices . . . no regime for further restricting fossil fuels would hold emissions constant, so climate change is what we should expect. . . . Are there long lead-time projects or policies that need now to be adapted to the prospects of changing climates? Water resources and related technology may have lead times of half a century; water is therefore a candidate for planning in a context of potential climate change. As forecasts for climate change become clearer, there may be strong indications for research and development related to agriculture, fisheries, and pests. Military planning will probably be alert to changes on land and sea. Certainly coastal planning should be affected by forecasts of rising sea levels. But nothing urgent is foreseeable yet [20].

In short, Schelling argues:

(1) The chances are very low that any single government, or any important combination of governments, will drastically reduce production and/or consumption of fossil fuel in an effort to reduce CO$_2$ emissions.
(2) Climate change is, therefore, inevitable and must be anticipated.
(3) But there is no urgency in terms of a policy response.

Yet the EPA and the NAS findings hold profound and doleful implications for the international policy community. If they are accepted as valid by scientific bodies generally, the effect of global fossil-fuel consumption has already gone beyond the point of no return: a global climate change is already irreversible. The policy options of *prevention* or *delay*, then, are now effectively closed out. The one option of *adaptation and adjustment* remains available, and policy establishments everywhere are left only with a choice as to what steps should be taken to implement this option and when implementation should start.

The EPA and the NAS studies are not necessarily the last word; other work in the US and elsewhere is in progress. The US Department of Energy, for example, has been sponsoring an elaborate, decade-long CO$_2$ research effort and its interim findings are scheduled to be available in 1986. It is conceivable that options for prevention or for delay may still be deemed technically practical and economically feasible. In any case, it will be useful, for our present purpose, at least, to reflect on some critical characteristics of these options as compared to the adjustment–adaptation option.

Strategies of prevention and delay are focused on the *cause* of CO_2-induced climate change: the strategy of adjustment–adaptation is focused on the *effects* of climate change. Each calls for a separate set of economic, technological, and social measures. But there is another, less obvious difference between the two: an attempt to deal with the cause of CO_2-induced climate change must take place on an international scale; there is little or nothing that any country can do on its own to influence the amount or rate of atmospheric CO_2 loading. On the other hand, it is possible to entertain the notion that individual nations can adopt effective, albeit costly, measures to mitigate or mute the effects of significant temperature increases and precipitation changes.

A strategy of adjustment–adaptation would involve special approaches in each country, depending on geographical and topographical situations, agricultural patterns, relative degree of poverty or wealth, etc. But, regardless of specific actions to take account of individual circumstances, a national effort to plan for and adjust to the most drastic climate change in modern history would touch virtually every facet of social and economic life: relocating, perhaps even restructuring, industry, rerouting highway and rail transportation, building dikes along low-lying coastal areas, moving populations, revising national immigration policies, shifting agricultural production, developing new regimes and new technologies for conservation and use of water, creating more resilient crop strains, providing new methods for control of pests, developing cheap and effective climate control devices for houses and factories, committing medical resources directed to heat-induced or heat-aggravated disease, reappraising geopolitical relationships, and even developing new international economic, scientific, and strategic arrangements. All of these issues, and many more, would have to be addressed by national policy establishments seriously intending to cope with a looming, seminal climate change.

In the end, the climate adaptation option may turn out to be no less complex to contemplate and plan, and no less costly to implement and administer from a national perspective than the global prevention option. It does, of course, have the advantage that a particular country can adopt it independently of others–or does it?

From the vantage point of rich, industrialized countries highly dependent on fossil fuels, a national adaptation strategy might seem to hold more promise than an international effort to prevent (or, more realistically, to delay) CO_2-induced climate change. But prudent policymakers will have to recognize that such a choice is not without international risks. The adaptation–adjustment option will force scores of poor, nonindustrialized nations to grope for survival while a handful of the more affluent societies spend vast sums to ride out the stresses of climate change. This is hardly a recipe for international harmony and tranquillity.

Water sharing, pest control, and immigration are already sources of tension between neighboring countries; they promise to become even more so in the circumstances envisaged here. More importantly, the administrative infrastructure, economic resources, and technical capabilities required for an effective national strategy of climate adaptation are beyond the capacities of most societies to marshall. For many countries living on the margin between bare subsistence and abject poverty, ugly perturbations of nature are already the stuff of disaster. A major flooding or a delayed rainy season can spell famine for a region of India or for the whole of Ethiopia. A program of dike building along the Florida coast or around the city of Leningrad is one thing, but such a program for Egypt's Nile Delta or the entire coastline of Bangladesh is another matter.

Moreover, for a host of Third World countries, economic development programs have been based on, and are being implemented on, the assumption of long-familiar patterns of temperature and rainfall. In certain regions of many countries—the wine-growing areas of France and Eastern Europe, the rice-growing areas of Southeast Asia, for example—certain crops have been grown and consumed century after century; it will not be easy from a cultural, economic, or political point of view for such societies to switch and adapt to, say, beans or potatoes.

It is true that mankind over the millennia has adjusted to and surmounted major natural and man-made calamities: indeed, both our remote and more immediate ancestors have been so adaptive and innovative that the world has become ever more prosperous, despite an unending train of devastating events. Nonetheless, periods of transition from one regime of nature to another are politically and socially unsettling. Looking back on such moments from centuries later is one thing. Living through them is something else again; the contemporary experience must have been harsh, tense, even violent.

If we move from the historic time scale to one that is more meaningful to today's generation of national leaders, the prospect of a seminal climate change occurring across the globe sometime during the next century cannot be regarded with detachment. That such a change may be inevitable should not mute concern for the social, economic, health, and geopolitical stress that will occur during the century or more of adjustment and adaptation. A prime task for all responsible national and international policymakers, then, should be to ease the world's transition into a new climate regime.

Timing and Nature of the Policy Response

Certainty versus Irreversibility

The looming specter of a seminal change in global climate is likely to present both observers and practitioners of science-for-public policy with a critical test. The range of questions to be dealt with runs the gamut from ethics to engineering. Societal, geopolitical, and ecological considerations will all come into play and virtually every nation in the world will be under profound, possibly unmanageable strains. However transitory the period of global adaptation to a new climate regime, domestic and external stresses will place long-established and familiar cultural patterns, economic relationships, and institutional arrangements at hazard. The call on the skills and wisdom of both scientific and policy-making establishments may be without precedent in the history of these communities (and would be rivalled only by the ghastly requirements following a nuclear war).

As scientists and policymakers try to come to grips with the enormity of this challenge, it is only natural that they will cast about for some guidelines or models that can be eked from previous recorded experience. The still-evolving international stance on the acid rain threat comes readily to mind. Here, too, is an environmental threat that has no respect for national boundaries and that endangers precious natural resources. Like the CO_2 problem, it cannot be dealt with by traditional national regulatory procedures. But, as we have seen, the acid rain policy experience, however tantalizing it may appear as an object lesson for those groping for an approach to the CO_2 question, is interesting, but not especially useful.

Perhaps the most valuable contribution acid rain has made to science-for-CO_2-policy has been to sensitize national and international policy establishments to the reality of transnational environmental threats. At the same time, however, the current preoccupation with acid rain in the US and elsewhere has made it more difficult for CO_2 researchers and analysts in the scientific community to seize the attention of policy makers. The expenditure of scarce time and considerable resources on addressing the current and visible effects of acid rain has had the effect of raising the threshold of policymakers' attention to the more serious, but not yet evident, problem of a CO_2-induced climate change.

The acid rain experience, however, underlines at least one important lesson for those concerned with other profound environmental challenges: policy establishments typically require a very high degree of certainty before embarking on costly corrective action.* And, since the very nature of scientific research and investigation has embedded in it some degree of uncertainty, hard-pressed policy establishments are likely to avoid making a decision until concrete evidence of consequential, deleterious effects is at hand. The certainty–uncertainty balance creates a great dilemma for both scientists and policymakers: on the one hand, increased certainty as to cause and effect increases the chances of effective, well-targeted policy responses:

---

*There are, of course, many other examples of too-little-too-late; problems appearing to be clouds no bigger than a man's hand seldom find themselves on policy agendas.

on the other hand, as the level of certainty increases, so do the odds on irreversibility with the result that policy choices narrow. No small irony, this.

Future science historians and policy analysts looking back on the CO_2 saga may conclude that the closing decades of the twentieth century were a period when the certainty–policy response trade-off became decisive in influencing the course of global climate. Indeed, the NAS and the EPA findings provide a quintessential case of this dilemma: there is general agreement that fossil fuels emit CO_2 and a consensus that heavy accumulations of atmospheric CO_2 will produce a "greenhouse" effect. There remains considerable uncertainty, however, as to both the timing of a global warming and the particular consequences of such an effect. But while policymakers wait for the uncertainty gap to be closed, the range of options available to them is narrowing.

A question worth pondering in this regard is: How certain must the scientific community be in engaging the policy community when both stakes and costs are enormous? In the case of CO_2, for example (again reverting to the EPA and the NAS reports), the difference in the estimate of the time when worrisome warming will occur is trivial: either the children or the grandchildren of this generation of policymakers will be affected. Indeed, if the 1° scenario is to be taken seriously, contemporary policy makers, themselves, may experience the mixed blessings of global warming.

What Next?

The questions for both scientists and policymakers raised by these considerations are thorny and numerous. Among them are:

(1) Is the scientific community prepared to deliver the verdict to the policy community that CO_2-induced climate change is an intractable problem, that a significant global warming is not still a matter of *if*, but rather, of *when*? Or is there substantial dissent among scientists from both the NAS and the EPA findings?

(2) If the consensus of the scientific community is dissenting, if it judges that there is a significant chance to prevent or to delay a consequential global warming for a significant period of time (and thereby allow opportunities for more gradual adjustments or possible scientific fixes), will the international policymaking community be ready to assume the costs involved?

    (i) What would policy establishments accept as a significant chance?

    (ii) What would be acceptable as a significant period of time?

    (iii) What are the costs involved?

(3) If the consensus is that the problem is intractable and, therefore, that the only strategy available is one of adjustment and adaptation, how much lead time for planning, research, and development will be prudent in order to ease national transitions into a new climate regime?

(4) What policies and programs would have to be pursued to ease the transition?

(5) Do the consequences of 1°C mean temperature increase warrant national and international policy attention?

(6) Can, in fact, a strategy of adaptation and adjustment to global climate change be realistically pursued at a national level?

(7) What international economic, institutional, and scientific arrangements would be necessary to assure that the century or more of transition to a newer climate regime would be as harmonious as possible?

(8) How can national and international policy establishments improve the process of interaction with national and international scientific communities to meet the unprecedented challenges of a CO_2-induced climate change?

References

1. Wetstone, G. (1985) A history of the acid rain issue, this volume Chapter 12.
2. Wetstone, op. cit., pp 238–241.
3. Wetstone, op. cit., pp 209–211.
4. Ravetz, J. R. (1985) Uncertainty, ignorance, and policy, this volume, Chapter 7.
5. Wynne, B. (1985) Uncertainty—technical and social, this volume, Chapter 8.
6. Clark, W. C. (1982) *Carbon Dioxide Review: 1982* (New York, USA: Oxford University Press).
7. New York Times (1983) 20 October p 1.
8. US Environmental Protection Agency (1983) *Can We Delay a Greenhouse Warming?* (Washington, DC, USA: US Environmental Protection Agency).
9. Carbon Dioxide Assessment Committee (1983) *Changing Climate* (Washington, DC, USA: National Academy Press).
10. US Environmental Protection Agency, op. cit., p xx.
11. Carbon Dioxide Assessment Committee, op. cit., p ii.
12. Statement (1983) by Dr. George Keyworth, Science Advisor to the President of the United States, 20 October.
13. Carbon Dioxide Assessment Committee, op. cit., p 21.
14. US Environmental Protection Agency, op. cit., p 1–17.
15. US Environmental Protection Agency, op. cit., p 4–8.
16. The NAS report used the 1°C scenario approach in an analysis of the effects of weather on wheat crop yields in the plains region of the US, see Carbon Dioxide Assessment Committee p 398.
17. Parry, M. (1984) The Impact of Climatic Variations on Agricultural Margins, in R. W. Kates (Ed) *Improving the Science of Climate Impact Assessment* (1985) (New York, USA: John Wiley).
18. US Environmental Protection Agency, op. cit., p 4–41.
19. Carbon Dioxide Assessment Committee, op. cit., p 3.
20. Carbon Dioxide Assessment Committee pp. 480–481.

CHAPTER 14

The Diversion of Water Resources into the Caspian Sea Basin

GRYGORY VOROPAEV

History of the Problem

Since the 1960s Soviet specialists have analyzed rates of water consumption in the Soviet Union and prepared forecasts for the forthcoming decades. This work was conducted along with the initial implementation of long-range plans for economic development, including the utilization and protection of water resources. It was established that the rates of water consumption were very high in all major branches of the economy, and that rates are forecast to remain very high up to the end of this century. Thus, during just two decades, from 1950 to 1970, the use and consumption of fresh water have increased more than two-fold.

The Soviet Union possesses an enormous reserve of fresh water. The annual volume of surface river flow is about 4700 km^3, while estimated reserves of underground water amount to 350 km^3, which exceeds the present consumption of water in all branches of the economy 15–18 times. However, there are at least three aspects of water distribution that give cause for concern. First, the spatial distribution of water resources is distinctly not homogeneous. A major share, 84%, is concentrated in Siberia, the Far East, and the northern regions of the European part of the country. The southern regions of the European part, Central Asia, and Kazakhstan—75% of the country's population and almost 80% of the production forces—contain just about 16% of the water resources available in the country. Second, the main consumption of water is for agricultural irrigation, which will impose major requirements upon water resources in the future as well. All arable lands that require irrigation are situated in the southern regions where water resources are already nearly exhausted. Finally, the largest lakes and inland seas are

Grygory Voropaev is Chairman of the State Expert Commission of the USSR State Planning Committee (GOSPLAN). He is also Director of the Institute of Water Problems, Academy of Sciences of the USSR.

Science for Public Policy

also situated in the southern regions. These are the Caspian Sea, the Aral, the Sea of Azov, the bays and firths of the Black Sea, and Lakes Issik-Kul, Balkhash, and Sevan, whose hydrologic and hydrobiologic regimes and even existence depend upon the amount, the regime, and the quality of fresh water inflow. In this respect, these water bodies can be looked upon as major consumers of fresh water resources, with all inflow being irreversibly consumed (mostly through evaporation from their surfaces).

This mismatch of water resources with respect to the distribution of consumers has given rise to suggestions concerning large-scale interzonal redistribution of river flow. It should be noted that the first suggestions and projects for territorial redistribution of river flow in the country were brought up as early as the last century and were actively advanced in the 1950s. However, the main purpose at that time was quite different. Projects were intended to provide a better transportation system and to increase the production of hydroelectric power. New approaches to the problem of water supply by territorial redistribution of river flow date from just two decades ago. Today engineering solutions have been found and research completed concerning partial diversion of northern rivers and lakes of the European part of the Soviet Union to the Caspian Sea Basin. One of the problems that received the most attention was that of predicting possible ecological consequences which the proposed partial diversion of river flow from the northern rivers might entail. The results of these studies served as a basis for the governmental decision concerning the problem as a whole.

Engineering Solutions

Studies of the problem took into account the engineering solution developed by a technical institute on the basis of technological and economic comparisons of different proposed plans. During the design process, many problems were addressed including the evaluation of water consumption development, choosing a scheme for the development of water systems and the diversion routes, the location of hydrotechnical installations, etc. The recommendation was to transfer, on average, up to 19 or 20 km^3 of water annually by the year 2000, the whole project being divided into three stages. The first stage would divert 5.8 km^3 per year, taken from the Onega River (Lacha and Vozhe Lakes) and the Upper Sukhona; the second stage, 3.5 km^3 per year from Lake Onega; and the third stage, 9 or 10 km^3 per year from the Pechora River. The engineering plan is shown in *Figure 14.1*, where diversion routes and locations of hydroelectric power projects are also shown. The stages are described in *Table 14.1*.

Water resources for the first stage will be provided by the River Onega, whose annual flow is 16 km^3 at its mouth and 3.4 km^3 at the proposed

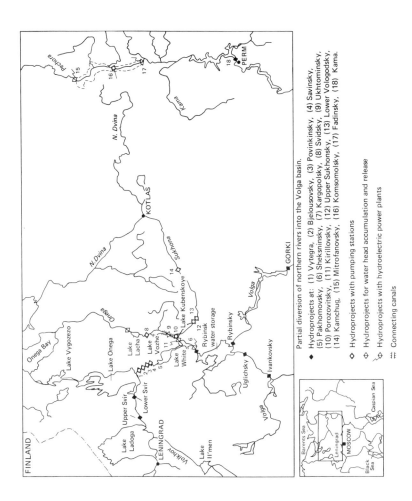

Partial diversion of northern rivers into the Volga basin.

Hydroprojects at: (1) Vytegra, (2) Bjelousovsky, (3) Povinkinsky, (4) Savinsky, (5) Pakhomovsky, (6) Sheksninsky, (7) Kargopolsky, (8) Svidsky, (9) Ukhtominsky, (10) Porozovitsky, (11) Kirillovsky, (12) Upper Sukhonsky, (13) Lower Vologodsky, (14) Kamchug, (15) Mitrofanovsky, (16) Komsomolsky, (17) Fadinsky, (18) Kama.

◆ Hydroprojects with pumping stations

◇ Hydroprojects for water head accumulation and release

◇ Hydroprojects with hydroelectric power plants

⋕ Connecting canals

Fig. 14.1. Engineering plan.

TABLE 14.1. Description of diversion stages

Indicators	Units	Stage 1	Stage 2	Stage 3	
		Lakes Lacha, Vozhe	Lake Kubenskoye, Sukhona River	Lake Onega	Pechora River
Mean annual volume of diversion	km^3	1.8	4.0	3.5	9.8
Mean annual flow at mouth	km^3	16	109	79	128
Mean annual flow at place of diversion	km^3	3.4	9.7	19.0	19.2
Net required elevation of water	m	11	7	81	30
Length of canals	km	42	64	134	108
Number of hydrotechnical stations	–	2	2	5	1
Number of hydroelectric plants	–	1	–	–	2
Power of pumping stations	MW	2	50	175	260
Flooded area, total	thousand hectares	0.7	11.8	0.2	21.7
Flooded land, agricultural	thousand hectares	0.2	6.2	0.02	5.1
Forests lost	10^6 m^6	0.03	0.57	0.02	12.6
People resettled		150	3700	500	16,000
Replacement housing costs	10^6 rubles	14	48	17	350
Total investment	10^6 rubles	75	361	240	1740

intake. Approximately 1.8 km^3 will be taken from the River's upper reaches, from Lakes Lacha and Vozhe. The water will flow freely along the Vandoga and Uzhitsa Rivers to Lake Kubenskoye and further, through the Kubensko–Sheksninsky Canal to the Sheksna water storage reservoir. This reservoir is connected with the Rybinsk water storage reservoir through which water flows into the Volga River. The second source of water for the first stage is from the Upper Sukhona, a tributary of the North Dvina. The annual flow of the North Dvina amounts to 109 km^3 at its mouth. It is planned to divert 4.8 km^3 of water from the Upper Sukhona, whose annual flow at the place of diversion is 9.7 km^3. For this purpose, several hydroprojects will be constructed, including the Kamchug hydroproject 300 km downstream from the Sukhona riverhead, the Upper Sukhona regulation and pumping hydroproject to transfer water from the Sukhona to Lake Kubenskoye, the Kubensko–Sheksninsky channel through the watershed with a discharge capability up to 800 m^3 per second; the Porozovitsky pumping hydroproject; and the Kirillovsky regulation hydroproject at the entrance to the Sheksna water storage reservoir (see Fig. 14.1). Because the difference in elevation is small, the annual amount of power needed to raise the required volume of water will be approximately 207 $\times$ 10^6 kilowatt-hours (kwhr).

During the second stage, the inflow to Lake Onega will be partially used. The net inflow to the lake amounts to 79 km^3 per year. It is planned to transfer 3.5 km^3 annually along the existing White Sea Canal and further to the Rybinsk water storage reservoir on the Volga through the Sheksna water storage reservoir. Water will be pumped to the watershed with a change in elevation of 83 m, requiring the annual use of 1 billion kwhr. The maximum discharge capability of this diversion will be 150 m^3 per second, so that there will be no need to change the existing capability of the Volga–Baltiysky water route.

The flow of the River Pechora will be used during the third stage. It amounts to 128 km^3 per year at its mouth and 19 km^3 per year at the place of diversion. At this point, up to 9 or 10 km^3 will be transferred annually to the Kama River, a Volga tributary. In addition, the Mitrofanovsky hydroproject with a water storage reservoir for year-to-year regulation of flow, the Komsomolsky pumping hydroproject, and the Fadinsky hydroproject with a hydroelectric power station to force the flow through the Kolva River to the Kama water storage reservoir are planned. The maximum discharge capability of this diversion route is equal to 600 m^3 per second.

Upon the completion of all three stages of diversion, some 19 or 20 km^3 of water will be transferred southward annually, thus allowing the irrigation of 4.5 million hectares of land, the production of about 2000 million kwhr of peak power annually at the cascade of the Volga–Kama hydroelectric power stations, and the stabilization of the water budget of the Caspian Sea, to keep its water levels close to 28.5–29 meters under average hydrometeorological conditions.

Research Problems and Methods

During research for this project several new problems were encountered, including an evaluation of the possible effects the planned river-diversion projects might have on the climate of both the Soviet Union and neighboring countries; long-term (up to several decades) prediction of environmental conditions over the several million square kilometers of territories affected by the partial transfer of water from the northern rivers and by its southward redistribution and utilization; evaluation of possible ecological consequences of river diversion, including changes in the productivity of aquatic and terrestrial biological systems in the respective regions; finding measures to prevent possible negative consequences of the partial southward redistribution of river flow; and estimation of the maximum permissible volume of diversion from the northern rivers and minimal additional volume of water required in the southern regions up to the end of the century.

Because of a lack of experience and the absence of an established methodological approach to solving similar complicated problems, special attention has been paid to methodological studies. Extensive use was made of systems analysis, the mathematical simulation of natural and combined natural and technical systems, field experiments, expeditionary and stationary observations, and statistical analysis of available information. More than one hundred national scientific institutes participated in the studies during 1976–1982 under a common scientific program.

The methodological approach was based on the following considerations: water resources, as a natural element of the biosphere, critically affect hydrologic and thermal regimes of land, water bodies, the atmosphere, the bioproductivity of the aquatic and terrestrial environment, and the living conditions of human society. At the same time, anthropogenic effects on natural processes in the biosphere reveal themselves mainly in the regime of bodies of water. Both the spatial and temporal scales of anthropogenic intrusion due to the planned diversion of rivers are exceptionally large. In fact, these measures involve natural processes at all levels of circulation of matter and energy fluxes in the biosphere. On the other hand, the diversion of rivers would take place with a general background of constantly increasing anthropogenic pressure on the environment. All types of mankind's economic activity clearly give rise to definite changes in the regime of terrestrial water resources and the character of the respective natural processes, which makes the separation of the effects of river diversion measures upon natural processes so difficult. The aquatic environment in the rivers and lakes to be diverted was therefore studied and predicted both under the conditions of the planned diversion and without any diversion. The general scheme of analysis and complex prediction of natural processes is shown in *Fig. 14.2*.

River Diversion and Climate

A partial diversion from the northern rivers will result in less inflow of fresh water into the Arctic Ocean. This fact gave rise to a hypothesis concerning possible changes in the thermal regime and circulation of moisture in the region, as possible climatic consequences of diversion projects. Similarly, the transfer of additional volumes of water to the southern regions and its utilization for irrigation will lead to higher

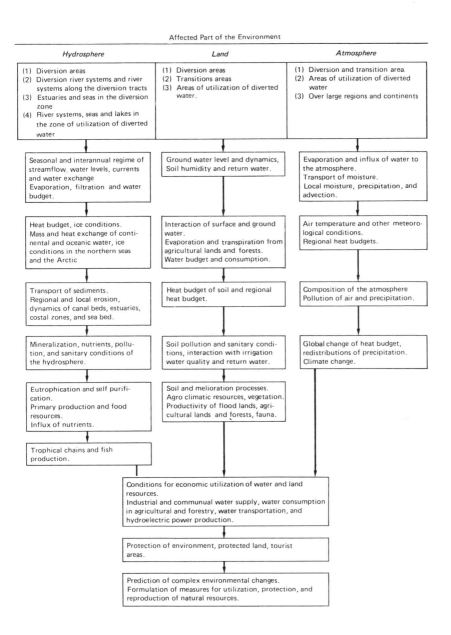

Affected Part of the Environment

Hydrosphere	*Land*	*Atmosphere*
(1) Diversion areas (2) Diversion river systems and river systems along the diversion tracts (3) Estuaries and seas in the diversion zone (4) River systems, seas and lakes in the zone of utilization of diverted water	(1) Diversion areas (2) Transitions areas (3) Areas of utilization of diverted water.	(1) Diversion and transition area. (2) Areas of utilization of diverted water (3) Over large regions and continents
Seasonal and interannual regime of streamflow, water levels, currents and water exchange Evaporation, filtration and water budget.	Ground water level and dynamics, Soil humidity and return water.	Evaporation and influx of water to the atmosphere. Transport of moisture. Local moisture, precipitation, and advection.
Heat budget, ice conditions. Mass and heat exchange of continental and oceanic water, ice conditions in the northern seas and the Arctic	Interaction of surface and ground water. Evaporation and transpiration from agricultural lands and forests. Water budget and consumption.	Air temperature and other meteorological conditions. Regional heat budgets.
Transport of sediments. Regional and local erosion, dynamics of canal beds, estuaries, costal zones, and sea bed.	Heat budget of soil and regional heat budget.	Composition of the atmosphere Pollution of air and precipitation.
Mineralization, nutrients, pollution, and sanitary conditions of the hydrosphere.	Soil pollution and sanitary conditions, interaction with irrigation water quality and return water.	Global change of heat budget, redistributions of precipitation. Climate change.
Eutrophication and self purification. Primary production and food resources. Influx of nutrients.	Soil and melioration processes. Agro climatic resources, vegetation. Productivity of flood lands, agricultural lands and forests, fauna.	
Trophical chains and fish production.		

Conditions for economic utilization of water and land resources.
Industrial and communual water supply, water consumption in agricultural and forestry, water transportation, and hydroelectric power production.

Protection of environment, protected land, tourist areas.

Prediction of complex environmental changes.
Formulation of measures for utilization, protection, and reproduction of natural resources.

Fig. 14.2. Factors considered in the analysis of the project.

evaporation and thus can change the thermal regime and moisture circulation over huge territories, which, in turn, might influence climatic processes. These considerations inspired special studies of heat and mass exchange over continental and oceanic regions in the north, possible changes in meteorological conditions in the regions of water removal and in the thermal budget, agroclimatic resources, and redistribution of water exchange budget elements in the regions that receive additional volumes of water. The studies included field experiments on land, rivers, seas, and bays, statistical analysis of data on meteorological conditions and water vapor flux, and numerical simulation of hydrodynamical processes and fluxes of matter and heat, atmospheric circulation, and water vapor transport.

It was found that partial redistribution of river flow, even on a much larger scale than planned, should not entail large-scale changes in the heat budget and atmospheric circulation. Changes of local character are possible and could be detected in aquatic and terrestrial environments over short distances (not exceeding several scores of kilometers) or up to a thousand kilometers in the atmosphere.

Additional inflow of water to the southern regions and the development of irrigation there will increase heat loss from evaporation, decrease the air temperature by 2–5°C, increase humidity in the surface layer by 2 or 3 millibars, with a resulting decrease in the net air temperature budget during the growing season. An estimate of possible change in water vapor transport over the territory of the country demonstrated that additional input of water vapor due to higher evaporation would be less than 1–2% of the current net water vapor transport of 2600–2800 km^3 per year over the European part of the country. This might cause a slight increase in precipitation over the Caucasus mountains (up to 10 millimeters, or 3 km^3 per year). It was also found that the compensating runoff of atmospheric origin cannot restore the unreturnable transfer of river flow for irrigation purposes.

According to our studies, the effects of river diversion on climatic processes cannot even be detected if the annual volume of diversion is less than 20 km^3. This is true even with respect to possible amplification of such effects due to the long-term influence of the project and possible feedbacks.

Environmental Changes in the Region of River Flow Diversion

As stated above, the volume of diversion at the project's first stage amounts to 5.8 km^3 per year; 1.8 km^3 taken from the Onega River (Lacha and Vozhe Lakes) and 4 km^3 taken from the Upper Sukhona River. All of this water goes to Lake Kubenskoye. The inflow into Lake Vozhe is mostly used to provide the 1.8 km^3 taken from the Onega. The normal water level of Lake Vozhe will be slightly lowered while that of Lake Lacha will remain close to natural conditions, though the periods of high water levels will be shortened.

The drainage of neighboring territories will be increased, which is favorable for their agricultural utilization. The changes will involve the seasonal distribution of streamflow and water levels at all reaches of the Onega, up to its estuary. The streamflow at the source will be decreased two- or three-fold during the dry season, water levels will be decreased, and the flow to the estuary diminished by 10 or 15% during dry years. The warming effect of fresh water will become less pronounced, and the dates of formation and break-up of the ice cover will be changed by 5 and 7 days, respectively. Water temperature will drop by 1.5°C during extremely dry years, while the ice-cover period will become slightly longer.

A partial removal of flow from the Onega will cause higher concentrations of pollutants in the river. However, the hydrochemical regime of Lakes Lacha and Vozhe will not be affected. The removal of water from the system of lakes that includes Lacha, Vozhe, and Kubenskoye will entail changes in the system of currents and a definite reconstruction of their hydrobiological systems, especially in Lakes Lacha and Kubenskoye. The loss in fish production could be rather high, up to 80 or 90%.

In order to take 4 km^3 of water from the Upper Sukhona, the Kamchug hydroelectric power station will be constructed to pump a part of the flow into Lake Kubenskoye, while the Sukhona will be transformed and its flow reversed. The water levels of Lake Kubenskoye will become controllable and the diminished flow from the river to the lake will allow control of the length of the flooding interval and water depth over the Sukhona Plain, thus improving the hydrological regime of floodlands along the river. The maximum discharge will change only slightly, while the average discharge will diminish markedly, especially downstream from the Kamchug hydroelectric power station. Discharges during the winter and summer dry periods will decrease substantially, causing diffficulties in navigation and timber rafting. Heat transport to the mouth will decrease slightly and the average dates of ice-cover formation and break-up will change by three days. Injection of water to Lake Kubenskoye will result in substantial intensification of water circulation in the lake though the quality of water might suffer and the oxygen regime might become worse in winter time. Fish production on the Sukhona, insignificant even now, will become still lower.

During the second stage 3.5 km^3 will be taken from Lake Onega annually. This will cause a respective decrease in the flow of the River Svir' the inflow into Lake Onega, and the flow of the Neva River. The water levels of Lake Onega, now at the normal level of the upper Svir', will remain practically unchanged though the exchange of water masses will intensify. The frequency of minimal flow occurrence for the Neva and Svir' during the dry seasons will increase. However, this will not affect navigation along the Neva. The analysis of year-to-year hydrology variations showed that this aquatic system would not undergo any substantial change. Partial diversion of flow might result in a slightly higher mineralization of water in the Neva and Lake Ladoga. The hydrochemical regime of Lake Ladoga will not deteriorate.

During the third stage, 9 or 10 km^3 of water are to be taken from the Pechora River. This will be done by constructing the Mitrofanovsky water storage reservoir and the Komsomolsky and Fadinsky hydroelectric power stations. The water is to be released through the Kolva to the Kama and further to the Volga. The water storage reservoir will cause major changes in the hydrology of the Pechora. Its flow downstream of the dam will be diminished by as much as 40 or even 70%, depending upon the volume of flow in each particular year. About 5000 hectares of an overall 40,000 hectares of meadows will not be flooded during moderately wet years. At the beginning of the dry season, water levels will fall by 2.5–4.0 or even more under unfavorable ice and streamway conditions. Navigation along the river and its tributaries will deteriorate drastically. The influence of the water storage reservoir and the water diversion will be felt to a lesser degree downstream, where more tributaries feed the flow, but it will remain substantial even at the river mouth where water levels will drop by 0.3m on average, the flow will diminish by 5 or 10%, the water temperature will drop by 0.5° or 1.0°C, and the dates of the formation and break-up of the ice cover will change by 5 or 7 and 2 or 3 days, respectively. About 5000 hectares of agricultural land will be flooded and the flow of several large tributaries will be affected by the high water levels of the reservoir. Migration of fish and navigation along the mainstream and tributaries will be cut off.

Water storage reservoirs and the diversion of flow will affect the hydrochemical regime of the river so that the quality of water will worsen. Changes in the regime of water levels in the river, disappearance of floods on the Pechora, deterioration of water quality, diminished flow, construction of dams—all these factors will change drastically the fishery conditions that now exist along the Pechora and in the Pechora Bay. The largest shoal of salmon in the European part of the country, which supplies up to 60% of the total catch, will probably be affected quite substantially along with other species of fish. Additional volumes of water entering the Volga through the Rybinsk water storage reservoir and the Kama River will not entail major changes in the hydrology of these streams. Changes in ice conditions at the high and lower reaches of hydroelectric power stations will probably be the most pronounced effects of the project on these rivers; water temperature will drop by 2° or 3°C in summer and increase by 0.5–1.0°C in winter. Polynia—areas of open water in sea ice—will occur more frequently in winter, and humidity and fogging are bound to increase.

Hydrochemical conditions in the Rybinsk water storage reservoir might get better, with a lower concentration of salts, nutrients, and oil pollutants. The chemistry of the Pechora will be affected only slightly, though the quality of its water will not be improved. No substantial negative impact of diversion on fishery production of the Volga water storage reservoirs and the river as a whole is expected.

Environmental Changes in Southern Regions

The southern regions where the additional volumes of water will be utilized include the Caspian Sea and the Sea of Azov, the Volga–Akhtuba floodlands and the Volga estuary, and new, irrigated lands in northern Caucasia and along the Volga. As mentioned above, the major goal of the river diversion scheme is the conservation of the unique fish production in the Caspian and Azov Seas under the conditions of growing water consumption and diversion of water resources in their basins. At the same time, our studies have shown that substantially larger volumes of additional water resources would be required to achieve this purpose. If, however, the volume of diversion were increased over 20 km^3 per year, the environmental changes would have been difficult to predict. Their evaluation might only be possible by making use of the experience gained in the initial stages of the river diversion scheme and through additional special studies, which cannot be done in less than ten or fifteen years.

These considerations made it necessary to choose only one of the two seas as the major recipient of water transferred to the southern region. For many reasons it was decided that more importance should be given to the conservation of the water budget of the Caspian Sea. First, the present water level of the Caspian Sea is close to the equilibrium state which corresponds to the present-day water budget, specifically to the inflow into the sea. Any additional diversion of water from the basin will make the level drop quickly even under average climatic conditions, thus diminishing the fish catch. The change over time of the Caspian Sea water level is shown in *Fig. 14.3*.

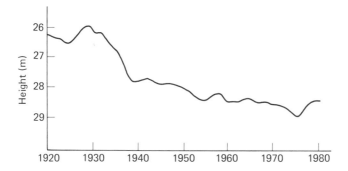

FIG. 14.3. Level of the Caspian Sea over time.

Second, the Caspian Sea still is and always was the largest producer of sturgeon in the Soviet Union and the world. It may remain the largest producer of sturgeon in the future with a simultaneous increase in the catch of other species. The Sea of Azov lost its former role as a major sturgeon producer during recent years. Its catch could not be restored, if at all, earlier than the end of this century. Third, the present water levels are closely interrelated with the economy of the region: both higher and lower levels are undesirable because they could cause definite economic losses.

The Soviet Government recently approved plans for the diversion of 5.8 km^3 of water annually from the basins of the Onega and the Sukhona Rivers into the Volga River and for the construction of the Volga–Don Canal to transfer 5 km^3 of water annually from the Volga into the River Don. This water will be used for irrigation in the northern Caucasus. Existing plans provide for the development of irrigation in the northern Caucasus and in the basin of the River Don, rather than in the Volga basin. This part of the diversion project cannot possibly affect the water budget of the seas during 1981–1985. However, termination of the development of irrigation in the Volga basin will result in a lower growth of water consumption in the basin and, consequently, in a more stable water budget and water level of the Caspian Sea during the forthcoming decade. Further increase of the diversion volume up to 19 or 20 km^3 per year, along with other measures aimed at reducing water consumption and controlling evaporation and outflow (by cutting off the northeastern shallows and controlling the outflow to the Kara Bogaz Gol) will help stabilize the water levels near to the present elevation, even under changing values of water budget constituents. The efficiency of all these measures will depend upon natural variations in the amount of water during the forthcoming period.

Decision Making Procedures

From our experiences we know that one should distinguish two stages in the obtaining and analysis of information and the related decision making when one deals with the investigation of large-scale scientific and technological problems. The first stage is the making of a preliminary decision on the basis of the data obtained. The decision making procedure is shown in *Fig. 14.4*. The procedure consists of a step-by-step analysis of the problem. If at any point a negative decision is reached, then the source material is sent back for further development and revision. If the decision reached is positive, the projects proposed are included in the draft of a long-range plan of national economic development. At the same time, further studies are carried out to prepare more detailed information on the projects. The information is used at the second stage of investigating a large-scale problem.

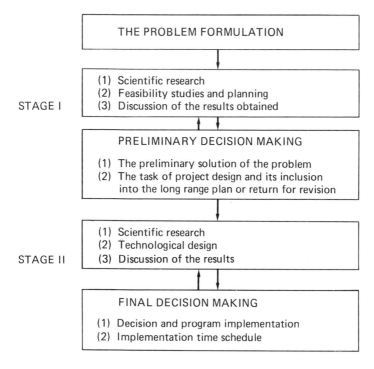

FIG. 14.4. The decision making procedure.

The second stage includes scientific research, technological design, and discussion of the results, leading to decisions on the preparation of program implementation measures and a time schedule (see Fig. 14.4). Revised data make it possible to specify technical details and consequently to set up a construction timetable.

In both stages continuous contacts and joint efforts between scientists, engineers, and the public take place. Most of the information needed is prepared by design and research institutions and various specialized scientific and technological councils participate in the discussion. Decisions are made by the ministries involved.

The redistribution of part of the river flow from the northern basins to the Volga basin can serve as an example. The decision making procedure is shown in *Fig 14.5*. Step 1: we formulated the problem of water transfer and specified the goals to be achieved by water transfer. Step 2: an integrated program of scientific research was developed. Over one hundred research and design institutions were involved. A scientific council on the problem was established. The results of these studies were widely discussed in scientific periodicals, newspapers, and by the public at large, as shown in Fig. 14.5.

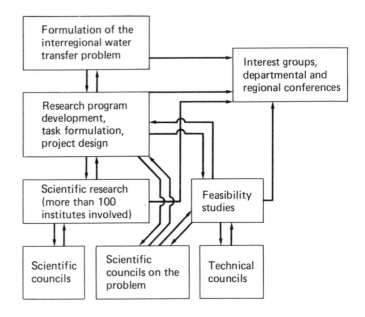

Ḟɪɢ. 14.5. The interaction of scientists, engineers, and lay people.

Then a decision was reached. The process is schematically presented in *Fig. 14.6*. The materials prepared in this process went to the USSR State Planning Committee (GOSPLAN), where the State Expertise Board within GOSPLAN scrutinized all the materials submitted. In addition, a temporary sub-commission of experts was set up, consisting of about 80 leading Soviet scientists. The recommendations they made were considered by the State Planning Committee and then by the Council of Ministers of the USSR. The final decision was made by the Council of Ministers.

Conclusions

High rates of water consumption and transfer of water have led to a substantial reduction of flow in many rivers in the southern and central regions of the European part of the Soviet Union. The quality of water has deteriorated, and unfavorable changes have occurred in the hydrochemical regime of river systems, water storage facilities, seas, and neighboring territories. A radical reconstruction of water utilization is necessary through the application of new techniques of water use in industry, agriculture, and the communal economy, by reducing normal expenditure of water per unit of production, introducing closed-circuit water systems, and reducing discharges of sewage water into river systems, seas, and underground layers.

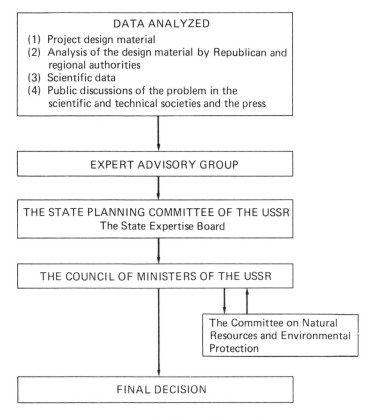

FIG. 14.6. The data analysis procedure.

These measures will reduce the demand for fresh water and, at the same time, help improve the quality of water and conserve the environment. New techniques that are being introduced now in all branches of the economy have proved to be highly efficient. Still, by themselves, they are hardly sufficient to solve the water problems of the southern regions, especially the southern seas. Water resources of the southern rivers should be increased at the expense of the northern rivers. The partial southward diversion of northern waters by the end of the century along with water protection measures presents a necessary measure for environmental protection that can prevent the deterioration of the Caspian ecosystem. Judging by the present-day ecosystems in the diversion zone and the existing knowledge of their possible response to changes in their water regime, the annual volume of water that can be taken from the rivers and lakes in the northwestern regions should not be in excess of 19 or 20 km^3 by the end of the century.

CHAPTER 15

Reports of Forum Panels

Editors' Note: The original Proceedings of the Forum on Science for Public Policy included reports of three panels which had been convened to synthesize and elaborate on points addressed in the formal essays. We have included these reports in this volume because they provide not only a degree of synthesis, but also some additional insights on the issue of scientific advice for policymakers.

H.B.
C.L.C.

Report of Panel 1

Chairman HARVEY BROOKS; *Rapporteur* LOREN GRAHAM

The first step toward the resolution of policy issues with high scientific or technical content is the placing of these issues on the agenda of political leaders and their scientific advisors. Unless the issues are recognized as important ones deserving attention, they will be passed over amidst the multitude of questions faced by governmental leaders.

What makes a society take off in response to a certain type of policy question involving science and technology? Why did a book like Rachel Carson's *The Silent Spring* attract such attention in the 1960s, but not earlier? If her book had not appeared when it did, would another one soon have had the same effect?

Upon examination of the recent history of such issues, we see that at certain moments the time is ripe for such controversies. Furthermore, there are two types of ripeness, which may be called scientific ripeness and political ripeness. There must be a concatenation of scientific developments and social receptivity before an event like Carson's book can have the impact that it did.

Harvey Brooks is Benjamin Peirce Professor of Technology and Public Policy at Harvard University, USA. He served on the US President's Science Advisory Committee from 1959 to 1964, was a member of the National Science Board from 1962 to 1974, and served as Chairman of the Committee on Science and Public Policy of the US National Academy of Sciences from 1967 to 1972.

Loren Graham is a Professor in the Program on Science, Technology, and Society at the Massachusetts Institute of Technology, USA.

Science for Public Policy

The scientific development which enhanced this impact was the refinement of scientific measuring techniques in such a way that low-level DDT and other polluting compounds could be detected and precisely measured. The social developments which prepared the way for a wave of interest in ecology in the 1960s are more difficult to isolate, but they probably derive from the fact that Western countries had just undergone a long period of industrial expansion that provided levels of affluence sufficient for environmental concerns to outweigh other, more traditional personal worries and also made the degradation of the environment visible to all urban residents.

If we see the importance of the concatenation of scientific and political events for placing such issues as ecology on the agenda of political leaders, we will then be able to understand more fully the fact that precursors to Rachel Carson are easy to find, but that these precursors did not attract much attention.

In the raising of such issues to prominence a variety of social and political phenomena play significant roles. The press and television are very influential in molding public attitudes, as the current attention given to acid rain by the popular German magazine *Der Spiegel* illustrates. Also, the cultural traditions of a country influence the receptivity of its citizens to certain kinds of emotional appeals; in Germany affection for forests and trees is perhaps stronger than in some other nations and influences the controversy over acid rain.

International institutions may also play an important role in placing such issues on the political agendas of other nations. Such organizations as the EEC, the UN, and IIASA itself have, at various moments, helped to spread or diffuse concerns about policy issues involving science and technology from one country to another.

Serendipity may also influence the moment when a certain issue of this type gets placed on the political agenda. An example is the concern over the ozone layer in the earth's atmosphere, which first became prominent in connection with the study of the effect of the supersonic transport planes on the atmosphere.

Finally, accidents have, on occasion, caused a certain type of issue to be placed much higher on the political agenda. A significant example is the incident at Three Mile Island in the US, which transformed the issue of the safety of nuclear power plants.

In connection with accidents, our Panel expressed the opinion that such accidents as Three Mile Island are not totally unforeseeable (and, in fact, the incident had been predicted, but the prediction did not attract much attention). With more careful attention to possible accidents, it might be possible to study certain types of science-for-policy questions before they are rudely forced upon our attention.

In order for scientific advice on policy questions to be effective it must be both technically accurate and politically persuasive. Adequate attention has not, in the past, been given to both halves of this requirement. We believe that IIASA might be able to make a contribution towards emphasizing both aspects of this process, and we propose the following experiment.

IIASA should choose a certain problem—say, acid rain in Europe—and set up two task forces which work simultaneously on the problem, each task force preparing a separate report. One task force would be composed of scientists and engineers, and would prepare a technical report on acid rain. The other task force would be made up of political leaders and journalists and would prepare a nontechnical report on acid rain designed to attract public attention and mobilize appropriate action. The two task forces would both work on their reports in proximity to each other so they would have constant contact and iteration, as they deemed useful. The two reports would then be compared. Furthermore, during the time that the two groups worked together, they might be observed by yet a third group made up of social scientists whose task would be to study how the two groups got on with each other, what disagreements they had, what different emphases they preferred, etc.

An important topic in considering science-for-policy questions is the role of the public. Several different models have been proposed for the public's role in the policy-making process. They include:

(1) The "jury" model.
(2) Public hearings.
(3) Selected public representatives.
(4) Referenda.

Although the members of our Panel differed somewhat in their preferences among these models, there was a rather general agreement that referenda are not usually a good way for resolving these issues. On the other hand, the jury model can work quite effectively when the members of the jury work closely with technical advisors or resource personnel.

The choice among these models will be influenced by the type of issue being discussed, and the reasons given for involving the public. The involvement of the public can serve several different functions, such as legitimation of the proceedings and gaining information about public attitudes and community standards. The latter function has been important in the US in the consideration of such questions as *in vitro* fertilization, on which public hearings were held in many cities.

Should the meetings of scientific advisors be confidential? Differences of opinions are inevitable on this issue. Confidentiality has both advantages and disadvantages. Among the advantages of confidentiality are that it avoids politicization of sensitive issues and it fosters a high degree of give-and-take among advisors. Among the disadvantages of confidentiality are that it obscures issues that may be important to the public and it may result in the disowning of experts' recommendations by the larger public who, because of the secrecy, may not understand the experts' recommendations or the reasons underlying them.

The Panel also discussed the dynamics of many controversies over policy issues involving science and technology. They agreed that these controversies are often initiated by dissident scientists who become alarmed about a certain issue and go public. After the controversy begins to grow, the scientists who initiated it are usually not suited to handle the interdisciplinary problems that emerge. The media become interested in the issue, and they often transform it from a rather narrow concern into a broad public debate.

The emotional responses of the public to these issues (such as nuclear power or the environment) are often distracting to the scientists, but sometimes these responses may play a positive role. They tell us something, however crudely measured, about the level of public concern on such issues. Furthermore, in at least a few cases the public response may even improve the technical advice by causing new issues to emerge. An example here may be the controversy over the pesticide 2,4,5-T in the UK which did not include sufficient attention to the hazards of sloppy usage of the pesticide until the farm workers involved had a chance to complain about the conditions of their work and to describe the behavior of the average farm worker when using such pesticides.

The role of the science advisor during such controversies was discussed in detail by the Panel. Two types of science advisors, each serving an important function, can be observed: (1) experts in particular fields, and (2) identifiers of experts on given questions.

The job of the science advisor is often to match the expertise of scientists to the political needs of government leaders. Furthermore, the science advisor needs to anticipate the course of the debate and bring in the appropriate experts rapidly, short-cutting, if possible, the natural course of the controversy.

Science advisors should also differentiate between long-term problems such as CO_2 and acid rain, and crisis management, such as the event occurring at Three Mile Island.

The science advisor will need not only to provide or find relevant technical advice, but he or she will also need to orchestrate and filter advice during the course of the controversy.

Another question considered by the Panel was the following: Does science for public policy reflexively influence science itself? In other words: Does attention to these issues result in different demands on science that may change the nature of science itself?

Although there was some disagreement on our Panel in response to this question, most members believed that examples of reverse influences could be found. Consideration of science for public policy increases the importance of what might otherwise be called "pedestrian science". Collecting data such as environmental base lines—an otherwise rather boring activity—becomes much more interesting at moments of ecological crisis or concern. Specialities like sanitation engineering, which earlier had low prestige, became more attractive.

The reward system of traditional science is not perfectly adapted to science for policy issues. As several people noted, Nobel prizes are not awarded for safety. Furthermore, tenure positions are not usually given to scholars as a result of their activities of this type. Nonetheless, there are some signs of recent changes in the reward system for scientists interested in policy issues. For example, the American Association for the Advancement of Science now gives awards to scientists who act in the public interest. Furthermore, some universities have set up new programs that provide faculty and research positions for scientists interested in policy issues.

The Panel discussed two different possibilities for improving the employment and reward system for scholars interested in policy issues, but never came to complete agreement as to which was best. Probably both are important. Some members of the Panel thought that it was best to try to persuade traditional academic departments in universities to accept scientists of this new type; others thought this hope was unrealistic, and believed that the creation of new science-for-policy centers of various sorts was a more promising idea.

Several American panelists pointed to the influence of legislation in reflexively influencing science in the US. Thus, the Toxic Substances Control Act, the Clear Air Act, and the Clean Water Act, have all made new demands on science and have evoked the production of scientists concentrating on new subfields. New offices like the Occupational Safety and Health Administration (OSHA) and the Environmental Protection Agency (EPA) have had similar effects, as have new ministries for the environment in some European countries. Several panel members noted, however, that lawyers seem to win more positions in these bureaucracies than scientists.

Another topic on which Panel members disagreed was the question: Should we change our research and educational system in order to create science for public policy? One or two members maintained that a new system and education was needed—and perhaps even a new form of philosophy of science—while others thought that the traditional educational system was

Science for Public Policy

adequate for the new challenge if graduates would be willing to take on the task of developing science for policy.

Uncertainty

At this conference many references have been made to the importance of scientific uncertainty as an issue affecting discussions of science for policy issues. In our discussions of this issue, several Panel members stressed the inherent relationship beween social consensus and scientific uncertainty. Most Panel members agreed that, on the issue of acid rain, less certain evidence is needed to catalyze political action if there is a broad cultural consensus about the value of preserving the forests, as there seems to be in the FRG. One of our Panel members went further and defended the generalization that on science for policy issues, "the broader the cultural consensus, the less certain the evidence can be and still warrant action."

The Panel also agreed that to talk about scientific uncertainty by itself is probably a mistake, since the concept of political uncertainty is also involved implicitly in all such discussions. One needs to look at scientific uncertainty plus political uncertainty and see how the two fit together. For example, the current rash of law cases against asbestos-producing companies in the US cannot be understood unless two types of uncertainties are seen side by side. There was the original scientific uncertainty about whether asbestos was harmful or not, a question that has changed as more scientific evidence has been collected. But there is also the political uncertainty about who should be held responsible if asbestos is judged harmful, the company that produces the asbestos (e.g., Johns–Manville, Inc.), or the companies that required their employees to work with the asbestos (such as ship-building companies in World War II).

Institutionalization of Policy for Science

The last broad topic considered by the Panel was the question of the appropriate institutions for producing science for policy. The Panel took note of the fact that there are almost no institutions where laboratory work, field work, and policy work are joined. But after discussion of this lack, we decided that the inclusion of all three activities is not absolutely necessary so long as the institution involved has a good network of communication with other institutions where laboratory and field work are conducted.

The Panel also noted that many institutions in the policy area synthesize old knowledge rather than produce new knowledge. In the US such institutions as the Office of Technology Assessment and the Congressional Research Service can be best described as knowledge-synthesizers rather than knowledge-creators.

The question of IIASA's role in producing science for policy was discussed by the Panel. We agreed that IIASA's work is mostly synthesis rather than creation, but we also argued that there was no need for IIASA to establish laboratories so long as it had good contacts with those elsewhere. The Panel also believed that the involvement of more social scientists would help IIASA in the area of science for policy.

What is the ideal type of institution for erecting science for policy? The Panel emphasized the following five criteria for such an institution:

(1) A methodological and theoretical approach.
(2) A core of self-selected policy problems.
(3) A component of work oriented to outside clients.
(4) A communication network with national laboratories and other appropriate research groups.
(5) Dialogue between natural and social scientists to produce analyses in a language that is understood by both scientists and policy makers.

An interesting institution discussed by the Panel is the Scientific Council for Governmental Policy in The Netherlands.* This successful organization has a permanent staff with five-year periods of tenure. The Scientific Council usually takes on problems that are considered too controversial for the regular government bureaucracies in The Netherlands. One interesting feature of this Council is that the government is required to give a response to its recommendations within a specified period of time, thus ensuring that the Council's recommendations will be considered by the government. Most of the work of the Council has so far been on social rather than technical problems. Two of its projects have been an effort to revise the social security system in a way that would make it less expensive and an effort to reform the educational system.

Several members of the Panel expressed surprise that the recommendations of this Dutch Concil were so well received by the public, even though the topics were highly controversial. This surprise led to a discussion of the question: Under what conditions does the public trust experts? The Dutch experience suggests that a high level of public trust of experts exists when the following conditions are met:

(1) An existing tradition of cultural reliance on scientific knowledge.
(2) Hope that a political impasse that has developed in the rest of the government bureaucracy will be broken by appealing to experts.
(3) The quality of the report itself is recognized as being very high.
(4) The history of the advisory group itself inspires trust.

*See the chapter by Theo Quené in this volume.

The Panel also discussed the example of the Academy of Sciences in Czechoslovakia. The Academy there often sets up special committees to study given problems. For example, a committee was recently established to study biotechnology that consisted of two representatives from the Academy, two from the Ministry of Agriculture, and two from the government.

The Czechoslovakian experience suggests that one of the greatest needs at the present time is for specialists on *implementation* of science for policy. In other words, it is not enough merely to devise new policy recommendations; those recommendations need to be accompanied by implementing mechanisms and personnel.

The Panel agreed that the problem of implementation is a general one that deserves much more attention. A great deal of technical regulation fails because of inadequate consideration of implementation. All too often policy advisors consider implementation as something that can be left to the politicians. A much wiser approach, however, is to look upon implementation as a part of the technical problem that the science advisor must help to solve. The best policy recommendation is useless if it can not be implemented.

Report of Panel 2

Chairman PIERRE AIGRAIN; *Rapporteur* JEROME R. RAVETZ

The Panel's deliberations were organized around the question of how issues are brought to the various policy agendas, and whether that process can be improved. We began with a taxonomic survey of the various sources of issues involved in the different stages of what can be a complex process, from the first discovery of an issue to its inclusion as an item for policy decision leading to action.

The endogenous sources, within the *establishment*, start with the *scientific community*; and here we distinguish between issues arising from the ordinary, communal processes of research and commentary, and those raised by an entrepreneur who alone realizes the importance of an issue and needs to struggle against indifference among colleagues. Another source is the *bureaucracy* itself, raising issues more or less routinely as it conceives of new problems or new roles. The *political community*, working at local, regional, or national levels, and internationally, motivated by ordinary or ideological concerns, will also bring issues to the fore. Exogenous sources include

Pierre Aigrain is a consultant to Thomson Brandt and Thomson CSF in Paris, France. From 1978 to 1981 he served as France's Secretary of State for Research.

Jerome Ravetz is a Professor of History and Philosophy of Science at the University of Leeds, UK.

individuals who initiate a campaign, leading to the creation of pressure-groups organized on an interest-group basis (local, industrial, moral/ethical, or ideological). All these foci of concern will interact with the *media*.

An important feature of the process, which may seem quite tortuous to those unfamiliar with it, is that as an issue matures and becomes salient, the presence of debate stimulates the production of new research, so that with improving knowledge the issue itself evolves and becomes more amenable to decision.

The first principle of the placing of items on the decision agenda is that the agenda is overcrowded. To get an item considered by those at the top requires tactical skill as well as some luck—this may be difficult for those trained in science to conceive or to accept. In particular, attention must be paid to the time structure of the cycle of decision making at any level, perhaps governed by the preparation of the budget on an annual basis, or by some more general national plan over a longer time span. The removal of an issue from a budget or plan, once entrenched in a special institution, may in some ways be more difficult than its placement there!

The media and independent pressure groups, although lacking formal constitutional status in most countries, play a strong and legitimate role in the process. Real issues may be forced to the attention of reluctant policymakers, though there is always the danger that hasty or sensationalist reporting may lead to false alarms.

The advisory role itself tends to be quite similar in its functions, over the different systems and styles of government, though of course the formal institutions will vary greatly. Policymakers need some person or small group who are personally close to themselves, whose judgment and integrity they can trust—this may be done formally or informally. The chief advisor must translate scientific materials into a form which is appropriate for that policymaker. This will involve the inclusion of aspects that are of social and political relevance (which seems to be difficult for those with experience exclusively in science). Also, the advisor must manage the biases that are explicit or implicit in the materials provided by the various advocates for special interests, as well as his or her own. The ethical problems in this task are challenging, particularly in the case of scientific advice where the materials are traditionally conceived as being neutral, objective, unbiased, factual. The solution does not lie in presenting materials as if they were in a pure-science research report, but rather in the maintenance of the personal integrity of the advisor. Honesty is essential in relations with the policymaker. But the advisor's usefulness depends also on his or her continued credibility with the scientific community, and for this it is essential that his or her work can be published, if not the details of the advice and its fate, then at least the strategic principles on which it is based. In this respect the science advisor is different from the traditional civil servant; and the placing of a professional scientist too close to decision making can impair his or her usefulness because of the loss of professional standing and credibility.

We should distinguish between advice and advocacy. At lower levels of decision making, as in ministries, scientific information is required as an input to an advocacy argument, in which the desired conclusion takes precedence over the presentation of a balanced case. But at the highest level, the advisor is rather like an assessor to a judge, and an important part of the task is in unpacking the advocacy arguments presented to the decision maker.

In the light of these general considerations, the Panel considered the problems of acid rain and CO_2. In the former case, the history is quite varied. In Sweden we see the full process, starting with entrepreneurial scientist efforts, proceeding through media and pressure group campaigns, receiving confirmation by the regular scientific community, eventually involving the Government and finally reaching international level at the 1972 Stockholm Conference. In this case, good tactics resulted in the issue being taken up in a goodwill gesture by a Head of State, so that it became an effective policy issue. France presented a strongly contrasting case: having a modest problem because of its geography and technology, and one which moreover was bound to decrease, its leaders could make a *beau geste* at little cost. The UK finds the issue embarrassing since up to now it has been a net exporter of the problem—and so research is the main action there. The FRG showed a rapid transition from quiescence to alarm, and regulatory action is already under way. In the US, the issue is uniquely divisive and complex, involving different regions, industries, and social values, and so the result up to now has been near-paralysis. In each of these cases, advice of the endogenous sort has been only one input among many, and not always the crucial one.

In the case of CO_2, it is far too early for there to be an agenda for action. But even the research agenda is not unproblematical. The natural locus for research is the World Meteorological Organization, and so the long-term research on CO_2 has been relegated there. Some practical help may come from those with a concern for environmental responsibility and no immediate acid rain problem: e.g., Japan. There research is being organized that can be fed into some future international effort.

I hope that the Panel and this rapporteur will be excused for a note of levity that crept in at the end of a long and intense session. We considered the serious international effects of the possible acidification of moorland water in Scotland, leading to changes in the composition of Scotch whisky. Would it be appropriate to prepare for an adjustment to this eventuality, using genetic manipulation techniques to make future generations tolerant of such a serious modification to the external and internal environment?!

In its discussion of uncertainty, the Panel distinguished among the various sorts that afflict scientific advice. Uncertainties in the political context of decision making are ever-present and indeed frequently extreme, but that is the stuff of politics, and not our special concern. Close to these are the inherent uncertainties in forecasts, particularly of the prospects of single, large technological systems. If these are to compete in a future market, then the possibility of their failing because of the emergence of competitive devices or systems, or of a change in the political climate, introduces more uncertainty still. A third sort of uncertainty, which seems in principle to be capable of control or management, is in the scientific information presented by advisors. In favorable cases this is temporary, occurring when an issue becomes salient and the scientific community has not yet caught up with techniques for monitoring or control.

The present political context of scientific uncertainty presents a paradox. Our technological culture has reduced the uncertainty that we face in coping with our environment most dramatically, and yet in recent years people have begun to feel very insecure and uncertain about the protections and even the benefits of our science-based technology. This is partly because the great successes of science have led to excessive expectations. Also, the new threats seem based on that same successful technology, and not on those parts of nature that we still hope to tame; and of course they extend to future generations. There is a real structural feature underlying these new fears—our technology is in some respects fragile, requiring high quality in design and maintenance if large-scale harm is to be avoided. The paradoxical quality of our new worries is revealed by the grossly incommensurable scales of risks that become salient for the public—automobile accidents are tolerated, while small-scale chemical hazards are not. But the operative feature in such risks is (as scholars have established in recent years) not the simple quantitative measure, but a complex of perceptions of the individual's fate in relation to institutions and nature.

The Panel gave closer attention to uncertainty in science itself, and in the political decision process. Uncertainty is least in the primary data (though in epidemiology or toxicology there can be quite serious problems); it is more serious in interpretation and theories; and worst in systems effects and future projections. Sometimes the sources of disagreement can be distentangled and consensus achieved on a band of numeral values in which a correct value of a parameter is likely to be located; but even such consensus cannot be guaranteed in all cases in a new and salient problem. Engineering designs, inevitably involving projections of behavior under field conditions and requiring simplified scientific models, can produce failures under even the best of circumstances. Scientists should be aware of uncertainties in their conclusions, however much they are attached to them, and should estimate and express uncertainties whenever possible.

In the political process, an important question is how well various actors can tolerate uncertainty. This may be a function of a simple cost–benefit calculation; the lower the cost of an error, the less critical is the assurance of correctness and certainty. But limited tolerance of uncertainty can impede the processes of advice and decision. Do politicians find scientific uncertainty difficult to accept or even to grasp? Opinions differed among the Panel, though it seems that in the US the personal need for scientific certainty is stronger. Also, individuals vary widely in their tolerance of uncertainty; scientists who need subjective certainty can be found in all fields and on all sides of policy issues.

Since political decision making is to such a great extent the management of uncertainty, the Panel found it useful to consider the differences in styles of advice and debate between various national centers, distinguishing very roughly between America and the others. In the US, government is relatively weak, nonhierarchical, and fragmented in structure. Competing centers of power conduct their debates to a great extent in the open, in a litigious, adversarial style, and with great attention to procedure. This produces a great variety of fora for debate, with corresponding sets of expert advocates, and a scientific debate running parallel to every political debate. This marketplace style runs right up to the top of the policy machine, making the task of science advisors there particularly challenging. But it does have the beneficial effect of stimulating research, both within agencies (where it is to a great extent subject to peer review) and in independent centers. The more consensual, closed, and hierarchical styles of Europe have lower procedural costs in administration, but fewer incidental benefits in public education. We may characterize such styles in terms of the ratio of advice to advocacy in each system.

Finally, the Panel considered the problem of uncertainty in connection with the two issues of acid rain and CO_2. It may be said that a ten-year span from inception to inclusion in an international policy agenda is not bad going. Indeed, a decade, more or less, may be a typical time-constant for the maturing of a science–policy issue, where research catches up to produce elements of a reliable policy for monitoring and mitigation. If this were accepted as a rough measure, then such a perspective would enable participants in these processes to evaluate their efforts at any given stage, and to follow more effective strategies. Further, the need for any international effort to accommodate national interests is brought out very clearly in this example. One important contribution that international organizations can make is to include scientists from reluctant nations in all its research efforts, so that the price of rejection of research findings by the government concerned would be significantly higher and their acquiescence in unpalatable policies facilitated.

Concerning CO_2, the Panel concluded that the main policy issue now is the design of an effective research effort. We can be sure that in view of the extreme uncertainties that afflict this issue, national interests will be difficult to contain. A constructive path at this stage would be consideration of the design of research at this and later stages, so that its results will be best adapted for use in the policy process as the problem matures.

Report of Panel 3

Chairman NIKOLAI EMANUEL; *Rapporteur* WILLIAM C. CLARK

Panel 3 explored an evolutionary or process perspective on the relationship between science and public policy. We believe that the reality of those relationships is distorted by the alternative view that portrays problems as being on or off agenda, and advice as being sought at one moment that was not being sought before.

The evolution of societies' treatment of problems like acid rain can be viewed as a process of interaction between the science, policy, and lay communities. The problem may be latent in any of these communities for a long time until it emerges into prominence and begins to interact with the concerns of other communities as well.

The subtle and complex nature of these interactions in the acid rain case has been well documented in Gregory Wetstone's chapter. In the case of the CO_2 problem, a few scientists were already engaged in relevant research even in the last century. Systematic research, however, was not undertaken until the International Geophysical Year of 1957. Since the mid-1960s, scientists have tried sporadically to make the carbon dioxide problem a focal concern of policymakers. They have had some local successes, but efforts to make the problem a matter of sustained concern in international policy discussions (e.g., the Venice Summit) have so far failed. Simultaneously, however, CO_2 and its greenhouse effect have increasingly become matters of concern for some public groups. An important role in this communication of concern from the science communities to the lay communities has been played by the media. In the US, television viewers have seen the country's most distinguished commentator interviewing Holland's chief dike-keeper, and asking what will happen to the tulips when the melting ice caps raise the sea level. The *New York Times* has published one (excellent) editorial on the greenhouse effect in each of the last several years.

Nikolai Emanuel is a member of the Presidium and Secretary of the General Chemistry Branch of the USSR Academy of Sciences, USSR.

William C. Clark is Special Assistant to the Director of the Institute for Energy Analysis, Oak Ridge, Tennessee, USA.

Other problems with even more varied histories are: What are the key factors shaping such evolving relationships? How can we better understand what is going on in the interactions between the science, policy, and lay communities? What can be done to improve the process of providing useful science for public policy? The Panel focused on two dimensions of these questions. The first concerns the most important events, actors, or agents that become involved in the interactions between science, policy, and lay agendas. The second concerns basic structural conditions relating to policy problems themselves and to the human institutions that deal with them.

Events, Actors, and Agendas

The Panel discussions emphasized that agendas of concern exist not only in the policy community, but also in the scientific and lay communities. It seems fruitless to speculate on when or why a problem first appears on one of these agendas. Much more important are the conditions that turn a problem from a minor concern of a few people into a major preoccupation of the leaders of the policy, science, or lay communities. We agreed that a problem can be said to have emerged into the upper levels of the policy agenda when responsible officials feel they must publicly address it. Similarly, a problem has emerged onto the science agenda when it becomes a focus for funding and for high quality, sustained research. The lay agenda can be viewed in the same way.

In the experience of the Panel members, communication regarding a problem can often occur among the science, policy, and lay communities in a low-key, low-level way long before the problem emerges into prominence on any of the respective agendas. Eventually, however, some problems do emerge as urgent concerns on the policy agenda. This emergence can be triggered by a number of events or actors, each exerting their influence in a number of subtle and complex ways.

The evolution of policy agendas is most dramatically affected by key events. Perhaps the most obvious and forceful of these are *accidents* of the sort represented by oil spills or nuclear reactor breakdowns; *discoveries* (whether they turn out to be correct or not) such as the role of asbestos in cancer or the effect of fluorocarbons on ozone; and new *observations* (whether correct or not) like the cancer epidemic or dying forests.

In addition to the role played by events, a variety of individuals and groups from within the science, policy, and lay communities can influence the evolution of agendas. In our discussion on acid rain, the following actors were noted as having played important roles from within the science community:

(1) *Distinguished leaders:* Individual scientists can—and have—made a difference in bringing problems onto the policy agenda. This usually

requires great stature and commitment on the part of the individual involved. Bernd Ulrich's role in discussions about forest damage in the FRG is a possible example.

(2) *Expert groups:* Groups of disciplinary experts can also be important. In Hungary, forestry professionals were among the first groups of scientists to recognize the possible policy implications of the acid rain problem. Based on their observations of tree damage, the foresters pushed their concerns both within the scientific and policy communities.

(3) *National scientific organizations:* In some countries, the scientific academies, research societies, and other panels and committees have been extremely influential in determining the movement of concerns from the science to the policy agenda. Examples given by Panel members showed that the role of such actors may be to block movement of scientific concerns from the science to policy agenda: treatments of the CO_2 question by the US National Academy of Sciences and the scientific review panels within the UK provide examples. In most cases, this blockage seems to be accompanied by a recommendation for more research and commitment to inform the policy community if significant new scientific findings emerge.

(4) *International scientific organizations:* These can also play an important role. For many small countries, the international organizations provide the only realistic source of legitimate scientific advice. For others, they offer an independent source of advice that can provide perspective on the opinions and activities of national scientific and government bodies.

(5) *Foreign science:* In several cases, scientific research performed and publicized in one country has been instrumental in moving a problem onto the policy agenda of another country. This is important not just because no country can do all science, but also because the scientific and policy establishments in some countries may not be willing to support certain forms of scientific research domestically.

Actors within the policy community can also play important roles in managing the relationships between science and the policy agenda. The following specific examples were raised by Panel members:

(6) *Government ministries and State committees:* These can be extremely influential through their powers to determine what research is funded and what scientific information is formally passed to other segments of government. In some countries, government study groups have been extremely effective in promoting research on acid rain and pointing out the implications to policymakers. In others, it is the relevant

government groups that have blocked the efforts of scientists to push acid rain onto the policy agenda.

(7) *Foreign policy considerations:* The acid rain case provides many examples of how a problem moves onto one nation's policy agenda because of the perceived concern of foreign governments with the problem. Note that this can occur in the virtual absence of any domestic scientific pressure to set policy on the problem.

Finally, the Panel members noted that actors and actions within the lay community (e.g. all those people who are neither scientists nor policymakers) had often influenced policy agendas. The following specific examples emerged from our acid rain discussions:

(8) *Interest groups:* These have been particularly important in places like the US (e.g., fishermen's associations protesting lake damage) and the FRG (the pre-election Greens).

(9) *Media:* As noted earlier, the media can be very influential in determining which problems achieve prominence on the policy agenda and which do not. Although sensationalist reporting is most often cited in this regard, sober analysis of trends and portrayal of background information can sometimes be even more powerful.

Panel discussions emphasized that, in any specific case, many of the actors and events listed here would be simultaneously involved in the emergence of a problem to a position of prominence on the policy agenda. In some cases, the process would follow a conventional pattern of scientific observation or discovery, followed by review within the scientific community, followed by orderly transition to government advisory groups, and so on. Often, however, much less obvious and predictable routes would occur. Several cases were cited where when an effort to move acid rain onto the policy agenda by the domestic science advisory route failed, another effort was mounted using international science, local interest groups, or the media. The history of failure in efforts to move the CO_2 question onto the policy agenda has not discouraged further attempts. This is probably more the rule than the exception, at least in pluralistic societies. Finally, surprising events—accidents, discoveries, or new observations—can at any time upset the orderly processes of agenda setting planned by scientists, policymakers, or public interest groups. The Panel surprised itself by its inability to give many specific examples where advisors had played a major role in the long-term evolution of policy agendas.

Structural Conditions

The vast diversity of routes by which acid rain has come onto (or been kept off) policy agendas in different countries warns against any simple interpretation of the agenda-setting process. When problems as different as acid rain and carbon dioxide are considered, the situation is even more complicated, and valid generalizations even more difficult to come by. The Panel attempted to reach some general understanding of their diverse experiences of efforts to provide useful science for policy. We therefore looked for fundamental structural features that seem to influence the evolution of relationships between science and policy. We believe that efforts to compare different experiences of providing science for public policy should explicitly recognize such distinctions. Some seem particularly important:

(1) *Spatial structure:* Problems will evolve very differently depending on whether they are local, regional, or global in character. For example, solid waste management, at least in the past, has tended to be a local problem. CO_2, in contrast, is perhaps the archetypical global problem (others might include the consequences of nuclear war or the ozone problem). Acid rain, like some earlier problems of transboundary air and water pollution, is an intermediate, regional-scale problem. Clearly, for each of these spatial scales, different scientific communities, political institutions, and channels of lay communication will be emphasized. Similarly, the relevance of national science advisors to the evolution of policy agendas is very different at each problem scale.

A significant feature of recent developments is the tendency of problems to move up-scale: waste management is increasingly a regional problem, and tall stacks are drastically extending the possible range of acid rain effects. This up-scale movement can be expected to induce significant changes in the communities that participate in the development of science–policy relationships. The question arises as to which institutional structures for science advice and communication are most effective at which spatial scales, and what breakdowns of science–policy relationships can be expected as problems shift scale from the perspectives of science, policy, and lay communities.

(2) *Temporal structure:* Problems will also evolve differently depending on whether their policy-relevant consequences are felt immediately or only predicted for the distant future. Acid rain belongs in the first category, CO_2 in the second. In the case of acid rain, politicians and public interest groups are often the leading actors, demanding advice from the scientific community that scientists are not ready to give. For

CO_2, the roles are generally reversed: some scientists are shouting warnings that relatively few members of the policy or lay communities are ready to hear. The consequences of different time constants of the various problems and institutions involved in the evolution of policy agendas needs much closer attention.

(3) *Communication:* A major structural feature stressed by several Panel members was the openness of lines of communication between leaders of the scientific, lay, and policy communities. Where all leaders know each other and freely exchange views, the evolution of relationships between science and policy is likely to proceed much differently than when such communication is impeded. This seems more a cultural issue than one of size or government style. Comparative analyses should be possible, both across nations and through time within nations as the social organization evolves.

(4) *Background concern:* Probably the most important structural feature noted by the Panel members in seeking to explain differences in the evolution of various science-for-policy issues was the level and development of background concern. Many stressed that acid rain could never have moved as quickly onto science, policy, and public agendas without the longer and more general history of concern for clean air in the science, policy, and lay communities. CO_2 may have an easier time moving onto the policy agenda because of the present concern there for acid rain. According to this view, novel concerns with little precedent should encounter greater resistance in all the communities. Again, the relevance of the evolutionary history of related problem concerns needs to be considered more explicitly in efforts to understand and influence the development of policy agendas.

An Annotated Bibliography of Selected Readings in English

MICHAEL DOWLING

Scientific Advice for Policy Making

Ashby, E. (1983) Scientists in the Whitehall village, *Minerva* **19**, 641–645.

In his reviews of Philip Gummett's *Scientists in Whitehall* and a House of Lords' report, *Science and Government*, Ashby makes several interesting comments on the nature of giving scientific advice in Britain. First, he argues that "there is no lack of capacity for giving scientific advice. What is lacking is initiative in asking for advice and a capacity for receiving it and using it." For example, he quotes the President of the Royal Society stating that government scientists rarely come to the Royal Society for opinions, advice, or facts. Ashby further criticizes current advice-giving arrangements because "even when advice is asked for and given, it is . . . either not followed or perhaps worse, it is not known what happens to it." Finally, he criticizes the obsession with confidentiality in the British civil service, which prevents access by scientists to the information they need in order to assess the relevance of advice to particular political problems.

Blume, S. S. (1974) Science and government, in S. S. Blume (Ed) *Towards a Political Sociology of Science* (New York, USA: Free Press)

In this chapter Blume examines the role of the scientist within the bureaucracy, including how scientific advisors are chosen, what departures from normative behavior are involved in their work, and what implications the "scientist as expert" role have on the scientific community itself. He concludes that elite scientific advisors necessarily become politicized by virtue of their association with government, which may lead to their alienation from the rest of the scientific community.

Michael Dowling was a Research Scholar at IIASA, Laxenburg, Austria and is now a Ph.D candidate at the University of Texas in Austin.

Brooks, H. (1964) The scientific advisor, in R. Gilpin and C. Wright (Eds) *Scientists and National Policy Making* (New York, USA: Columbia University Press).

In this essay Brooks makes a distinction between "science for policy" and "policy for science"; the former is concerned with matters that are basically political or administrative but are significantly dependent on technical factors, the latter is concerned with the development of policies for management and support of scientific research and development. He makes further distinctions between five advisory functions of scientific advisors or advisory committees:

(1) To analyze the technical aspects of major policy issues.
(2) To evaluate specific scientific or technological programs for the purpose of aiding budgetary decisions.
(3) To study specific areas of science and technology for the purpose of identifying new opportunities for research or development.
(4) To advise on organizational matters affecting science.
(5) To advise in the selection of individual research proposals to be supported.

Brooks, H. (1975) Expertise and politics—problems and tensions, *Proceedings of the American Philosophical Society*, **119**, 257–261.

In examining the relations between the expert scientific community and the political community, Brooks makes several key observations. First, he points out that one of the problems that the scientist has in participating as an expert in the political decision process relates to the use of tentative evidence and provisional conclusions. Provisional conclusions in basic science have few consequences and can be discussed rather freely. However, tentative propositions in the political arena are not always recognized as such, but often become the basis for drastic political action. Brooks concludes that "the particular facts which are selected and the way they are presented to the public may have much greater political impact than the mere facts themselves, so that the scientist holds enormous power in his hands".

Brooks, H. (1976) The Federal Government and the autonomy of scholarship, in C. Frankel (Ed) *Controversies and Decisions* (New York, USA: Russell Sage Foundation).

In this essay on the relationship between social science research and policy making, Brooks observes a hazard relevant to natural science experts as well. This hazard is the tendency in Western countries, especially the US, to appeal to value-free knowledge and scientific advice as a means of achieving political consensus. As a result, experts often present their political preferences as disguised technical recommendations, and politicians seek experts who can cloak their goals with the respectability of scientific objectivity. At work in such situations is a mutually reenforcing temptation. On the one hand, the scientific expert is flattered that the politician is interested in what he has to say and excited by its apparent relevance to policy issues. On the other hand, the politician seeks sharp scientific answers to shift the burden of a decision to the expert so that a controversial decision can be defended on the science rather than the values involved.

Ezrahi, Y. (1977) The antinomies of scientific advice, *Minerva*, **14**, 76–77.

In this book review Ezrahi criticizes the tendency of recent analysts of politics and science to treat the political and scientific components of scientific advice separately. Such a separation, he contends, presupposes "a process through which agreements on relatively clear and mutually consistent goals were attained". He argues that, on the contrary, there often exists a conflict between scientific standards and political ends. "Scientifically proper advice might constitute a basis of politically unacceptable decisions; politically legitimate and acceptable decisions may be inconsistent with scientifically based proposals for rational and effective policy." This observation leads to the critique of the notion of public interest science espoused by Joel Primack and Frank von Hippel in *Advice and Dissent* (see Books on Science for Public Policy section below), which he claims is based on the "undemocratic notion of experts who are accountable only to an abstractly conceived idea of the public, and free from the constraining institutions and conventions which constitute the authority of elected officials".

Ezrahi, Y. (1980) Utopian and pragmatic rationalism: the political context of scientific advice, *Minerva*, **18**, 111–131.

Ezrahi describes two contrasting views of the relationship between scientific knowledge and policy making. One view, which he calls utopian rationalism, regards any political considerations in the making of policy to be obstacles that must be overcome on the way to a progressive rationalization of decisions and actions. In contrast, pragmatic rationalism considers the political components of public policymaking to be inherent ingredients in the democratic political order. The utopian rationalist outlook is limited to only one of four possible relationships between politics and scientific knowledge, namely, the situation in which both political objectives and relevant scientific knowledge are unambiguous and agreed-upon. He points out that the relationship is really better described as a 2 × 2 matrix where the possibilities are agreement on goals with scientific consensus, agreement on goals without scientific consensus, scientific consensus with disagreements on goals, and neither scientific consensus nor agreement on goals. He discusses a number of cases to illustrate these possibilities.

Gummett, P. (1980) Advisory elites and problems of scientific advice, in P. Gummett (Ed) *Scientists in Whitehall* (Manchester, UK: Manchester University Press).

In discussing the use of scientific advice in the British civil service, Gummett argues that scientists, if they are to guard against manipulation and retain control over the use of their advice, need political as well as scientific skills. Political skills are required, first in deciding how to present and how to make explicit, assumptions in scientific data. In addition, in issues involving science and politics, the scientific components may not be the most important, so scientists must at least understand the nature of politics. Finally, he outlines the qualities an expert must possess in order to survive and be useful in government. They include: political sensitivity, proximity to the decision maker, the ability to condense and simplify scientific information into clear and concise advice, the ability to seek advice from other scientists before advising a decision maker, and the ability to seek approval not only of the decision maker but also of those who will implement and benefit from a decision.

Habermas, J. (1970) The scientization of politics and public opinion, in J. Habermas (Ed) *Toward a Rational Society* (Boston, USA: Beacon Press).

Habermas argues that experts and politicians cannot isolate themselves and their decision making procedures from the public. Instead, the implementation of technical decisions is increasingly dependent on mediation by the public as a political institution. In order to increase this public participation, Habermas contends that scientists are "compelled to go beyond the technical recommendations that they produce and reflect upon their practical consequences". Communication between experts, politicians, and the public will lead to a "rational society . . . only to the extent that science and technology are mediated with the conduct of life through the minds of its citizens".

Hammond, K. R. (1978) Toward increasing competence of thought in public policy formation, in K. R. Hammond (Ed) *Public Policy Formation* (Boulder, USA: Westview Press).

Hammond argues that policy makers and their science advisors use a weak, incompetent mode of thought when forming public policy. He describes and advocates a more powerful mode of thought focused on variables rather than objects, and aided by the use of conventional statistical description, computer simulation, and decision analysis.

Jones, R. V. (1972) Temptations and risks of the scientific adviser, *Minerva*, **10**, 441–451.

In this historical account of scientific advice in Britain during World War II, Jones identifies temptations and risks that are equally applicable to the scientific advisors of today. First, he admits that scientific advice can be slanted in several ways. He relates an example where he deliberately put a scientific case more strongly than the evidence warranted in order to influence a decision he felt was important. He also points out the tendency to slant evidence toward the less risky of two positions and even suppress evidence that may be awkward or detrimental to a scientific argument. He further identifies the temptations of the advisor to "say what the chief wants to hear" or to draw attention to a danger by presenting overly pessimistic views of a situation. Finally he argues that if scientists deviate from objective advice they should be aware of the issues at stake and the personal responsibility involved.

Lakoff, S. A. (1977) Scientists, technologists, and political power, in I. Spiegel-Roesing and D. de Solla Price (Eds) *Science, Technology, and Society* (London, UK: Sage Publications).

Lakoff begins his essay by tracing the historical development of the relationship between scientists and those who hold political power. He then criticizes the belief held by many scientists that because they are trained in the scientific method, they approach all problems, including political ones, with rigor and objectivity. In fact, scientists also bring into play their own sets of values and biases when trying to solve policy problems that have technical components. He goes on to distinguish three roles for scientists involved in policy, as advocates of support, as advisors, and as adversaries. Finally he points out the dangers involved in public interest science, and concludes that although scientists and technologists are likely to have a significant impact in shaping the view of those who make decisions, only in rare cases will the views of scientists exclusively determine an outcome.

MacRae, D. (1976). Technical communities and political choice, *Minerva*, **14**, 169–190.

MacRae advocates the development of technical communities to improve the use of expert advice in the policymaking process. He reviews the shortfalls of a system based largely on advice given by academic, "pure" scientists who are not controlled by the usual peer review system. In addition, he observes that laymen cannot easily assess conflicting views offered by pure scientists on scientific matters affecting policy. He argues that the credibility of technical advice in selecting policies may have to be established on bases other than those prevailing in the basic scientific communities. What is needed, MacRae claims, are technical communities analogous to scientific communities, but expressly interested in the use of expert knowledge in choosing among policies.

Margolis, H. (1973) *Technical Advice on Policy Issues* (Beverly Hills, USA: Sage Publications)

Margolis examines the role of technical advice in making national security decisions. In Part One of his study, he comments on the politics of technical advice as illustrated by three cases: the Skybolt missile, the Serpukhov computer, and the anit-ballistic missile. In Part Two, he addresses the specific problem of technical advice to the Secretary of State of the US.

Moss, T. (1982) Is there a scientific basis for environmental decision-making?, *Annals of the New York Academy of Sciences*, **387**, 29.

Moss examines the role of science in environmental decision making from the point of view of a scientific staff assistant to the US Congress.

Nichols, R. (1972) Some practical problems of scientist advisers, *Minerva*, **10**, 603.

Nichols argues that scientists as advisors have three responsibilities:

(1) To be completely open and honest.
(2) To make clear distinctions between facts and values.
(3) To recognize that evaluative statements from scientists have less weight than the views of elected or appointed officials and nonscientists.

Such criteria, he admits, create a hard path for scientists to follow.

Nowotny, H. (1981) Experts and their expertise: on the changing relationship between experts and their public, *Bulletin of Science, Technology, and Society*, **1**, 235–241.

Through examining two cases, the nuclear power debate in Austria and a comparison of carcinogen regulation in the US and the UK, Nowotny argues for "greater awareness into the social nature of the influence to which experts and their expertise are subject and a greater sensitivity in facing the limits to their expertise". She rejects the positivistic notion of value-free science, removed from "political contamination". She concludes that only by increasing the public's understanding of the strengths and weaknesses of scientific expertise will an ever-increasing trend towards public distrust of science be reversed.

Perl, M. L. (1971) The scientific advisory system: some observations, *Science*, **17**, 1211–1215.

Perl describes the science advisory sytem in the US as those scientists and engineers who help the government make decisions on technical questions by serving on committees attached to the executive branch and semigovernmental institutions, like the National Academy of Sciences, and by working for Congress. He criticizes the advisory system for being largely ineffective or ignored, which he attributes to its diverse functions, to the limits of its influence, and to the need for confidentiality and legitimization.

Price, D. K. (1974) Money and influence: the links of science to public policy, *Daedulus*, **103**, 97–133.

In the first section of this essay, Price looks at federal financial support for science in the US, i.e. policy for science. In the second section he examines arrangements by which scientists influence policy and programs, i.e. science for policy. He concludes that the legitimacy of science as a guide to public policy is under serious challenge as a result of the tendency of politicians to demand too much in return for financial support, and of scientists trying too hard to influence policy decisions without losing their aura of privileged academic freedom.

Primack, J. (1980) Scientists and political activity, in S. A. Lakoff (Ed) *Science and Ethical Responsibility* (Reading, USA: Addison Wesley).
Primack discusses the science advisory system in the US and points out four major problems:

(1) The science advisory system is generally not capable of stopping a bureaucracy from doing something it already has decided to do.
(2) The mere existence of the system implicitly supports the *status quo*. Scientists with strong dissenting views are usually excluded from advisory committees.
(3) Scientists often talk past each other on controversial issues when the real concerns of the debate are nonscientific.
(4) The science advisory system is controlled by officials, often for political purposes.

He argues for more public interest science as a supplement to, and not a replacement for, the established advisory system.

Revelle, R. (1975) The scientist and the politician, *Science*, **187**, 1100–1105.

Revelle believes that the real crisis in industrialized countries may be a loss of faith in the inevitability or even the possibility of human progress. He argues for more cooperation between politicians and scientists in the search for ways out of this dilemma. Scientists, who have long accepted the idea that they should advise politicians, should also be open to advice *from* politicians concerning the kinds of scientific and technical advice needed and the conditions under which it should be given. Finally he argues for the formulation of a "National Policy of Science and Technology" as a guide to legislative and executive action in the US.

Schmidt, H. (1982) Science and politics, *Interdisciplinary Science Review*, **7** (4).

Former German Chancellor Schmidt, in commenting on the social responsibility of the scientist, observes that the flood of information and overspecialization in science has led to the absence of any attempts to develop a universal scientific perspective. He criticizes the influence of expert advisory committees that too often results in both scientists and politicians trying to evade the responsibility for decisions.

Weingart, P. (1977) Science policy and the development of science, in S. S. Blume (Ed.) *Perspectives in the Sociology of Science* (New York, USA: Wiley and Sons).

Weingart examines how certain political issues with a high scientific component evolve and what role scientific information and political goals play in putting a problem on the policy agenda. He then examines how such problems are processed into the formulation of a political program and, finally, how political programs influence scientific research. As an example he uses the evolution of the Program for Environmental Protection of the FRG.

Weingart, P. (1982) The scientific power elite—a chimera. The deinstitutionalization and politicization of science, *Scientific Establishments and Hierarchies: Sociology of the Sciences*, **6**, 71–87.

Weingart rejects as outdated the notion of a scientific establishment or power elite that dominates the science advisory system. He argues that because much systematic knowledge useful for policy making is produced in government science installations, industrial research laboratories, and management staffs, and only to a small extent in academic institutions, science has lost its institutional identity, which used to be associated with universities and academic settings. Today, the involvement of scientists in politics, which has been interpreted as a scientification of politics, has led to a politicization of science as well.

Zuckermann, Sir Solly (1980) Science advisers, scientific advisers and nuclear weapons, *Proceedings of the American Philosophical Society*, **124** (4).

Zuckermann traces the history of, and compares, science advice to the President of the US and the Prime Minister of the UK. He examines the effectiveness, or lack thereof, of this advice, especially concerning the control of nuclear weapons.

Scientific Conflict and Consensus

Brickman, R. (1984) Science and the politics of toxic chemical regulation: US and European contrasts, *Science, Technology, and Human Values*, **9** (Winter).

Brickman contrasts the role of science in the US and Europe in setting public policy for toxic chemicals. He argues that, in the US, disputes over toxic chemicals involve the politicization of scientific debate, use of experts by opposing sides, and the reliance of administrators on science to give decisions an aura of authority. In Europe, however, decision making for technically complex issues takes place in an environment characterized by less intensive public scrutiny, deference to the bureaucracy, and little pressure to bolster decisions with scientific argumentation and formal analysis. These different approaches, in part, reflect institutional differences in the make-up and power of advisory committees, the role of the courts, and mechanisms of public participation.

Brooks, H. (1984) The resolution of technically intensive public policy disputes, *Science, Technology, and Human Values*, **9** (Winter).

Brooks examines the problems involved in resolving public policy disputes with high scientific and technical content when the experts disagree. He points out that even when experts strive to be impartial, policy preferences nevertheless significantly influence the interpretation of data and evidence when uncertainties are present. He further observes that many disputes with high scientific content hinge on which side should bear the burden of proof in the appraisal of a technical situation. He advocates the "smoking out" of a disagreement by requiring opposing sides in a debate to state, in advance, what types of experiments, evidence, or analysis would convince them to alter their policy positions on a controversial issue. Finally, he examines the roles of distributional issues and public participation in such disputes.

Casper, B. (1976) Technology policy and democracy, *Science*, **194**, 29–35.

Casper criticizes the proposed science court (see Kantrowitz below) for attempting to separate the political and scientific components of technical controversies. He argues that "new adversary forms concerned with technology policy issues should address all questions relevant to a choice among policy options, political and ethical as well as scientific and technological". He suggests organizing adversarial congressional hearings with expert advocates of different policy alternatives appearing together to present their own views and cross-examine each other.

Casper, B. and Wellston, P. (1982) Science court on trial in Minnesota, in B. Barres and D. Edge (Eds) *Science in Context* (Cambridge, USA: MIT Press).

A case study of a failed attempt to put into practice the science-court proposal on a dispute involving high voltage transmission lines in Minnesota.

Collingridge, D. (1980) The role of experts in decision-making, in D. Collingridge (Ed) *The Social Control of Technology* (London, UK: Frances Pinter).

Collingridge criticizes the traditional model of expert advice which holds that for any set of data there is only one interpretation or one theoretical explanation of the data that is superior to all others, so that disagreement between experts can only be the result of bias on the part of one or the other groups of experts. Collingridge instead asserts that for any given set of data there are a number of conflicting interpretations; therefore, experts can be expected to disagree, especially given the uncertainty surrounding data on complex scientific problems. On the basis of this model, the scientist is much more an advocate actively engaged in a policy debate. The expert's task is to offer and defend interpretations of data, which when coupled with commonly shared values, lead to the policy options favored by the sponsor of the expert. Finally, he offers a methodology for monitoring decisions made under scientific uncertainty or ignorance so that, if the decision proves to be wrong, corrective action can be taken.

Cournand, A. and Meyer, M. (1976) The scientist's code, *Minerva*, **14**, 79.

Cournand and Meyer, in discussing the scientist's code or general norms of scientific activity, examine the conflict between the traditional concept of scientists as "rational, open-minded investigators seeking objectively for the truth", and the more recent conception of science as a product of craftmanship, intuition, social processes, and persuasion. They reject the notion that the standards of objective scientific method are ideals rarely attained in practice and distortions of the real nature of science. Rather, they argue that objectivity "is an essential aspiration of scientists, even though the meaning of the concept may be imprecise and in its relationship to science open to alternative interpretations".

Edsall, J. T. (1981) Two aspects of scientific responsibility, *Science*, **212**, 11–14.

In this paper on scientific responsibility, Edsall examines the role of scientists in matters of public policy. He discusses the case of Rachel Carson and the resulting furor over her book *Silent Spring*. He concludes that "scientific facts and value judgments are so closely interwoven that it is exceedingly difficult to disentangle them, and the inferences to be drawn are inconclusive. Scientists can honestly disagree as to what inferences can be legitimately drawn from the facts." He also argues that "the passion for getting at the truth should be the dominant passion for scientific workers when they are trying to act as responsible scientists".

Hammond, K. and Adelman, L. (1979) Science, values, and human judgement, *Science*, **194**, 389.

Hammond and Adelman review the debate surrounding the input of scientific and value judgments into the policy process. They argue that judgment is a human cognitive activity and is therefore subject to scientific analysis. They propose a methodology for integrating scientific information and social values and give an example of its successful use.

Jasanoff, S. and Nelkin, D. (1981) Science, technology, and the limits of judicial competence, *Science*, **214**, 1211.

Jasanoff and Nelkin examine the problems involved in resolving scientific and technological controversies in the US courts. They review recent litigation, the burdens on the judicial process, and some proposed reforms.

Kantrowitz, A. (1975) Controlling technology democratically, *American Scientist*, **63**, 505.

In this essay Kantrowitz outlines his science-court proposal, calling it an "institution for scientific judgment" that, he argues, should be created to aid the US Congress in making decisions on scientific and technological issues.

Longino, H. (1983) Beyond 'bad science': skeptical reflections on the value-freedom of scientific inquiry, *Science, Technology, and Human Values*, **8** (Winter) 7–17.

In this paper Longino offers a new analysis of some of the issues included under the rubric of "science and values". She makes a distinction between two sets of values: contextual values are those influencing the choice of particular areas of research, questions to pursue, etc.; constitutive values are the source of the rules that determine what constitutes acceptable scientific practice or method. Longino criticizes the classical understanding of the relation between knowledge and values which holds that, although social and cultural values (contextual) determine which areas or aspects of the world are to be illuminated by application of the scientific method, the conclusions, answers, and explanations revealed through this methodology, are not governed by those values. Through the review of several case studies she shows how nonepistemological, personal, social, or cultural values have affected scientific practice.

Mazur, A. (1973) Disputes between experts, *Minerva*, **11**, 243–261.

This article compares the controversies over health effects of radiation and fluoridation of drinking water. Mazur shows that scientific conclusions are not unambiguous and even data accepted as valid by two parties can be disputed in interpretation. Such disputes usually become polarized into two distinct positions and often become very acrimonious. Mazur is in favor of a science-court mechanism to resolve such controversies, but also suggests bargaining and the explicit mapping of differences as possible alternatives.

Mazur, A., Marino, A. A., and Becker, R. O. (1979) Separating factual disputes from value disputes in controversies over technology, *Technology in Society*, **1**, 229–237.

In this article the authors defend the science-court proposal and claim that it is possible to separate fact and value components of a technical controversy. They examine the case of high voltage transmission lines in Minnesota and call it a "largely successful attempt" to separate facts from values. This view is in contrast to the account given by Casper and Wellstone (op. cit.) who judged the effort a failure.

Mulkay, M. (1978) Consensus in science, *Social Science Information*, **17**, 107–122.

This article argues that scientific knowledge is open to sociological analysis. Mulkay examines scientific consensus, and finds that agreement among natural scientists occurs much less often than is usually claimed. He further finds that the creation of scientific consensus is a social process, which does not necessarily depend on the application of clear-cut, independent intellectual criteria. Finally, he argues that the standards used in judging the adequacy and value of scientific knowledge claims are constantly negotiated and renegotiated in the course of social interaction.

Nelkin, D. (1975) The political impact of technical expertise, *Social Studies of Science*, **5**, 35–54.

Nelkin compares the controversies that surrounded the building of a nuclear power plant in New York and the addition of a runway to Logan Airport in Boston, and examines the roles played by experts and expert advice. She finds that policy makers often find it more efficient and comfortable to define decisions as technical rather than political, but that such technical debates are often based on different criteria and interpretations of available data. She further shows that in these two cases the existence of technical debate, rather than its substance, stimulated political activity.

Nelkin, D. and Pollak, M. (1980) Problems and procedures in the regulation of technological risk, in C. H. Weiss and A. H. Barton (Eds) *Making Bureaucracies Work* (Beverly Hills, USA: Sage Publications).

This essay examines various experiments that have been tried in the US and Europe to resolve disputes on scientific issues. Nelkin and Pollak describe two basic models, advisory and informational, which are subdivided into elitist and participatory forms. They then examine the problem of legitimacy for such mechanisms by discussing protests that evolved in these cases concerning areas of problem definition, participation, direction of the mechanism, distribution of technical expertise, and openmindedness of government.

Nichols, K. G. (1979) The de-institutionalisation of technical expertise, in H. Skoie (Ed) *Scientific Expertise and the Public* (Oslo, Norway: Norwegian Council for Science and Humanities).

Nichols argues that administrative authorities have employed technical expertise to depoliticize political controversy. This practice has resulted in a widening of the distance between experts and the general public, and led citizen groups to increasingly rely on their own experts, who are often used as a political weapon to undermine the credibility of government-appointed experts. The resulting conflicts between government and citizen experts lead Guild to call for new, more effective institutional mechanisms by which citizens and experts together can seek to ascertain the limits of available technical and nontechnical knowledge and the appropriate conditions for decision making on issues involving high risks and uncertainty.

Nowotny, H. (1975) Controversies in science: remarks on the different modes of production of knowledge and their use, *Zeitschrift fuer Soziologie*, 34–45 (English).

This article attempts to address the question of why disagreements in science persist. Nowotny argues that controversies arise not only when cognitive differences exist, but when these differences come to matter. Illustrations are provided from the history of science and anthropology.

Nowotny, H. and Hirsch, H. (1980) The consequences of dissent: sociological reflections on the controversy of the low dose effects, *Research Policy*, **9**, 278–294.

In examining the controversy over low-dose effects of radiation, Nowotny and Hirsch observe that the existing trend of political integration of science has resulted in conflict and dilemmas for the scientists involved. In particular, they explore the role played by dissenting scientists in such controversies.

Robbins, D. and Johnston, R. (1976). The role of cognitive and occupational differentiation in scientific controversies, *Social Studies of Science*, **6**, 349–368.

The authors claim that analyses of conflicts between experts and the relationship between political institutions and the scientific community should be informed by a conception of scientific knowledge not as absolute or given, but as socially constructed. They argue that the scientist advises and informs outsiders in conformity with a professional ideology, an admittedly neo-Kuhnian perspective. This argument is illustrated by the controversy surrounding safe environmental lead levels.

Roberts, M., Thomas, S., and Dowling, M. (1984) Mapping scientific disputes that affect public policymaking, *Science, Technology, and Human Values*, **9** (Winter) 112–122.

Despite a growing number of acrimonious public policy issues with scientific and technical content, none of the various suggestions for resolution of such disputes has proven successful for long-term use. In this paper the authors look at the existing mechanisms and a number of recent controversies, and ask where and when consensus is a reasonable goal, and when is clarifying the issue and educating the public a limited but practical goal.

Rushefsky, M. (1982) Technical disputes: why the experts disagree, *Policy Studies Review*, **1** (4) 676–685.

This article examines the 2,4,5-T controversy as an example of a scientific dispute based on epistemological differences between the scientists involved. Rushefsky proposes a framework for analysis based on three dichotomies: acute/chronic, which refers to whether scientists concentrate on long- or short-term effects; chemical/biological, referring to a scientist's main area of interest; and classical/romantic, which separates the methods people use to analyze a given problem. He finds that science-court mechanisms are not very useful and suggests that such adversary models would be better suited to mapping areas of disagreement rather than forcing consensus.

Weinberg, A. M. (1972) Science and trans-science, *Minerva*, **10**, 207–222.

Weinberg makes a distinction between two kinds of questions that are posed in the language of science: genuine scientific questions that can be answered by normal scientific methods, and trans-science questions that involve value judgments and political decisions beyond the realm of science. He argues that such questions must be separated and dealt with individually and that the failure to do so has led to a decrease in the credibility of scientists. He advocates more public participation in attempts to resolve trans-scientific questions.

Dealing with Scientific Uncertainty

Ashby, E. (1976) Protection of the environment: the human dimension, *Royal Society of Medicine*, **69**, 721.

Ashby discusses the problems of dealing with uncertainty in making political decisions to protect the environment. He distinguishes between three kinds of uncertainty:

(1) Uncertainty about facts.
(2) Uncertainty about public perception of these facts.
(3) Uncertainty about future consequences.

He concludes that decisions on the protection of the environment are not just deductions from scientific and economic data, but include unquantifiable social values. Such social values are difficult to assess, which may lead the decision maker to make decisions not in the public interest.

Bazelon, D. L. (1979) Risk and responsibility, *Science*, **205**, 272–280.

Judge Bazelon examines the difficulties in regulating hazardous activities that involve substantial risks. He recognizes and addresses the problem of sorting out facts, inferences, and values in the scientific evidence used to support risk regulation, and identifies two different kinds of uncertainty that plague such regulation. One kind of uncertainty exists because many of the scientific activities being regulated are on the frontiers of science. The other kind of uncertainty comes from a refusal to face the hard questions created by this lack of knowledge. As he stated in a recent court decision: "To the extent that uncertainties necessarily underlie predictions of this importance on the frontiers of science and technology, there is a concomitant necessity to confront and explore fully the depth and consequences of such uncertainties." He argues that the courts can play a substantial role in addressing these issues by "fostering the kind of dialogue and reflection that can improve the quality of decisions."

Brooks, H. (1976) The Impossibility of Proving Impossibilities, Speech at the University of Pennsylvania, Philadelphia, USA: 14 April.

In this lecture Brooks discusses the problem of burden of proof in decisions concerning technology that involve uncertainties. He observes that historically the burden of proof has shifted from those who are opposed to a particular technology to those who promote it. "In a remarkably short period we have moved from a market characterized by 'let the buyer beware' to a market characterized by 'let the seller beware'." This shift is shown in a number of areas, including nuclear power, chemicals in the environment, and occupational hazards. He goes on to analyze the public skepticism that has grown concerning the power of science, and the difficulty that the public has in accepting the fact that science or scientists cannot give precise answers to questions of safety.

Finally, he argues that people will increasingly recognize that safety cannot be determined in isolation; that is, acceptable risks will involve comparisons of the risks between alternative ways of reaching similar social objectives.

Collingridge, D. (1980) Decision-making under ignorance, in D. Collingridge (Ed) *The Social Control of Technology* (London, UK: Frances Pinter).

Collingridge makes a distinction between decisions taken under uncertainty that can be handled by Bayesian decision-theory techniques, and decisions made under ignorance where such techniques are not applicable. He goes on to present a framework for making decisions under ignorance and analyses several historical examples. The central idea of this framework is that under conditions of ignorance, a premium ought to be placed on decisions that can swiftly and easily be recognized as wrong and that are easy to correct.

Haefele, W. (1974) Hypotheticality and the new challenges: the pathfinder role of nuclear energy, *Minerva*, **12**, 303.

Haefele uses the concept of hypotheticality to describe hazards that cannot be verified or disproved on the basis of operating experience or experimentation, but rather must be described through inference and hypothesis. An example of such a hazard is the debate concerning the effects of low-level ionizing radiation that Haefele argues has influenced the "strange and often unreal features" of the public debate on nuclear reactor safety.

Majone, G. (1982) The uncertain logic of standard setting, *Zeitschrift fuer Unweltpolitik*, **4**, 305–323 (in English).

Majone discusses the dilemma of scientific uncertainty surrounding the setting of environmental and occupational safety standards. He points out how standard setters must often resort to "rules of thumb" because they are unable to find clean, theoretical solutions to the problem of setting standards at some safe level.

Ramo, S. (1981). Regulation of technological activities: a new approach, *Science*, **21**, 837.

Ramo offers a proposal for a new investigatory agency that would determine the negative effects of a technological activity. In addition to this agency, Ramo suggests that a separate, politically appointed decision board be created that would consider negative evidence and make decisions balancing negative effects against the benefits of the proposed activity.

This is another example of an attempt to separate the fact and value components of decisions involving risk and uncertainty through a new institutional mechanism.

Ravetz, J. R. (1978) Scientific knowledge and expert advice in debates about large technological innovations, *Minerva*, **16**, 273.

In discussing the role of scientific knowledge in debates about large technological innovations, Ravetz points out the difficulties in trying to analyze complex issues without a precise, established body of knowledge. The first problem is projections of the future consequences of technological decisions. "No matter how much is extrapolated from past experience, any description of a future state must involve an element of faith." Second, in scientific work involving the natural environment, information may be lacking, and to start collecting information from the time the problem is defined may be too late. Finally, even when data exist, it is often uncertain and therefore does not meet the expectations of the public and politicians who want scientists as experts to provide the hard facts.

Samuels, S. W. (1981) The uncertainty factor, *Annals of the New York Academy of Sciences*, **363**, 271.

Samuels discusses the uncertainty factor inherent in policy decisions based on scientific evidence. This uncertainty is present in three stages in moving from evidence to a decision; uncertainty in scientific observations, uncertainty in the cultural interpretation of scientific data, and finally uncertainty in the moral integration necessary to act. He argues that elimination of uncertainty is impossible, as it is "a condition of the universe in which we live". What is needed is elimination of unnecessary risk, which requires decisions based on moral standards that go beyond the calculus of cost/benefit analysis.

Tversky, A. and Kahneman, D. (1974) Judgement under uncertainty: heuristics and biases, *Science*, **185**, 1124–1131.

Tversky and Kahneman examine the psychological principles that govern the perception of decision problems and discuss how the evaluation of probabilities and outcomes produce predictable shifts of preference when the same problem is framed in different ways.

Tversky, A. and Kahneman, D. (1981) The framing of decisions and the psychology of choice, *Science*, **211**, 453.

In this article Tversky and Kahneman contend that in assessing the probability of an uncertain effect, people rely on a limited number of heuristic principles that reduce the complex tasks of assessing probabilities and predicting values to simpler judgmental operations. They observe that these heuristics are quite useful, but may lead to severe and systematic errors.

Wynne, B. (1980) Technology, risk and participation: on the social treatment of uncertainty, in J. Conrad (Ed) *Society, Technology, and Risk Assessment,* (London, UK: Academic Press).

Wynne argues that one of the key elements in the assessment of technology is the way uncertainties of various kinds are handled. He contends that unless uncertainties are acknowledged and dealt with openly, they will lead to distrust and damage to the credibility of decision making institutions. He argues that public participation is not as essential as public identification with such decisions. "This implies that open, i.e., widely socially visible and searching discussion of conflicts, uncertainties, and alternative choices would be sufficient—decisions made in public rather than by the public." He contends more open decision making processes would "not secure any political utopia, but . . . would raise to view a model which could secure constructive political development rather than political degeneration".

Managing Global Problems and the Role of Scientific Institutions

Brooks, H. (1977) Potentials and limitations of societal response to long-term environmental threats, in W. Stumm (Ed) *Global Chemical Cycles and their Alterations by Man* (Berlin, FRG: Dahlem Konferenzen).

Brooks observes that there are several characteristics of long-term environmental problems that determine the likely or possible societal responses. They are summarized as follows:

(1) By definition long-term environmental effects lie far in the future, so that their assessment and control almost always involves trade-offs between the interests of current and future generations.

(2) Predicted effects are usually subject to a high degree of uncertainty and are difficult to prove to the satisfaction of all experts. This raises unique problems in establishing a consensus necessary for action.

(3) Even when physical or chemical effects can be established with fair confidence, there usually exist much larger uncertainties about biological and ecological effects, and even greater uncertainties with respect to social consequences. These latter uncertainties will

usually also take much longer to resolve, thus further complicating the problems of decision making under uncertainty.

(4) When effects are long term and cumulative, the costs of delaying action often appear small compared with the immediate economic costs and social dislocations that might result from actions or policies which many would consider premature.

(5) Long-term environmental problems can seldom be dealt with by single, discrete actions or policies, but respond only to continuing, sustained effort, supported by steady public attention and visibility. This requirement is in conflict with the crisis orientation of most politics, especially democratic politics.

Evan, W. M. (1981) Some dilemmas of knowledge and power in W. M. Evan (Ed) *Knowledge and Power in a Global Society* (Beverly Hills, USA: Sage Publications).

In the introduction to this volume based on a conference discussing the role of international scientific and professional associations (ISPAs), Evan asks "What impact, direct or indirect, do such organizations have on world affairs?" His answer is some impact but not enough. He argues that ISPAs should try to enlarge their scope of influence in international policy making by seeking more resources for scientific research, and finding more effective mechanisms of lobbying intergovernmental agencies.

Galey, M. (1977) Trends and dimensions in international science policy organization, in J. Haberer (Ed) *Science and Technology Policy* (Lexington, USA: Lexington Books).

In this paper Galey makes an effort to define international science policy, to distinguish several different types of international science policy, to discuss the various frameworks in which such policy is made, and finally to indicate what appear to be the major trends in the development of international science policy since the 1950s.

Gvishiani, J. (Ed) (1979) *Science, Technology, and Global Problems.* (Oxford, UK: Pergamon Press).

This book contains the proceedings of the International Symposium on Trends and Perspectives in Development of Science and Technology and Their Impact on the Solution of Contemporary Global Problems, held in Tallinn, USSR. It includes statements and papers (by Eastern and Western scientists) on various aspects of scientific cooperation in solving global problems by Eastern and Western scientists.

Keohane, R. O. and Nye, J. S. (1975) Organizing for global environmental and resource interdependence, in *Commission on the Organization of Government for the Conduct of Foreign Policy* (Washington, DC, USA: US Government Printing Office).

This report by Keohane and Nye assesses US governmental performance in areas of global environmental and resource interdependence. They argue that the characteristics of these issues require mobilizing scientific knowledge to provide warnings and create conditions that ensure adequate responses. They propose an extensive, extra-governmental system organized around a "Global Systems Critical List of Problems and Opportunities" that would inventory potentially long-term catastrophic effects, arising from the unmanaged or mis-managed development of global systems. The critical list study system would involve the US National Academy of Sciences, the Congress, the State Department, and the President's Science Advisor to coordinate policy responses to problems on the list.

Kapitza, S. P. (1982) Interdisciplinary cooperation essential, *Interdisciplinary Science Reviews*, **7** (4) 257.

Kapitza contends that what is lacking in dealing with global environmental and resource problems is an international mechanism for the appreciation of the findings of scientific reports and studies, and "the political will for implementing these recommendations." As a first step he advocates the development of public attitudes on these issues.

Myers, N. and Myers, D. (1983) How the global community can respond to international environmental problems, *Ambio*, **12** (1), 20–26.

Norman and Dorothy Myers argue that new mechanisms are required for dealing with rapidly emerging supranational environmental problems. They criticize the effectiveness of UN efforts in this area, and believe that much potential lies within certain institutions of the private sector, particularly multinational corporations and nongovernmental organizations.

Scharlin, P. (1982) The United Nations and the environment: after three decades of concern, progress is still slow, *Ambio*, **11** (1) 26.

Scharlin offers a critical review of UN activities in the field of the human environment over the last 35 years. She concludes that progress has been too slow and more concrete action is called for if we are to mitigate the forces that are altering the Earth's life support systems.

Sebek, V. (1983) Bridging the gap between environmental science and policy-making, *Ambio*, **12** (2) 118.

Sebek observes a wide gap between the scientific assessment of environmental problems and their legal and administrative regulation and enforcement. He analyzes what he sees as the main deficiencies and makes several recommendations to promote stronger links between policy makers and scientists on such issues.

Skolnikoff, E. (1977) Science, technology, and the international system, in I. Spiegel-Roesing and D. de Solla Price (Eds) *Science, Technology, and Society* (London, UK: Sage Publications).

Skolnikoff reviews the international significance of developments in science and technology in such areas as food and population, energy, and environment. He points out that science and technology have traditionally been seen by governments as a means of serving national interests. This orientation has had very undesirable effects including "lack of anticipation and understanding of the international changes wrought by science and technology, poor ability to cope with issues as they impinge on international affairs, little understanding of how science and technology might be directed to avoid or ameliorate issues, and enormous surprise and fear when the overall magnitude of the changes which science and technology have worked are realized." He argues that all of these issues require that they be dealt with by nations in an international environment, with some form of international negotiation and agreement. However, he is not encouraged by the record of existing international governmental organizations in carrying out these functions.

Case Studies

Brooks, H. (1982) Stratospheric ozone, the scientific community and public policy, in F. A. Bower and R. B. Ward (Eds) *Stratospheric Ozone and Man*, Vol II, (Boca Raton, USA: CRC Press.

Clark, I. D. (1974) Expert advice in the controversy about supersonic transport in the United States, *Minerva*, **12**, 416.

Gillespie, B., Eva, D., and Johnston, R. (1979) Carcinogenic risk assessment in the United States and Great Britain: the case of aldrin/dieldrin, *Social Studies of Science*, **9**, 265–301.

Nelkin, D. (1971) Scientists in an environmental controversy, *Science Studies*, **1**, 245–261.

Neustadt, R. E. and Fineberg, H. V. (1983) *The Epidemic That Never Was: Policy-Making and the Swine Flu Scare* (New York, USA: Vintage Books).

Priebe, P. M. and Kaufmann, G. B. (1980) Making governmental policy under conditions of scientific uncertainty: a century of controversy about saccharin in congress and the laboratory, *Minerva*, **18**, 56.

Voropaev, C. and Kosarev, A. (1982) The fall and rise of the Caspian sea, *New Scientist*, 8 April, 78.

Wynne, B. (1982) *Rationality and Ritual: The Windscale Inquiry and Nuclear Decisions in Britain* (London, UK: The British Society for the History of Science).

Zum Brunnen, C. (1974) The Lake Baikal Controversy in I. Volgyes (Ed) *Environmental Deterioration in the Soviet Union and Eastern Europe* (New York, USA: Prager).

Books on Science for Public Policy

Ashby, E. (1977) *Reconciling Man with the Environment* (Stanford, USA: Stanford University Press).

Boffey, P. M. (1975) *The Brain Bank of America* (New York, USA: McGraw Hill).

Feyerabend, P. (1978) *Science in a Free Society* (London, UK: NLB).

Gilpin, R. and Wright, C. (Eds) (1964) *Scientists and National Policy-Making* (New York, USA: Columbia University Press).

Golden, W. T. (1980) *Science Advice to the President* (New York, USA: Pergamon Press).

Gummet, P. (1980) *Scientists in Whitehall* (Manchester, UK: Manchester University Press).

Kuehn, T. J. and Porter, A. L. (Eds) (1981) *Science, Technology, and National Policy* (Ithaca, USA: Cornell University Press).

Lakoff, S. A. (Ed) (1966) *Knowledge and Power* (New York, USA: The Free Press).

Mazur, A. (1981) *The Dynamics of Technical Controversy* (Washington, DC, USA: Communications Press).

Nelkin, D. (Ed) (1979) *Controversy: Politics of Technical Decisions* (Beverly Hills, USA: Sage Publications).

Price, D. K. (1965) *The Scientific Estate* (Cambridge, USA: Harvard University Press).

Primack, J. and von Hippel, F. (1974) *Advice and Dissent: Scientists in the Political Arena* (New York, USA: Basic Books).

Ravetz, J. R. (1973) *Scientific Knowledge and its Social Problems* (Middlesex, UK: Penguin Books).

Rose, H. and Rose, S. (1970) *Science and Society*, (Middlesex, UK: Penguin Books).

Salomon, J-J. (1973) *Science and Politics* (London, UK: Macmillan).

Schooler, D. Jr. (1971) *Science, Scientists, and Public Policy* (New York, USA: The Free Press).

Spiegel-Roesing, I. and de Solla Price, D. (1977) *Science, Technology, and Society* (London, UK: Sage Publications).

Teich, A. H. (1974) *Scientists and Public Affairs* (Cambridge, USA: MIT Press).

Zuckerman, Sir Solly (1971) *Beyond the Ivory Tower* (New York, USA: Taplinger Publishing Co.).

An Annotated Bibliography of East European Literature

Compiled by the Scientific Information Service of the Polish Academy of Sciences

Articles

Frieske, K. (1980) Politicians, experts and—who else? *Science of Science,* **1** (4) 385–397.

The paper discusses problems of scientific consultation, stressing the need for controlling the relationship between experts and decision makers by the so-called social environment, i.e. the active, self-conscious part of society. In the author's opinion, the idea of the common good could be the axiological basis of such a control.

In the Polish historical situation, the intelligentsia promoted this idea.

Frolov, I.T. (1983) The topical philosophical and social problems of science the technology, *Voprosy Filosofii,* (6), 16–26.

The article opens the collection of materials for the Seventh International Congress on Logic, Methodology and Philosophy of Science. It analyzes the most urgent problems from the thematic and practical viewpoints, which emerge at the junction of different sciences, and also new trends of the unity and interaction of social, natural, and engineering sciences. The author shows the importance of broad philosophical and methodological approaches to studies of these problems, including their world-outlook basis. He criticizes scientific and technocratic views, the narrowness of which reduces the perspectives of the development of our civilization to only scientific and technological progress.

Problems associated with the human approach to scientific and technological progress, internal aspects of scientific cognition and its social, ethical, and humanistic aspects are discussed. Particular attention is given to the philosophical aspects of the global problems of our time.

In this connection the author analyzes the latest reports of the Club of

Rome, in particular *Micro-electronics and Society. For Joy and For Woe (1982)* The great philosophical and humanistic importance of this report is emphasized.

Haraszthy, A., Szànto, L., and Stolte-Heiskanen, V. (1981) The relationship between science policy, autonomy and the climate of research groups in two countries, *Science of Science*, **1** (2), 163–179.

The basic properties of science policy and administration in Finland and Hungary are described, with research activity discussed on the basis of empirical data of research groups.

In Hungary, there is a centralized science policy, being an integral part of the general economic policy; in Finland science policy is divided into sectors and not integrated into the general social policy.

In Hungary, institutions concerned with science policy have greater influence on guiding research and the choice of research problems, and the results of the teams' work are controlled by research institutes. In Finland, these institutions have not much say in the matter of the direction of research, and the control over research is extra-institutional.

Mikulinsky, S. R. (1980) Science policy in the socialist countries, *Science of Science*, **1** (1), 17–30.

The article discusses the main principles of scientific policy of the socialist countries, which challenge scientific knowledge to work out long-range programmes for the development of science and technique. These science of science investigations demand such a direction of development that they may supply theoretical and methodological bases for guiding the process of development of science in order to enhance the social effectiveness of scientific activity.

Monchev, N. (1980) The scientific policy in the management system of scientific and technological progress, *Science of Science*, **1** (4), 321–335.

Scientific policy is examined as a combination of planned activities, a system of measures, methods, and means of the legislative, executive, and public organs for the development of science and for the intensification of its interaction with other social systems.

An analysis is made of the ideological, economic organizational–management and social–psychological problems of science policy.

The role of science policy in the management system of scientific and technological progress under conditions of intensive development of the national economy is studied as an element of the general policy of the socialist state.

Rudniański J. (1983) Men of science and men of power: some similarities and differences, *Science of Science*, **3** (4), 379–387.

The author analyzes some features of men of science and men of power, essential from the viewpoint of the further development of our civilization. The chief similarity consists of an unemotional, cool view of reality, while the main differences lie in the fundamental criteria of values, regarded as supreme, and in objectives determined by these criteria, or, in the particular case cited here, in the different types of expansion. The author argues that neither men of science nor men or power, whatever criteria of values and aims they might accept, are free from responsibility for the development of man and his further existence.

Szakasits, G. D. (1980) Some problems of the process of science becoming a direct productive force in Hungary, *Science of Science*, **1** (1), 43–53.

The process of science becoming a direct productive force in Hungary has posed several problems for analysis and solution for the specialists of science management, sociology of science, and of economies of R & D. These problems are reflected in the activities of the Hungarian Science of Science Association, acting within the framework of the Association of Scientific Societies, as presented in this paper.
The paper refers to experiences in realizing the science policy directives of the association and the Hungarian Government, and describes the assistance that the Hungarian Science of Science Association has given in the introduction of science to the sphere of industrial production via discussions of related scientific problems.
From the discussions that have taken place in the association, this paper describes the most important statements and results of the research program entitled "Interrelation of science and technology in the Hungarian industry", and gives an account of the debate on "Social and economic conditions improving the efficiency of creative scientific and technological activities". This is followed by an analysis of the connection between the five-year R & D plan now being prepared, and planning of the national economy in general. This is presented within the framework of the problem of whether science can be planned, and the statements are based on experiences gained so far.

Shulze D. (1980) The determination and differentiation of the term strategy of science, *Science of Science*, **1** (2), 163–171.

The paper discusses the concept of strategy of science, the term science being understood in the broadest sense, which includes not only basic research but also scientific—technical research and development. The concept of strategy of science refers to long-range development tendencies and processes, and encompasses both the objectives of that development and the means that subserve development. The strategy of science is formed by the ruling class and reflects the general strategy of that class. The general strategy of science, moreover, distinguishes the strategy of scientific policy, the strategy inherent in science itself, strategies of scientific and technological progress, and strategies of science management. The meanings of these concepts are analyzed in detail and discussed with examples drawn from science policy in various socialist countries.

Szczepański, J. (1980) The role of science in the rebuilding and development of Poland, *The Review of the Polish Academy of Sciences*, (1–2) 91–103.

The author argues that in developed societies science constitutes a very important factor, which, through various mechanisms of its relations with economy, education, politics, and culture, has helped to form the society's organization, the conditions and standards of everyday life, etc. This influence of science upon social life greatly depends, of course, on the scholars themselves, on the quality of their work, the range and results of the research they undertake, as well as on the organization of the state, its economy and the system of that economy, on the intellectual level and imagination of state leaders and managers of the economy, on the use to which the results of research are put, and on how far and how deeply these results can influence the everyday life of people.

Books

Cemodanov, M. P. (1982) *Trends of Development of Sciences and a Factor of Intensification (Koncepcii nauki i faktor intensifikacii)* Novosibirsk, 198 pp. (in Russian).

The author examines the character of industrialization processes and the intensification of scientific research in developed socialist societies, and their relationship with the intensification of national economies. He describes the nature of social functions of science performed in developed socialist societies and the role of science in the intensity of national economics. He displays also an analytical picture of modern scienciometric trends in Western European countries and the USSR, considering the improvement of models of the relationship between science and output processes as a means of intensification of research.

International Cooperation in the Domain of Science, Technology, and Output Processes: Legal Aspects (1982) (*Mezdunarodnaja naučno-technicêskaja i proizvodstevennaja kooperacija. Pravovoe aspekty*). Moscow 304 pp. (in Russian).

The monograph is a presentation of legal problems concerning international cooperative links in the domain of science, technology, and output processes, arising from the cooperation between countries of one social-economic system (here the example of CMES countries is given) and those based on different social and economic structures. The article gives also legal aspects of cooperative links between countries of various systems operating in the Third World countries.

The main emphasis is placed on the problems of the development of ties between various industrial bodies and firms, which are immediate users of those cooperative links. It contains an analysis of contracted cooperative agreements.

Kapitza, P. L. (1977) *Experiment—Theory—Practice (Eksperiment—Teorija—praktika)* Moscow, 351 pp. (in Russian).

This is an impressive book which contains a collection of lectures written by P. L. Kapitza, one of the greatest scientists of this century. The book begins with chapters devoted to the author's own research work in the field of physics. Another chapter contains several papers on major figures in the growth of the exact sciences, from the time of B. Franklin to that of L.D. Landau. In chapters III and VII Kapitza deals with some general questions of science and the relationship between science and technology, and science and society. The main points of these papers concentrate on the problems of the organization and planning of research work. Kapitza analyzes also questions of the future of mankind and the role of science for future generations.

Science and the Current Problems of the Development of National Economies. General Assembly of the Academy of Sciences of USSR December 13–14. 1979 (1980) (*Nauka i aktua 'lnye problemy razvitija narodnogo chozjajstva. Sessja obsščego sobrania AN SSSR 13–14 dékabria 1979 r.*) Academy of Sciences of the USSR, Moscow, 164 pp. (in Russian).

This book contains a series of articles presented during the General Assembly of the Academy of Sciences of USSR and generally devoted to the role of science and improvement of the effectiveness of managing and intensification of development of the country.

An introductory paper was delivered by A.P. Aleksandrov the others by M.K. Bajbakov, P.N. Fedoseev, V.A. Kotelnikov, G.I. Marchik, B.E.

Paton, and others. The main topics of these articles were devoted to the problems of development based on oil and raw materials, power engineering, machine building, metallurgy, chemistry and other branches of industry, the improvement of means of transport, reasonable utilization of labor, oil, and energy resources, improvement of economic managing mechanisms, and the immediate role of science in all these processes and in the general and complex program of development of science and technology for the next 20 years.

Selected Problems on the Policy of Science under Conditions of Developed Socialism (Symposium on the Problems of General Theoretical Development of Science and Technology). (1979) (nekotorye problemy rozrabotki strategii nauki v uslovijach rozvitogo socializma. Simposium po time Obščeteoretiěskie voprosy rozvitija nauki i techniki). Prague, 165 pp. (in Russian).

This book is a review of a series of reports delivered during the Symposium of the CMEA member countries held in Czechoslovakia (May 1977). The Symposium was held within the frame of a coordination program for scientific and technical research for 1976–80. An important problem discussed during the Symposium was designation of scientific policy under conditions of developed socialism (policy of development of science, under conditions of scientific and technical revolution, international social and economic integration, various aspects of links between science–technology output processes: problems of effectiveness of scientific research, influence of fundamental research on the process of modeling new relationships in science, technology and output, and development of an idea of science policy).

    The Symposium was attended by specialists from Bulgaria, Hungary, GDR, Poland, USSR, and Czechoslovakia.

List of Participants

Prof. Pierre AIGRAN
8 Square Henry-Pate
Paris 16 eme
75016 FRANCE

Prof. John ASHWORTH
Vice-Chancellor
University of Salford
Salford M5 4WT
UK

Dr. Christopher BERNABO
Executive Director
National Acid Precipitation
  Assessment Program
722 Jackson Place, N.W.
Washington, DC 20506
USA

Dr. Ronald BRICKMAN
2032 Belmont Rd., N.W.,
  No. 620
Washington, DC 20009
USA

Prof. Harvey BROOKS
Aiken Computation Laboratory
  Room 226
Harvard University
Cambridge, MA 02138
USA

Dr. Frantisek CHARVAT
Deputy Director
Institute of Philosophy
  and Sociology
Yilska 1
11000 Prague 1
CZECHOSLOVAKIA

Dr. E. CHERKASOV
Deputy Secretary of the Soviet
  Committee for Systems Analysis
c/o Committee for Systems Analysis
Presidium of the Academy of Sciences
  of the USSR
Prospect 60 Let Octyabria, 9
117312 Moscow
USSR

Dr. William C. CLARK
Oak Ridge Associated Universities
Institute for Energy Analysis
PO Box 117
Oak Ridge, TN 37830
USA

Dr. Chester L. COOPER
IIASA
Special Advisor to
  the Director

Dr. Marion Graefin DOENHOFF
Zeitverlag Gerd Bucerius KG
Pressehaus
Postfach 106820
D-2000 Hamburg 1
FRG

Prof. Loren GRAHAM
Massachusetts Institute of
    Technology
Bld. E-51/128
Cambridge, MA 02139
USA

Michael DOWLING
IIASA
Science for Public
    Policy Forum

Dr. Elizabeth HELANDER
Director of Research
The Academy of Finland
Ratamestarinkatu 12
SF-00520 Helsinki 52
FINLAND

Acad. Nikolai EMANUEL
Deputy Director
Institute of Chemical Physics
Academy of Sciences of the USSR
Kosygin Street 4
117334 Moscow
USSR

Prof. C. S. HOLLING
Director of IIASA

Univ. Doz. Dr. Heinz FISCHER
Minister
Federal Ministry for Science
    and Research
Minoritenplatz 5
A-1010 Vienna
AUSTRIA

Prof. Donald F. HORNIG
Interdisciplinary Programs
    in Health
Room 1308
Harvard School of Public Health
665 Huntington Avenue
Boston, MA 02115
USA

Dr. John H. GIBBONS
Director
Office of Technology Assessment
United States Congress
Washington, DC 20510
USA

Prof. Zdzislaw KACZMAREK
Scientific Secretary of the
    Polish Academy of Sciences
Palace of Culture and Science
PO Box 24
PL-00 901 Warsaw
POLAND

Acad. Leonardas KAIRIUKSTIS
Director
Lithuanian Science Research
  Institute of Forestry
Girionys
Kaunas, Lithuania SSR
USSR

Prof. Yoichi KAYA
Chairman
Department of Electrical
  Engineering
The Faculty of Engineering
The University of Tokyo
7-3-1 Hongo, Bunkyo-ku
Tokyo 113
JAPAN

Prof. Dr. Istvan KISS
General Secretary of the
  Hungarian Committee for IIASA
Bureau for Systems Analysis
  of the State Office for
  Technical Development
PO Box 565
H-1374 Budapest
HUNGARY

Acad. Kalman KULCSAR
Hungarian Academy of Sciences
Bureau for Systems Analysis
  of the State Office for
  Technical Development
PO Box 565
H-1374 Budapest
HUNGARY

Prof. Hans LANDBERG
Chairman
Swedish Council for Planning
  and Coordination of Research
FRN - Forskningsradsnamnden
Box 6710
S-11385 Stockholm
SWEDEN

Prof. Giandomenico MAJONE
IIASA
Institutions and Environmental
  Policies Program

Dr. Helga NOWOTNY
European Center for Social Welfare
  and Training Research
Berggasse 17
A-1090 Vienna
AUSTRIA

Prof. Ir. Theo QUENE
Chairman
Netherlands Scientific Council
  for Government Policy
2 Plein 1813
NL-2514 JN The Hague
THE NETHERLANDS

Dr. Jerome RAVETZ
Department of Philosophy
University of Leeds
Leeds LS2 9JT
UK

Erland ROST
Editor
Ny Teknik
Box 27315
S-10254 Stockholm
SWEDEN

Prof. Grygory VOROPAEV
Director
Institute for Water Problems
USSR Academy of Sciences
13/3 Sadovaya-Chernogryazskaya St.
103064 Moscow
USSR

Dr. Jean-Jacques SALOMON
Directeur
Centre Science,
Technologie et Societe
 - CNAM
292 rue Saint-Martin
F-75003 Paris
FRANCE

Dr. Gregory S. WETSTONE
Director
Air and Water Program
Environmental Law Institute
1346 Connecticut Ave., NW
  Suite 620
Washington, DC 20036
USA

Dr Brian WYNNE
University of Lancaster
Bailrigg
Lancaster LA1 4YN
UK

Dr. Guenter SCHUSTER
Hoehenweg 32
D-5300 Bonn 1
FRG

Index

283